SHELL SHOCK

D1375056

SHELL SHOCK

Wendy Holden

With special thanks to Sally Lindsay and
Robert Coldstream for their invaluable
research and High Moral Fibre

First published 1998 by Channel 4 Books
This edition published 2001 by Channel 4 Books, an imprint of Macmillan
Publishers Ltd, 25 Eccleston Place, London SW1W 9NF and Basingstoke.

Associated companies throughout the world.

ISBN 0 7522 1945 6

Text © 1998 Wendy Holden

10 9 8 7 6 5 4 3 2 1

A CIP catalogue record for this book is available from the British Library.

Commissioning Editor: Charlie Carman
Editor: Charlie Carman
Typeset by: Keystroke, Jacaranda Lodge, Wolverhampton
Printed by: Mackays of Chatham Plc, Chatham, Kent

This book accompanies the television series Shell Shock made by
Blakeway Productions for Channel 4.
Executive producer: Denys Blakeway
Producer: Julia Harrington

Wendy Holden is an experienced author and journalist. She wrote for the
Daily Telegraph for over ten years, and has written twelve books to date.
She lives in Suffolk with her husband and four dogs.

Contents

Acknowledgements

Too many people have contributed so much to this book to allow me to remember or even know them all. Sally Lindsay and Rob Coldstream have already had a special mention in dispatches for their outstanding cheerfulness under heavy bombardment, but Julia Harrington, Denys Blakeway and all those hardworking souls in the Woodstock Studios' trenches also deserve a large vote of thanks. The remarkable Charlie Carman at Boxtree deserves a gallantry medal for keeping up morale and so very much more; Dr Martin Deahl and Hazel Orme should be decorated for trying to make sense of it all; General 'Mad Mark' Lucas and his wonderful lieutenant Sally Hughes drew up the battle plans, and Chris, my inimitable batman, surpassed himself in dangerous and difficult circumstances. But those to whom I gladly award the most prestigious ribbons are the numerous kind contributors to the documentary and to the book, people whose expertise, life experiences, or those of their family members, have qualified them to speak with courage, eloquence and humility about a most harrowing time. Thank you all.

Chapter One

Who are these? Why sit they here in twilight? . . .
These are men whose minds the Dead have ravished.
Memory fingers in their hair of murders,
Multitudinous murders they once witnessed . . .
Always they must see these things and hear them,
Batter of guns and shatter of flying muscles,
Carnage incomparable, and human squander
Rucked too thick for these men's extrication.

'Mental Cases' Wilfred Owen

Few have been able to express the horrors of the battlefield quite so well as the soldier poets of the First World War. Their graphic descriptions of watching friends die, killing fellow human beings or leading others to their deaths make salutary reading. The stark beauty of their poems and essays eloquently depicts the process by which the human spirit can take only so much of the monstrosities of war before something cracks.

For the doctors entrusted with the care of those whose minds eventually gave way in the 1914–18 war, there was little medical history to go on and few clear guidelines. There had never been a war on the same scale, and no one had ever seen anything like the varying degrees of mental breakdown among soldiers or experienced it in such massive numbers. The symptoms were wildly diverse, from total paralysis and blindness to loss of speech, vivid nightmares, hallucinations and memory loss. Some patients declined eventually into schizophrenia, chronic depression and even suicide. The medical consequences of severe trauma to the moral and mental state on the battle lines were, it seemed, unquantifiable. There was no telling who would be affected or why and the military and the medical establishment were caught completely off-guard.

The effect of terrors on the minds of servicemen has been chronicled as far back as the early Greeks and in just about every conflict since. But it was during the First World War that it was first recognized as a problem that necessitated serious military-medico diagnosis, not least because the sheer numbers of men affected could not be spared from the front lines, as the Europe-wide conflict continued to claim countless lives. The long-term well-being of those who were stricken was considered very much a secondary issue to the manpower crisis. Thorough analysis of the problem was thought vital only in as much as it could distinguish genuine sufferers from malingerers – those hapless men whose debilitating mental symptoms labelled them as cowards and in some instances led to their execution.

Thanks largely to the requirements of an efficient war machine to stem the flow of sick men being sent home, the science of military psychiatry was born, designed to reduce men's moral objection to war and to counteract the dramatic and often fatal effects of combat on the minds of servicemen. Progressing far beyond its initial remit, its extraordinary findings about the workings of the mind have been widely adopted throughout modern psychiatric practice ever since.

Although it may seem difficult to imagine now, in its earliest days, the fledgling study of the relationship between war and madness represented nothing short of a revolution in military attitudes to the fragility of men. In Edwardian Britain particularly, the 'stiff upper lip' mentality prevailed throughout all classes. Fresh from the strait-laced Victorian era, men were still viewed as utterly unassailable, particularly when the honour of the country was at stake. Mass mental breakdown simply wasn't on the agenda.

Not that such human frailty should have come as a complete surprise. Warfare had long been recognized as one of the most extreme human experiences, imposing huge stresses on the minds of combatants torn between instincts of self-preservation and military duty. Descriptions of strange behaviour in the face of battle were recorded by Homer and in early Chinese literature. Virgil wrote of visions of 'wars, horrid wars and the Tiber foaming with much blood'. William Shakespeare's *Henry V* called upon the God of battles to 'steel my soldier's hearts, possess them not with fear, take from them now the sense of reckoning', and Lady Percy tells Hotspur of his night terrors in *Henry IV Part I*:

> *In thy faint slumbers I by thee have watch'd*
> *And heard thee murmur tales of iron wars; . . .*
> *Thy spirit within thee hath been so at war,*
> *And thus hath so bestirr'd thee in thy sleep,*
> *That beads of sweat have stood upon thy brow . . .*
> *And in thy face strange motions have appear'd,*
> *Such as we see when men restrain their breath . . .*

The history of war-related illness encompassed seventeenth-century German soldiers in the Thirty Years War between the Catholic Habsburg emperors and their mainly Protestant enemies, where stress-related disorders were attributed to homesickness, or *heimweh*; the revolutionary French troops of the late eighteenth century and those who fought in the Franco-Prussian War of 1870. In the American Civil War (1861–5) in which more than three million Americans served and more than 60,000 were killed, the trench warfare conditions endured by the troops were similar to those suffered by the servicemen in France and Flanders five decades later. Trenches undoubtedly offered shelter, but they also imprisoned the fighting men, immobilizing them and inducing a powerful urge to escape. In the war between the Confederacy and the Union, the phenomenon of mental breakdown among soldiers became known as 'mind wounds' and in diaries and journals, letters and historical reports, it is clear that many men who took part were haunted by their experiences long after the last battles were fought.

S. Weir Mitchell, an American physician attached to the fighting forces, wrote that even the most gallant soldiers had become 'as hysterical as the veriest woman', and were suffering from weight loss, exhaustion and fatigue. He advocated heavy massage and prodigious feeding to build up their strength in battle. The Union Army had no label for the condition that could help explain or legitimize the puzzling behaviour of some of its men. No category short of lunacy could account for their symptoms and many were either sent to an asylum for the rest of their natural lives, dispatched on the journey home where – left to fend for themselves – they died of hunger or exposure, or were hanged as malingerers.

The *American Journal of Medical Science* in 1864 noted drily: 'The great majority of malingerers consists rather of men who exaggerate real maladies of trifling character, or who feign disease outright . . . The depletion of our ranks is not so much by feigned epilepsies, paralyses and the like . . . as by those cases of disease . . . by which men add invented symptoms, or continue to assert the existence of those who have passed away.'

In 1860, William Hammond, a Union surgeon who became one of the pioneers of nervous and mental diseases in his age, did his best to fathom the condition he described as 'nostalgia', in which veterans continually relived horrible events. He wrote later: 'The cases were of amazing interest. At that time I had eighty epileptics, and every kind of nerve wound – palsies, choreas, stump disorders. Thousands of pages of notes were taken . . . massage was used to restore action to limbs in which healing nerve wounds left the muscles palsied or for the rigidity of splinted cases.' Other soldiers found to have 'irritable heart' problems were said to show signs of an increased heartbeat and aroused feelings of alarm triggered by reminders of combat. He treated all those afflicted by keeping them busy with nonstressful work away from the front line of battle.

Hammond complained that many of his patients were too immature; some were just sixteen. 'Youths of this age are not developed,' he concluded, 'and are not fit to endure the fatigues and deprivations of military life. They soon break down, become sick and are thrown upon the hospitals.' He recommended that the recruiting age be raised to twenty and that those affected should be discharged from duty. He also criticized the lack of psychiatric screening in the draft process. His generals were not so charitable and urged the government not to be soft on the alleged victims of nostalgia. They suggested the formation of a 'malingerer's brigade', of men accused of cowardice, with its members wearing a distinctive uniform and performing only the dirtiest and hardest of duties as punishment.

That idea, and others like it, was quickly abandoned when it was realized that no one was immune to the horrors of war; even senior officers succumbed. Many of those broken by their experiences took to drinking as a palliative. Whisky in the US Civil War became to the Army of the Potomac what marijuana became for the American Army in Vietnam. The actions of one senior officer, Colonel Raymond Lee of the 20th Massachusetts Volunteers, prompted Lieutenant Henry Abbott, a junior officer in his ranks, to write to his father about him in 1862: 'Colonel Lee . . . is undoubtedly very much shaken in his intellects, it seems the horrors of Antietam, his previous fatigues and his drinking completely upset him. He didn't give any orders, he wouldn't do anything . . . he was livid and shaky, just like a little child, wandering away from home.' Another Union captain wrote poignantly of a deserter in his charge: 'His eyes are in mourning for his loss of character.'

Even between the wars, instances of mental disorder began to attract some public interest. In the latter part of the nineteenth century, any display of instability was attributed to 'railway spine theory' in which the controversial new steam trains were blamed for allegedly causing a violent blow or shake to the spinal column while travelling. A surgeon in the Boer War noted in 1900 that he had seen many cases of 'functional impairment of sensory and motor power associated with psychical symptoms akin to nervous shock or those observed after railway accidents'.

During the Russo-Japanese War of 1904–5, and particularly the siege of Port Arthur, the Russian psychiatric services were inundated with two thousand cases of 'insanity'. Special lunatic asylums were set up in the provincial hospitals of Siberia, and the Red Cross was summoned for additional assistance. Symptoms described included psychoses, paralysis, epilepsy, dementia and hysteria.

By the time the First World War loomed, there had been adequate historical warning of what might come, but little genuine concern. It was widely felt that there was no need to worry about such an unpalatable issue during peacetime, especially when the proportion of early psychological casualties had been so small compared to that of the wounded or physically sick. In any event, the view was that the astonishing advances in military technology would give a whole new meaning to the term conflict. Servicemen armed with the very latest in weaponry would surely be able to defend the Empire swiftly and without fuss. When hostilities broke out on 4 August 1914, the nation rose to the challenge and embraced arms gladly.

The vast majority of the idealistic young men who marched joyously to the battlefields of Europe were among the million or so who volunteered for military service spurred on by the moustachioed Lord Kitchener, British secretary for war and Boer War general whose rallying cry was: "Your Country Needs You." Before too long the new 'Pals Regiments' comprising friends and neighbours from villages and towns across the country signed up *en masse* and were dispatched to conquer the imperious Germans.

In the space of four years, Britain raised a vast citizen army virtually from scratch. There was very little training and no time to instil the men with much regimental or filial loyalty. Military chiefs simply didn't see the need: this war was widely expected to be short and sharp. The trenches were only ninety miles from London, the fighting could be heard all along the south coast. Officers boasted that they could have breakfast in the trenches and dine at their club in the evening. 'Over by Christmas' was the popular belief; a quick bloodying of the Boche nose before a victorious return to 'Blighty'.

The medical profession and the military showed scant concern for the possibility of psychological casualties. As war impended a doctor in the *British Medical Journal* advocated alcohol as an instant salve for any problems that might arise, while an officer of the 29th Division claimed that the cure for fear was a minute tied to the barbed wire at the front. In France, the government's most eminent doctors, invited to consider whether the strain of warfare was likely to lead to nervous disorders, concluded that mental disorder among men worn out by the fatigue of battle was 'extremely rare' and unlikely to be a problem. But all hopes of being home for Christmas were soon dashed when early British attempts to turn the German flank failed. Following the retreat at Mons and the first battle of the Marne by the autumn of 1914, the war had settled into static immobility, each side facing the other from their water-filled trenches.

War on the western front was different from any war fought before. It had become ever more destructive, and so, too, had its impact on the minds of servicemen. The nerve-shattering properties of the new killing machines that dominated the fighting – aeroplanes, tanks, and rapid-firing heavy calibre artillery – brought mental resistance to saturation levels. Tremendous advances in metallurgy, the production of superior gunpowder and the rapid development of weaponry, allowed for the firing of steel-jacketed bullets at a range and velocity never before achieved.

Modern chemical industries produced high explosives, which were used for the first time and on an industrial scale. Sustained shelling and bombing caused horrific injuries far beyond those suffered previously. In the battle of Verdun alone, the opening German artillery barrage lasted ten hours and expended two million shells. By the end of the battle, ten months later, nine villages had been pounded to dust, and the heavy artillery shells had ploughed the ground to a depth of more than twenty feet.

Paul Dubrille, a French Jesuit serving in the infantry, wrote graphically: 'To die from a bullet seems to be nothing; parts of our being remain intact; but to be dismembered, torn to pieces, reduced to pulp, this is a fear that flesh cannot support . . . The most solid nerves cannot resist for long.'

Throughout Belgium and France the British forces were continually harried and suffered heavy casualties. Men had an average four hours' rest per day and became mentally weak from the continual strain of always being in range of the relentless German guns. In what quickly became a war of endurance and little heroism, soldiers were said by Charles Moran, later Lord Moran, medical officer to the 1st Battalion of the Royal Fusiliers, to 'wear out in battle like their clothes'. From the outset, Allied deaths reached epic proportions. The spirit-sapping mud, rain and freezing conditions in the trenches further compounded the misery, adding to the sense of immobility and helplessness, and giving rise to mental desolation surpassing all previous experience, especially to such inexperienced and barely trained troops. This was not the glorious battle expected by so many, it was a siege, and the letters home detailed the misery of life within its grip.

Captain Herbert Leland, of the 3rd (Reserve) Battalion South Staffordshire Regiment, who was in his mid-forties and had seen military service in Africa, wrote to his wife:

> Mud, muck, misery and melancholy reign supreme, and the pitiless bombardment adds to the general discomfort . . . The continual roar of the guns, the whirr of the machine guns, the ground shakes as if by earthquake and it never ceases day or night . . . I was all over the Front this morning; you could not believe the scene of desolation. The shell holes and mine craters actually touch one another, wire entanglements levelled to the ground. Wagons; limbers lying shattered along the road, rifles, equipment, shells strewn everywhere, and the long line of stretcher bearers passing slowly back to the dressing station. One poor devil, I could not help noticing, his leg was practically blown off, just hanging from the knee. He was lying back with eyes closed and a cigarette sticking out of the corner of his mouth. The walking cases were also most pathetic. Up to their eyes in mud, limping and helping each other along as best they could.
>
> This kind of weather takes all the enthusiasm out of one. You never saw such a miserable looking lot of poor devils in your life . . . we are up to our eyes in mud and water. The men frequently sink to their waists and have to be hauled out . . . we have no chance . . . of drying ourselves and consequently a great majority are suffering from colds and coughs.

Captain Leland wrote of rats the size of rabbits plucking the hair from men's lice-ridden scalps at night to line their nests, and of filthy pools of stagnant water being the only medium for washing. On a brief respite from the trenches, he wrote: 'We have come back from Hell and are resting in Hades.'

Tom Leland, Captain Leland's grandson, said, 'My grandfather was experienced in fighting and the privations of war but when he got to France, he found the conditions in the trenches so different from anything that he had experienced before. It was the vast numbers of men involved, the vast numbers of casualties, and the continuous noise of barrages. It was non-stop, both the incoming shells and the shells going out, and it took a lot of getting used to. The conditions shocked him – the noise, the mud, and the numbers they lost. He found that going over the top wasn't so bad – there were moments of terror and exhilaration in fighting and you had the adrenaline rush – but being back in support, with the continuous noise, the continuous shelling, and seeing the numbers of wounded coming back. He never hardened to the horrors.'

Richard Trafford, a coal miner from Ormskirk, was just fifteen years old when he signed up to the 9th Kings Liverpool Regiment. He had bluffed his way into the Army and joined up with his workmates from the colliery. Their first experience of warfare was the battle of Loos. He went on to fight in the bloody battle of the Somme and at Passchendaele. 'I hadn't the slightest idea what I was letting myself in for,' he said. 'It was a bit of a shock for a young lad, but you don't think, you carry on with the rest. The Germans had that many machine-guns that the bullets were coming past our ears thick and heavy like bees buzzing, and the shrapnel was dropping on our steel helmets like hailstones. If you weren't shot or killed by shrapnel you were drowned in the shell holes. You were half drowned half of the time.

'I felt like running away many times, I felt like a rat going for the next hole. You never knew whether the next bullet or lump of shrapnel was going to hit you. You're jumping over bodies, there were that many thousands and when you got to the barbed wire, you couldn't get through. You've corpses lying in front of you, you've men coming behind you with fixed bayonets. You can't go back, you've got to go forward, and that's when you come up against the wire. If there was anywhere you could run to, you'd get away, but there wasn't. So you had to get used to it and get on with it or go mad. It was all in the mentality of the individual. The epitaphs for those who were killed for their actions should be changed from "shot for cowardice" to "killed in action". They had been through a lot.'

Many servicemen admitted afterwards that they joined up primarily for a 'square meal and a decent pair of boots', to get away from an unhappy home or to find a life more stimulating than working in a factory or on a farm. They thought it would be like school camp and saw it as an opportunity to travel, to be with their workmates and to be regarded as heroes by the folk back home. The peer-group pressure was enormous and those who stayed behind were regarded as pariahs, 'conchies' – conscientious objectors – or handed a white feather, the symbol of a coward. But little did those naïve young men who enlisted know what was in store for them in the battlefields of Flanders.

Guy Botwright, a platoon commander of the Labour Corps at seventeen, explained: 'It wasn't what we had expected. I was just a young boy, football and games in my head. It was the first time I'd ever seen death and it was so terribly shocking. It was not just men either, mules used to drag the eighteen-pound guns and so many of them were killed or wounded. I thought it was the most dreadful thing, those animals having to suffer. You were living in a land of impossibility – death, blood, mud, pouring with rain, boiled with sun. It was very difficult to face. It was a case of "I'm not going to see this, I'll run away from it" sort of business, but of course you never did, and in my case I was in charge of a large number of men. I was responsible. I'd trained for it and loathsome as it was, there I was.'

By September, just one month after war broke out, the first cases of men suffering from some sort of mental breakdown began to arrive back in Britain. Tens of thousands more were to follow. No one had expected them and no arrangements had been made. Placed in beds set aside for the physically wounded in normal military hospitals, they quickly deteriorated. The doctors literally did not know what had hit them.

At that time psychiatry was still very much on the fringes of the acknowledged medical establishment, and was characterized by a muddle of conflicting theories, diagnoses and treatments. The work of Sigmund Freud and his fellow psychoanalysts in Vienna, such as Carl Jung and Alfred Adler, although considered shocking and exciting was still regarded with much scepticism. Freud's analysis of dreams and his insistence on finding repressed sexual desires in almost every response had alienated many. The London Society for Psychoanalysts, set up in 1913, had attracted only a dozen members.

But many Freudian theories were soon to be taken much more seriously, particularly his belief that serious psychological conditions such as war neuroses – or 'neurasthenia' as it was widely known – could be cured by making a patient confront his experiences and recall painful memories under hypnosis. Freud extended this idea to 'free association', allowing the patient to lie on a couch and ramble his or her thoughts when in a relaxed state, coming to a diagnosis after adding information gleaned from dreams and childhood recollections. Such techniques were later to become vital tools in the battle for the minds of the First World War participants, men who were largely wholly unsuited to homicide and for whom the fear of death and the horror of mutilation had pushed them to the brink of mental illness for the first time in their lives.

As increasing numbers of strangely silent or stuttering men shuffled home from the front, the doctors dispatched them to newly opened neuro-logical wards, such as those at the established military hospital, the Royal Victoria Hospital at Netley near Southampton, Hampshire, or the 4th London Territorial Hospital in Denmark Hill. Nursing staff were advised to wash and feed them, let them sleep and comfort them as best they could. After a few days or weeks of rest, the men were expected to make a quick recovery before being returned to the front. But as more and more of the pale, tremulous young men filled the beds, with peculiarly similar symptoms of tormented nightmares and hallucinations of what they had recently witnessed, the doctors realized they had an epidemic on their hands, and one for which there was no quick fix.

The case of Private 'M', a twenty-three-year old soldier with two years' service, was reported as a typical example by Arthur Hurst, a major in the Royal Army Medical Corps (RAMC), who ended up at Netley. Hurst wrote that the young man was quite fit until a year into the war, when he suddenly had to be forcibly prevented from going over the parapet to attack some German mortars firing on his trench. He became dazed and lost the power of speech, communicating only in writing. 'He believed he was still in the trenches which were being heavily shelled; his pupils were widely dilated and he sweated profusely. His pulse was 140. Convulsive tremors of the head, trunk and limbs constantly occurred. In his dreams he saw the ghosts of Germans he had bayoneted come to take revenge on him.'

Repatriated to England, Private M became paralysed from the neck down, lost all memory and had still not regained his speech by the time he was examined by Major Hurst. 'He had no idea who or what he was and had no knowledge of the meaning of words. During the following months he learned a kind of pidgin English, but the meaning of every word had to be taught, and he used each word in his limited vocabulary for a variety of meanings. He did not recognize any of his relations. He delighted in childish toys and in a general way his mind was that of a year-old child.' Suddenly, and without warning, nearly two years after he first fell ill, Private M's power of speech returned in the middle of the night after a severe headache. 'He felt something snap in his head, and immediately afterwards he talked quite normally and his memory of his home and past life flowed back. He soon remembered his experiences in France, but his life in the hospital was almost a blank, as it seemed to him that he was in France only a few days ago. 'He remembered "feeling funny with a buzzing in his head",' wrote Hurst. 'Then something in his head was suddenly relieved, the buzzing stopped and his memory returned.'

Faced with such extraordinary symptoms, and in so many men, the doctors warned the military in no uncertain terms that the mystery plague was fast becoming a serious problem. It was generally agreed that preventive measures had to be taken before mass panic broke out in the ranks and the war was lost. In recognition of the seriousness of the situation, the War Office invited doctors from all over Britain to help examine the cases flooding back from the front. Almost anybody with an idea that they could help was accepted. The military gave this disparate collection of neurologists, budding psychoanalysts and anatomical specialists a free hand to treat their puzzling new patients however they liked – anything to get the sick soldiers fighting fit and back to the trenches.

The initial medico-military view was that the doctors would find that the men they examined probably represented the normal proportion of those who might have become mentally ill in civilian life. With over a million men in the British Expeditionary Forces, there was bound to be a certain percentage unhinged. But as the reports on the human guinea-pigs began trickling back to the War Office, one thing became clear: whatever it was these men were suffering from, it appeared not to be inherent or innate but a response to the war itself. Senior officers were among those affected, and most of the patients had previously been perfectly ordinary men who had never before suffered from any sign of mental imbalance. In the face of the prolonged horror of war, the doctors said, it seemed the soldiers' minds were simply giving way. And the horror showed no signs of abating.

In October 1915, the Allies attempted an attack on the Germans across the Flanders plain in what became known as the first battle of Ypres. It was abandoned after seven weeks of fighting and little success. At this point the British Army was said to be composed of 'tired, haggard and unshaven men, unwashed, plastered in mud, many in little more than rags'. The following month, the so-called 'race to the sea' attempt to turn the German flank also failed and the mobile war truly turned into trench war, providing the worst possible conditions for the exhausted men at the front.

The German armed forces were indefatigable; in training and organization, the best in Europe. Moreover, they were inspired by a high degree of patriotism and a belief in a great destiny, as yet unfulfilled. With France and Britain unprepared for a drawn-out conflict, and the Allied soldiers led by generals who still believed in the vital role of the cavalry, the balance was tipped largely in Germany's favour. Outnumbered and outmanoeuvred, the British servicemen, who had anticipated a short war, were forced to accept that they faced a long and bloody conflict in which their chances of survival were reducing almost daily. That fear alone caused many to collapse under the mental strain.

Among those recruited to help cope with the steady flow of soldiers being sent back from the front was a middle-aged professor called Charles Myers, the former editor of the *British Journal of Psychology*. Myers was one of a group of gentleman intellectuals specializing in primitive people and their psychology, who lived among tribesmen and missionaries in Malaya and Borneo to learn about their customs and mentalities. It was fascinating work, but Myers and his colleagues were soon to find France and its effects on men's minds every bit as interesting.

Joan Rumens, his daughter, explained: 'My father was busy in Cambridge, researching primitive Australian music, but after a few weeks he couldn't concentrate and felt he should be making some better contribution to the war effort. He went up to the War Office in 1914 but they turned him down because he was too old to join up, but he took himself off to France as a civilian and went to the Duchess of Westminster Hospital in Le Touquet as a registrar. In early 1915 when the casualties started coming in, he was commissioned into the Royal Army Medical Corps as a captain and sent to work in more specialized hospitals in France. He was very concerned about the conditions out there and moved from hospital to hospital very close to the front line where he did what he could for these traumatized men coming out from the firing line.'

In December 1914, two months after his arrival in France, Myers treated one soldier who had been trapped in barbed wire in no man's land – the neutral ground between the entrenched hostile forces. Several shells had burst right next to him, causing him no physical damage, but ever since he had been partially blind, and had lost the senses of taste and smell.

> He had been in the best of spirits until the shells burst about him [Myers wrote]. An eye-witness said his escape was a sheer miracle. Immediately after the shell burst in front of him his sight became blurred. It hurt him to open his eyes and they burned when closed. At the same moment he was seized with shivering, and cold sweat broke out, especially around the loins. He was crying the whole time and wondering whether he was going blind. He kept turning over in his mind the succession of events from the beginning of the advance to the bursting of the shells.

Myers concluded that the shattering noise caused by the explosion of the eight-inch shell, showering the soldier with hot shards of metal, must have had some physical effect. 'I was inclined to lay some emphasis on the physical shock produced by the bursting of the shell,' he wrote. He believed such an explosion could have caused 'an invisibly fine molecular commotion in the brain'. In other words, some sort of physical concussion, damaging the nerves. In an article in the medical journal the *Lancet* a few months later, he coined a rather more catchy phrase for the condition: 'shell shock'.

The term spread like wildfire through Britain and in the trenches. From then on it was applied to a whole host of odd medical phenomena, which doctors didn't know how else to account for. Once the phenomenon had a name, it gained in credibility and the cases that had begun as a tiny trickle at the outset of war, arousing the interest only of the medical community, started to flood in thick and fast.

The *British Medical Journal* and the *Lancet* sensed the excitement among their readers and followed the development of the situation closely, being among the first to raise the worrying spectre that the numbers of cases could be an indication of mass hysteria in the troops. Doctors, invited to publish their findings openly, continued to report strange symptoms and elusive side-effects of what they also described as 'temporary nervous breakdowns'. A *BMJ* article in 1915 stated that such a condition

> *occurs in those who have been strong and well and is ascribed to a sudden or alarming physical cause, such as witnessing a ghastly sight or undergoing a harassing experience. As a result of such shock the patient becomes nervy, unduly emotional and shaky, and most typical of all, his sleep is disturbed by bad dreams of experiences he has passed, of shells bursting, of duels between aeroplanes, or the many harassing sights of war in the trenches. Even the waking hours may be distressful from the acute recollection of these events revolving in his memory. Headache, slight mental depression and fine tremor may be accompaniments to these symptoms.*

Numerous examples were cited of British officers and lower ranks suffering from the aspect of shell shock termed 'hysterical paralysis', the sudden inability to move a limb despite there being no physical cause. There was a sergeant with a paralysed trigger finger, which prevented him from firing his weapon, and an officer ordered to lead his men in a suicidal raid who found he could no longer speak.

The term hysterical – previously related to a condition believed to be suffered only by faint-hearted women – brought an uncomfortable element into the debate: it implied that the soldiers had become over-emotional and suggestible, all the things that men are not supposed to be especially when called upon to defend their country in a time of national crisis. Sensing the hostility to such a word among the chiefs of staff, the doctors tended to use it only in reference to the lower ranks. Officers were not permitted to suffer from anything so unmanly as hysteria: they were 'neurasthenic'.

One medical editorial postulated: 'The question remains whether physical factors such as fatigue, hunger, the strain of responsibility, repeated air concussion from high explosives . . . in some unrecognized fashion so impress the nervous system as to pave the way for the action of such a force as autosuggestion.'

With such an abundance of conflicting symptoms and suggestions, the War Office received no clear suggestions from the many doctors they had mobilized. Explanations were limited: the soldiers were either hysterical – not a palatable thought during national crisis – or they had something physically wrong with their nerves caused by exploding shells, which made their limbs and senses not work properly. The various advocates of the different branches of medicine each rushed to examine the cases and to propound their own theories, which only added to the confusion.

The neurologists quickly claimed the condition as their own. The study of the nerves was the fashionable new science of the era, rather like genetics is now. Professor Lepine in France and Charles Mercier in the UK, supported by Major Frederick Mott, a doctor with front-line experience, and William Turner, consultant neurologist to the Army, agreed with Myers's initial diagnosis that there must have been some sort of organic or physical cause of the shell shock, which, when healed, somehow allowed 'emotional disturbance' to remain. Others, including Myers, were beginning to have their doubts.

Lieutenant Colonel Ian Palmer, a senior lecturer in military psychiatry, explained the term's appeal: 'It made much sense. It captured exactly what was happening. There were lots of shells around. There were lots of blasts, lots of shock, and people – after being blown up or buried after an explosion – were in a state of shock. It was a wonderful term because it described it perfectly. However, because it did, many different conditions became subsumed under the one term. Eventually, the term became too attractive. Myers wrote of people coming out of the line and, when asked what was wrong with then, they said, "Oh, I have shell shock," and because of that the term lost its validity later on.'

To the intense irritation of the neurologists, Myers eventually rejected his early connection between shell shock and 'organic molecular commotion' in the brain because not all the evidence concurred. He agreed that cerebral haemorrhage could be involved in some instances, but insisted that sometimes 'emotional disturbance' was sufficient cause. This outlandish theory recognized the psychological nature of the physical presentation of war stress for the first time, and was later responsible for the setting up of a modern system of diagnosis and treatment.

The arguments abounded and there was no shortage of new subjects for examination. As one psychologist remarked, experimentation on that scale in peacetime would have been possible only on animals. Psychiatry was still in its infancy, a melting pot of different ideas and its practitioners were little more than amateur enthusiasts, but faced with such a unique situation, a whole generation of medical men became fascinated by the phenomenon and surveyed the scene with a mixture of compassion and relish. Reputations were to be made – or lost – in diagnosing and treating the condition. Dozens turned into hundreds of cases being repatriated and doctors of every nationality were reporting on what they were seeing, although many had to be reminded constantly that their mission was not research, but to return the servicemen to the war and solve the manpower crisis.

John MacCurdy, an American doctor who examined many soldiers, wrote of the classic case in a US medical journal:

> *The face of the patient is drawn, showing signs of fatigue, while emotional strain is exhibited by chronic frowning with considerable wrinkling of the forehead. Occasionally they had nervous mannerisms such as grimacing accompanied by a withdrawal of the head, suggesting the starting back from something unpleasant. A frequent problem was hopelessness and shame for their own incompetence and cowardice, accompanied by obsessive thoughts about the horror they had seen on the battlefield.*

He regarded the symptoms as the inevitable reaction of forcing thousands of everyday civilians into the horrors of war with no real means of fighting back.

> *There are millions of men – previously humdrum, sober citizens with no obvious traits of recklessness of bloodthirstiness – not only exposing themselves to extraordinary hazards [but] engaged in inflicting injuries on fellow human beings without the repugnance they would have shown in performing similar operations on the bodies of cats and dogs.*

There was no such repugnance from the British medical establishment. At the Royal Victoria Hospital in Netley, which became a clearing hospital from where servicemen would be sent on to other, more specialist establishments according to their diagnosis and rank, doctors fell over themselves to prod, poke and classify individual cases, even filming many of the worst-affected for posterity. One ghostlike, grainy film of pale faces with luminous eyes exists to this day. Filmed partially by the famous Pathé brothers, it chronicles mostly cases from Netley but also from Seale-Hayne Hospital in Newton Abbot, Devon and an unknown London establishment, and shows assorted soldiers in a desperate state of trembling, twitching and paralysis before and after treatment. Their conditions were all clearly categorized and sometimes given outlandish names, such as 'hysterical stump orator', or 'hysterical slippery gait'. In what was almost certainly an early promotional film, almost all the patients shown made a near-complete recovery, working happily on farmland afterwards, basket-weaving, taking part in physical-fitness training or staging mock battles for the cameras.

Shell shock, it seemed, knew no nationality boundaries. Across Europe, medical men struggled to identify the problem and treat those whom it afflicted. The Germans were overwhelmed by thousands of cases and their doctors, who called the condition *kriegsneurose* – literally, war nervousness – were doing all they could to get their own men back to the fighting lines. The French, who named the phenomenon *la confusion mentale de la guerre*, were among the first to try to differentiate between cases, treating many near the front line, often by radical means and death threats, much to the condemnation of many who complained of torture to the government in Paris. Only the most serious French shell-shocked were sent home. The British sent the majority home and got worse results.

By December 1914, only four months after the war began, as many as 10 per cent of British officers and 4 per cent of other ranks were estimated to have suffered some sort of nervous or mental breakdown. With so many men affected, the War Office sent its consultant neurologist, William Turner, to France to investigate. A month later, he came across Myers, already doing his pioneering work in the field, and was much impressed. Three months later the War Office officially recognized the term 'shell shock' and appointed Myers 'specialist in nerve shock', later promoting him to consultant psychologist to the British Expeditionary Force, replacing Turner in overall charge of arrangements for shell-shocked men.

Myers, who did not include neurology in his qualifications and had previously been conducting a personal crusade, had no choice but to accept. It was a matter of some irony to him that he had initially been turned away by the very military establishment now asking for his help. He noted in his diary: 'I had no asylum experience, nor had I a specialist's knowledge of neurological diseases. But an Army officer has to obey orders. They arose in my case partly from the fact that there was no one else available in France.'

In Britain, shell-shock fever continued to grow. Rumours abounded about the strange new condition, lowering public morale still further as Christmas came and went. Families of men repatriated as mere shadows of their former selves demanded to know what had happened. By early 1915, a series of newspaper articles began to appear about shell shock, exposing readers to radical new views about the workings of the mind and summarizing the various methods of treatment. *The Times* was the first British newspaper openly to address the problem. One of the first such articles, headlined 'The Wounded Mind', spoke of hysterical blindness; another 'Wounds of Consciousness' addressed the symptoms of deafness and paralysis. Other such articles were widely read and fuelled the consuming popular interest.

Both in and out of the War Office, the subject continued to be the topic of much heated debate and speculation. Pacifists, who had been against the war in the first place, turned public fears to their own advantage, claiming it was the intrinsic immorality of the war that was causing so many men to suffer mental breakdown. The more patriotic accused sufferers of pretending to be ill just to get away from the danger of the front. Whatever the view, there was growing concern that the number of men diagnosed with the condition was still rising rapidly and there appeared to be no sign of a 'cure'.

Although shell shock was on everybody's lips, the term itself was a complete misnomer, to Myers's lasting embarrassment. He and his colleagues had been thrust headlong into psychological medicine, a specialism still in its infancy, and found great difficulty in trying to change people's attitudes to mental disorder, or even to accept his redefined diagnosis. 'Too many men, it was realized, had never been near an exploding shell. The cause wasn't physical at all, it was their psychological problems that had accounted for their disastrous mental state,' Mrs Rumens said, recalling her father's angst. 'He wasn't at all happy with the term being applied to this quantity of young men who had suffered such tremendous traumas through their experience of the war, whether it was the landing of shells nearby or just through the ghastly conditions of life in the trenches.'

The real cause, it was emerging, was something that everyone was less willing to acknowledge: the sheer horror of the war. Trapped in the stinking trenches, bombarded day and night, the men on the western front continued to endure intolerable conditions, expecting death at any minute and, in some cases, longing for it. At times, the mud turned into a glue-like quagmire, sucking both the living and the dead into its deep craters. There was rarely time or space to bury those killed and if the bodies could not be carried away by the overworked stretcher-bearers, they lay where they fell in the trenches, slowly decomposing – rotting companions for the rats and those still alive. With scant rest and nothing but mud and bodies to look at, or a soggy Woodbine to smoke beneath the parapet of the trenches, it was little wonder that so many men were pushed to their mental limits.

Second Lieutenant Siegfried Sassoon, a young cavalry officer and poet serving with the Royal Welsh Fusiliers, who later became an icon of the First World War, graphically described the scene in his diary: 'Stumbling along the trench in the dusk, dead men and living lying against the side of the trenches – one never knew which were dead and which living. Dead and living were nearly one, for death was in all our hearts.'

Captain Leland, writing to his wife in a letter that would have first been censored by a senior officer, said:

> I told you about the patrol I lost. Well, they are all accounted for. All dead, thank God, and not missing. I am sending a party out to bring them in tonight. I hear from my runner's report that they have been stripped. After what I have seen, no German will ever say 'Kamerad' to me . . . We are quite willing to play the game, but when they take one of my men, strip him, shoot him, and throw him over the parapet for me to pick up I see red. I have not been feeling too well lately . . . How I do wish I could tell you some things. I dare not, of course, for you would never get my letters . . . I am absolutely deaf and as weary as a kitten.

Leland's grandson, reading the letters now, reflected on his grandfather's position. 'All the indications were there that he was starting to find it all too much. He was a very sensitive man and realized what was happening. Initially it was the effect of near misses which dazed him. In one case, he said he was out of it. He doesn't remember anything for two hours and then there was a bad taste in his mouth, deafness, a vicious headache and a quivering of the hands.

'Later on, the effects became cumulative and there were instances of a few hours, then days, but gradually, with time, a never-ending break. You can see how weary he was, how his hands would shake. He couldn't sleep. His temper was vile. He had this ringing in his ears the whole time. He needed a rest, he needed leave but it was never convenient and gradually the more he needed it, the less he would ask for it.

'From his letters it was clear he was having quite a battle with himself. He reckoned it was other people's duty to send him back when necessary, but he would ask for no favours. He had this great sense of duty and he felt that he should be there. Although he realized the effect of shell shock on himself, he fought against giving in to it and was pretty disparaging about others who did. There was a case of one of the soldiers who shot himself in the foot to get out of it and he commented, "It was better the chap killed himself." And during shelling another officer's nerves had completely gone and my grandfather said he could have hit him. Being a proud military man, the effect of giving in to weakness and being taken out of battle without being physically wounded was something that he was very ashamed of. And he was conscious that his wife and family might feel shame. It wasn't done.'

Pat Barker, the novelist whose bleak *Regeneration* trilogy so perfectly captures the unmitigated misery of the First World War, wrote of one soldier's mind 'bulging as a memory threatened to surface'. She added: 'These men had been trained to identify emotional repression as the essence of manliness. Men who broke down, or cried, or admitted to feeling fear, were sissies, weaklings, failures . . . fear and tenderness were emotions so despised that they could be admitted into consciousness only at the cost of redefining what it meant to be a man.'

Most of the symptoms witnessed during the First World War have been seen in veterans of every war since. Amnesia, nightmares and flashbacks are familiar today as indications of trauma. But faced with these strange manifestations in previously normal people for the first time, the medical staff of the 1914–18 war were baffled and, in many cases, overwhelmed. Some early sufferers appeared so debilitated by their symptoms that they weren't diagnosed shell-shocked but insane and sent home to lunatic asylums, with no real prospect of recovery. By the time there was more understanding about what had caused them to break down in the first place, many were past saving.

The War Office, frustrated with lack of progress, decided in true military style that the best way to tackle the problem was to quantify and qualify it. It insisted that the doctors came up with precise classifications and duly identified four types of war neurosis:

1. Shell shock, caused by an explosive shock to the central nervous system.
2. Hysteria, causing partial or complete loss of control over sensory perceptual motor functions.
3. Neurasthenia, caused by prolonged intense physical or mental strain, the symptoms of which were chronic fatigue, headache, exhaustion and loss of appetite.

4. Disordered action of the heart, or 'soldier's heart', manifested by palpitations, giddiness or fainting.

Many of the latter sufferers were mistakenly diagnosed as suffering from organic disease and ended up in non-specialist hospitals.

Once the problem had been classified, the powers-that-be set about identifying the basic steps to a 'cure', wrongly assuming that the enormously wide range of symptoms would benefit equally from identical treatment. Basic orders were issued for those working on the psychoneurosis wards.

1. Each patient on admission to have a hot drink.
2. Each patient to have three full meals a day unless otherwise ordered.
3. Do not discuss the symptoms with the patient.
4. No one is permitted in these wards unless assigned for duty.
5. The rapid cure of these patients depends on food, sleep, exercise and the hopeful attitude of those who come in contact with them.

Similarly, all neurosis patients arriving in Britain received a standard cure of isolation, rest, massage and a milk diet. A number of doctors experimented with relaxation therapy, even trying 'the controlled use of rum', which was, unsurprisingly, popular among patients. Doctor after doctor propounded their own theories based on whether they believed in the neurological or the psychological diagnosis, many of which were tried and tested by others before being rejected, however outlandish.

A handful relied on the strict Freudian view of war neuroses, which was that the experience of an all-male environment with a high level of emotional intensity, coupled with the experience of battle, aroused homosexual and sadistic impulses normally repressed, and led to breakdown. Others claimed that the hysterical manifestations were based on suggestion – the patient did what the doctors expected of them. The idea then was to prove to a patient that there was nothing physically wrong, that it was all in their minds, and use suggestion to remove symptoms, such as repeatedly saying that a 'miracle doctor' was coming to cure them before dressing up an orderly in a white coat and having him lay his hands on the patient. Another method was to tell the men that an operation would cure them before they were given a small dose of ether to render them momentarily unconscious. When they came to, the symptoms were often gone. These methods certainly produced some dramatic cures, but were not so successful in the long-term. Many patients promptly broke down again or suffered a relapse as soon as they returned to the front and heard gunfire.

Siegfried Sassoon was among those who was diagnosed unfit for duty, although many believed the diagnosis in his case to be politically based. His heroism in the trenches, for which he received the Military Cross, led him to a heartfelt hatred of war, which he wrote about fulsomely, in an open letter resoundingly denouncing the war and in other missives from the front: 'Shell shock: a delayed effect of horrible memory you can't forget. How many a brief bombardment had its long-delayed after-effect in the minds of these survivors, many of whom had looked at their companions and laughed while inferno did its best to destroy them. Not then was their evil hour, but now; now in the sweating suffocation of the nightmare, in paralysis of limbs, in the stammering of dislocated speech.'

Fearing the effect of such anti-war sentiments from an officer who was clearly still in full possession of his faculties, the Army diagnosed him as suffering from shell shock and sent him back to Britain. The popularity of his published works did nothing to endear him to the hard-pressed War Office at a time when the combined effects of the death toll and those injured or sent home had led to an acute manpower shortage. The British Expeditionary Forces had lost 21,747 officers and 490,673 other ranks by the end of 1915. An untold number had been sent home. The crisis called for urgent measures, so the Army set up a system designed to process the men as quickly as possible before sending them back to what Sassoon called 'the sausage machine'.

Until now, most recognized shell shock cases had been repatriated to Britain, from where it took several weeks, if not months, to return. That was all to change. The first stop for cases stretchered from the front remained a regimental aid post, where they were examined by a battalion medical officer. Under plans put forward by Charles Myers and his colleagues, the men were sent from there to a casualty clearing station for classification and emergency attention, before being sent to a base hospital, a few miles back from the front if it was deemed necessary.

Admitted to the peace of a ward for monitoring, the patients' neuroses would worsen. One soldier was reputed in an MO report to 'curl up under the bedclothes and from time to time look out as though peering over the parapet of a trench, stare wildly around him and hide under the clothes again'. Another, whose fellow soldiers reported that his brother had been killed standing beside him in a trench, used to sit up and shout, 'He's gone! He's gone!'

The idea of the base hospitals and clearing stations was that the cases could be categorized quickly into mild or serious. Many men were simply exhausted, others were deeply traumatized. Making these distinctions was a major breakthrough. Despite initial Army resistance at being encumbered with what it considered lunatic cases in military areas, the new system meant that mild cases could be rested then returned to their posts, without being sent home. This was similar to the system the French and Germans had been operating for the previous year and the British now followed their example. It was a method for which Myers claimed a 31 per cent success rate at the casualty clearing station he established at St Omer, the general headquarters of the British Armies in France.

He also set up a base in Boulogne for patients to be screened for sending back to Britain. They were kept in the attic of a general hospital, which was itself a converted hotel. Here the monumental task facing him became clear. His base effectively became a dumping ground for any soldiers who were problematic, from lunatics to bedwetters to thieves. As in previous wars, there had been little screening of recruits and conscripts, so those who signed up represented a cross-section of the community, including the genuinely insane and people of very low intelligence. These latter were the first to break down. The Army didn't want to have to shoot them all as deserters so it sent all the insane, imbecilic, epileptic and criminal patients awaiting evaluation to Myers, so that he could class them as 'mental' and ship them back to Britain. This practice severely hampered his endeavours.

Myers wrote in his diaries: 'It was obvious that much harm was being done to the shell shocked by being segregated in the same ward as the demented, maniacal or suicidal. Naturally, they feared they too were destined for a lunatic asylum. It seemed to me undesirable that innocent men who had mentally broken down under strain of warfare should be closely associated with those accused of murder, attempted suicide [then a criminal offence], theft or desertion.' For the first time since war had broken out, he realized, the doctors recruited into the RAMC were being used by the military to rubber stamp disciplinary decisions, a grim task for them, although not altogether surprising bearing in mind that they were constantly being reminded not to forget the 'A' in RAMC.

Lieutenant Colonel Palmer explained: 'The dilemma for the medical officer, and for every MO subsequently, was and is should they evacuate someone out of the line who does not have a physical problem? Because for every one you take out of the line, that's one less person to fight. This was a major problem at a time of national crisis. It was like not having enough bullets. Warfare is a group endeavour and anything which detracts from the group's ability to achieve its goal or aim needed to be looked at. The group's health needed to be maintained. As much as you need bullets, guns, uniforms and food, you need men. If you don't have men you can't fight and this had never happened before. It had been learned from previous wars that disease and injuries could certainly cut the manpower down, but now they had to accept that the psychological response to warfare could do the same, and they had to do what they could to stop it. Doctors became the moral arbiters of fitness to fight, and the pressure on them must have been quite difficult.'

Myers's daughter said: 'The medical profession didn't understand the meaning of shell shock, that it was a result of psychological problems. My father had arguments with the adjutant general and the head of medical services out there. He felt that part of the problem was that these men were not suitable to be fighting men, but had been selected because of the rush to enlist.' Myers was almost certainly right, but there was another, much more frightening, aspect of the influx of shell shock cases yet to be faced. His problems and those of his fellow doctors were only just beginning.

Chapter Two

I could not look on Death, which being known
Men led me to him, blindfold and alone.
'The Coward' Rudyard Kipling

Shell shock, although officially recognized as a medical condition by the War Office, had always been confused with either cowardice or real madness, and in some quarters always would be. Ignorant of the true horrors of the trenches, British official and public opinion held that any soldier who gave up the fight or otherwise behaved in an unmilitary manner was a coward and a disgrace. In the minds of the top brass, men were either wounded or well; there was no middle ground. Crucially, shell shock was not admissible as a plea in a court-martial for crimes of cowardice or desertion – for which the ultimate penalty was death.

As Myers wryly remarked in his diaries: 'From the military standpoint a deserter was either insane and destined for the madhouse or responsible and should be shot.' Either way, it was felt, the man was probably better off dead. While deeply sympathetic to the plight of men who were genuinely ill awaiting court-martial for cowardice, Myers was also astute enough to realize that the term he had invented then spurned had quickly become the perfect excuse for the small percentage of malingerers who were simply fed up with war and wanted to go home. He reported that in certain units it had 'become fashionable, if not catching' to have shell shock. His MOs accused many soldiers of 'funk' and said there were a great many 'dirty sneaks' abusing the system. Recognition of this opened up a military nightmare. 'Extremists in one direction argue that such symptoms are so closely akin to malingering that they demand the adoption of the strictest disciplinary measures,' Myers wrote. 'Extremists in the other direction would subject them to a prolonged course of psychoanalysis, or would tend to indiscriminately pamper them. The truth, of course, lies within these extreme attitudes. Each case must be treated on its own merits.'

Some servicemen undoubtedly pretended to be shell shocked or exaggerated their symptoms when caught going AWOL (absent without leave), but whether there was any genuine neurosis underlying their actions in the first place was almost impossible to gauge. Faced with the inescapable fact that, as the war dragged on and the death toll broke all expectations, the statistical probability against them surviving the next battle was gaining by the hour, desperation set in. Soldiers pretending to be ill might truly have been on the verge of mental illness, a symptom of which was their uncharacteristic attempt at pretence. Others, petrified at the realization that they were likely to be killed, may have been trying it on to see how far they could get. After all, what did they have to lose? An anonymous contributor to an in-house magazine at one British military hospital summed it all up when he penned the two-line poem:

> Shall I mutter and stutter and wangle my ticket,
> Or try another flutter and go back and stick it?

There were risks involved, whichever diagnosis the doctors chose. One soldier accused of desertion was hypnotized and declared mentally well, a state of mind for which he was later shot. Others, who laid the symptoms on too thick, risked being sent to one of the secure units of a lunatic asylum, from which there might be no escape. It was a stark choice – a chance of life in the trenches or a brutal regime of cold baths and padded cells.

A personal account written by J. W. Rowarth, a member of one of the Irish regiments who had seen several months of active service, gives a telling insight into the mind of the malingerer. 'I started to scheme, how the hell can I work my ticket and get out of this bloody war,' he wrote. 'I had heard from a bloke that patriotism was the refuge of a coward. If that is right, I admit I am a coward, a bloody bleeding coward and I want to be a live coward rather than a dead blasted hero.' After running away and then lying down in a ditch, as if wounded, Rowarth was taken to hospital and questioned closely by the neurologists. 'My thoughts now were on whether I could fool the doctors,' he wrote. 'To every question they asked, I replied, "I don't remember." The doctor said, "We cannot keep him here, he requires special treatment," saying something like "amnesia, shell shock". He wrote on my card "Evacuate".'

Richard Trafford, the veteran who was only fifteen when he first saw service in the trenches, believed it was easy to tell the genuinely afflicted from those who were feigning illness. 'The ones that became shell-shocked were mentally disarranged, they weren't with you half the time, they were in a world of their own, it was like seeing a person in a fit,' he said. 'I don't believe there was any of our men cowards. It's surprising what you'll do when you get shell-shocked, they weren't responsible for their actions. A man doesn't join the Army to fight for his country and then run away.'

One fellow soldier in particular, he remembered, suddenly ran from the trenches shouting, 'The Germans are here, the Germans are here!' and disappeared. The rest of his unit assumed he had been shot. 'We heard nothing else about this fellow, until I was on home leave and I saw him coming across the road in post office uniform, all smiles. I said, "How the hell did you manage to get back home?" and he told me all about it, said he was put on a train back home and when he got to England, they discharged him and said he wasn't fit to go back to the regiment, he was shell-shocked.'

Some offices had little sympathy for those affected, especially once it became apparent that a number were play-acting. Alastair Crerar, a second lieutenant in the Royal Scots Fusiliers, who survived three days wounded in no man's land before crawling back to British lines, wrote to his mother from hospital: 'We get entertainment in the ward from a shell-shock case who raves away at his men to "Dig, dig" to and calls his servant "six feet of misery". I don't know how many of his men he's threatened to shoot but I think them all; I think he did shoot his sergeant.'

The difficulty for the doctors and senior officers was that shell shock was so arbitrary. Some men seemed more susceptible than others, and it simply couldn't be predicted who would crack, why or when. Much seemed to depend on the individual and how much service a shell-shock victim had seen. One man, who lost all his brothers and was four times buried alive by shells, only broke down on the final occasion. Another gallant infantry officer, who had seen his brigade of over three thousand men wiped out twice, leaving him as the only surviving senior officer, ran away and 'cried for a week' when his quartermaster brought up all the horses and it dawned on him for the first time that there were no officers left to ride them. Others cracked up as soon as they reached the front – or even before they got there.

Many of the regimental medical officers reflected the sceptical opinions of the top brass and seemed to pride themselves on not recognizing battle neurosis. There were rare instances of medical officers who wrote 'fatigue' on a man's records, out of sympathy for the stigma he could face at being classified shell-shocked, but the majority had no such scruples. For the most inflexible in the military, a deserter was either mad or bad.

Harold Hills, a neurologist to the Fourth Army, was one of the many doctors appointed to sit in on court-martial cases and offer his opinion of the men charged with cowardice or desertion. He wrote:

> I had about eighty so-called 'shell-shock' cases, and they certainly were a mixed lot. Their only common factor was the absence of physical signs that would explain their physical peculiarities. Any signs of organic trouble, I passed to the physician. Neurologist was a curious term: in those days, mental symptoms were regarded as shameful so the term was given to make it acceptable to the troops. My work was interesting, but all the time at the back of my mind was the thought of the court-martials.

Dr Hills's first encounter with such a life-and-death decision was easily avoided. He classified the soldier in question as a 'chronic alcoholic, not responsible for his actions', and the court ordered him to be sent to a hospital. He soon learned the ways of the judicial process. 'If I called a man a "paranoiac" or "schizophrenic" I was not questioned – anyone with such horribly named diseases ought to be in hospital. I found it hard to get across to the board the idea that a grown man could have the mind of a child and – childlike – could not hold out. The court always gave prisoners the benefit of the doubt and many of them got off, not because of my arguments but because I was the Doubt.'

Dr Hills himself began to suffer from war neurosis and developed a dread of bombing, which caused much amusement at staff headquarters. His superiors began to question his judgements and suggested that he was sending too many patients to the base hospital. Stung by the criticism, he ordered a return to the front for one soldier, who promptly turned his gun on him and threatened his life before doing as he was told.

Charles Myers was also called upon to attend court-martials and offer his expert opinion, which his daughter Joan Rumens said he found difficult. 'My father found it very distressing, when he had to attend those committee decisions as to whether a man was a deserter and had to be shot or not. That affected him very deeply because he realized the reasons behind some of these disastrous cases were psychological.'

As the war lumbered on into another year, there appeared to be no end in sight for those at the brunt end of conflict. Battle after battle added to the store of horrific memories piling up on both sides. Between April and May 1915, at the second battle of Ypres, the grim conditions surpassed all previous experience. A German officer described the scene: 'The whole countryside is yellow,' he wrote. 'The battlefield is fearful. A curious sour, heavy, penetrating smell of dead bodies strikes one. Bodies of cows and pigs lie, half decayed; splintered trees, the stumps of avenues; shell crater after shell crater on the roads and in the fields.'

Chlorine gas was used for the first time at Ypres with devastating results. The Germans opened five thousand cylinders releasing 168 tons of the greenish yellow gas, killing five thousand Allied troops who had little or no protection against it. Men died choking on the green-yellow clouds as their colleagues looked on helplessly. The Allies had been warned, by prisoners-of-war, of the presence of gas cylinders in the German trenches, and yet were taken by surprise.

Like all new weapons, from the crossbow to the atomic bomb, it was passionately denounced as vile and inhumane, but within five months the Allies retaliated with their own poison gases, eventually coming up with three different types – chlorine, phosgene and mustard gas – each offering a different way in which to drown the victim in his own lungs, blind him or do both, with the additional effect of burning and blistering his skin. Gas masks did not become standard issue until 1916 and British soldiers had to rely on dampened handkerchiefs or a prevailing wind to save them. If the wind suddenly shifted direction, the soldiers were accidentally gassed by their own side, so they had to be on constant guard.

Not surprisingly, the threat of a gas attack, drummed home by regular drills, pushed even the most stoic to the brink. One study found that only 40 per cent of those who said they had been gassed actually had. The rest suffered from 'anxiety neurosis due to fear of gas'. Wilfred Owen, one of the best-loved of the war poets, vividly describes a gas attack and its aftermath in 'Dulce et Decorum Est':

Gas! Gas! Quick boys! – An ecstasy of fumbling,
Fitting the clumsy helmets just in time;
But someone still was yelling out and stumbling,
And flound'ring like a man in fire or lime.
Dim, through the misty panes and thick green light,
As under a green sea, I saw him drowning.
In all my dreams, before my helpless sight,
He plunges at me, guttering, choking, drowning.

The German troops were equally affected by shell shock and the fear of gas, if not more so, but the German High Command regarded shell shock as a violation of military discipline and an indication of weak will-power. Faced with such a label, there were numerous suicides among those affected, who would rather die honourably than be accused of a lack of patriotism. However, there was sympathy from some quarters. In his work *Hysteria and War Service*, published in 1915, the German neurologist Professor Gaup went a long way towards persuading the authorities that the affected men were not malingering. He wrote:

> There is no justification for calling every instance of this a case of malingering or simulation. These are quite capable men of irreproachable character whose nervous system is positively unfitted for the hardships and horrors of war. They have enthusiasm and the best of intentions but these cease to inspire them when the horrors and terrors come. Their inner strength rapidly decreases and it only requires an acute storm to break upon the nervous system for their self-control to vanish completely. The exhausted mind then feels that it is no longer master of the situation and therefore takes refuge in disease.

At a Berlin conference on the subject, doctors argued against sending men home, claiming it was detrimental to their recovery and that they should be kept near the front. Sigmund Freud, giving evidence to the Austrian war ministry, outlined the basic moral-ethical dilemma facing the soldier.

> Psychoanalysis . . . has taught . . . that peacetime neuroses can be traced back to disturbances in a person's emotional life. The same explanation has now been generally applied to those suffering from war neuroses . . . the immediate cause of all war neuroses was a soldier's unconscious inclination to remove himself from the aspects of military service that are dangerous or offensive to his feelings. Fear for his own life, resistance to the command to kill others, revolt against the total suppression of one's personality by superiors were the most important emotional sources that nourished the inclination to shun war. A healthy soldier in whom these emotional motives were to become powerfully and clearly conscious would either desert or report himself sick. But only a small fraction of war neurotics were actually simulators: the emotional impulse against military service that arose in them and drove them to be sick operated in them without their being conscious of it.

Dr Fritz Kauffman, a psychiatrist at the German psychiatric hospital at Ludwigshafen, devised his 'surprise-attack method' for curing shell shock in one session. Using high-dosage electric shocks for several minutes at a time on limbs affected by hysterical paralysis – treatment that even his colleagues regarded as inhuman – Kauffman conducted his experiments in an atmosphere of strict military discipline, with orders barked at the patients.

During each treatment he advised his patients to recover quickly. Faced with such a painful alternative, progress was almost instantaneous. His treatment became popular throughout Germany, despite the occasional death from an accidental overdose of electrical current. Kauffman admitted that his methods were harsh and merciless, but claimed that the matter was cut and dried: 'The powerful impression of pain,' he wrote, 'suppresses all negative mental desires.' In essence, his patients would be cured, whether they liked it or not.

During the summer of 1915, with the advent of warmer weather and a lull in the proceedings, the opposing armies remained relatively static, although with the endless shelling, patrolling and sniping, the British still sustained casualties at a rate of about three hundred a day. The gaps were quickly filled with raw recruits, men who had previously not qualified for enlistment and who had been cajoled into leaving their comfortable civilian lives. Some were under eighteen or over forty, medically borderline or previously considered too mentally unstable to cope with the stresses of war.

With so many lives lost already and the prospect of even more men going off to battle, there was still considerable public concern about the fate of those who might come back shell-shocked. Against all previous experience, the military authorities were forced to continue to seek the advice and help of civilian therapists and to consider their ideas about what should be done. The pressure was on to find some answers, but the doctors still couldn't make up their minds. In May 1915, the *Lancet* described shell shock as 'a matter of serious difficulty and considerable importance'; three months later, in an article entitled 'Nervous Manifestations Due to the Wind of High Explosives', it blamed violent explosions.

The Mental Treatment Bill, put before Parliament in May 1915 by Cecil Harmsworth, under-secretary for home affairs, was designed to alleviate some of the pressure on the military hospitals and 'to facilitate the early treatment of mental disorder of recent origin arising from wounds, shock and other causes'. To speed up the processing of the influx of shell-shock cases, the Bill advocated the removal of the need for certification of mental breakdown. 'This Bill will enable a man who, in the service of his country, has suffered a nervous breakdown, to accept the treatment without being certified, but only for a period not exceeding six months and under conditions which should provide security against misuse,' the *Lancet* reported.

In September of the same year, in response to questions in the House of Commons, the under-secretary for war made a public statement. All military mental and nervous cases, he said, were being sent to twenty-three military hospitals in the UK, plus Springfield House in Tooting, south west London, the newly requisitioned Red Cross Hospital at Maghull near Liverpool and the

Napsbury War Hospital for the most severe cases who needed an asylum setting. Until then, all such cases had remained in military care while being treated but rumours abounded that some were to be discharged as unfit and transferred to the care of the Lunacy Commission.

The under-secretary admitted that 'The subject of the disposal of the more serious mental cases has been receiving consideration and has caused the authorities considerable anxiety.' In view of the growing numbers of incurable cases, he declared, it would be impossible to continue with the present situation indefinitely. He announced that from then on any shell-shocked soldiers with 'general paralysis, chronic epilepsy or chronic insanity' would be dealt with in accordance with the King's Regulations relating to the removal of a 'lunatic soldier' – effectively kicking them out of the armed forces and into the care of their families, the community or the local asylum.

Meanwhile, those in command of the men at the front were continuing to provide near perfect conditions for shell shock. They had decided to mount a counter-attack against the Germans for Ypres, aided by what became known as 'the accessory' – chlorine gas. The disastrous battle of Loos, which began a few days later, became renowned as one of the most grossly foolish attacks by totally inexperienced troops. The chlorine gas released by the British either dissipated harmlessly before it got to the German lines or was blown back on to the first wave of Allied troops, knocking them out of the battle. There were immense losses: between September and November, more than 95,000 casualties for the capture of a few thousand yards of land. Even the official history books damned it as 'a useless slaughter of infantry'.

General Sir Douglas Haig was brought in to replace Sir John French as commander-in-chief, but any hopes for a softer line were soon dashed. Haig announced that the only way to wage the war was to kill Germans 'in a war of attrition'. He urged his commanders: 'Gather together every man and gun and wear down the enemy by constant and if possible by ceaseless attacks.' And so the war of attrition continued: the Big Push, Haig called it. It became known by the troops as the Big Fuck-up.

The British Expeditionary Forces now numbered 987,200 – more than ever before – and with many more being trained at home. But still it wasn't enough, and the manpower problem was becoming acute. In January 1916 voluntary enlistment ended and conscription began, raking in hundreds of thousands of untrained recruits, young men who would be still more vulnerable to war trauma. The need for troops was so severe that the height requirement was dropped to five foot three inches. The cycle of death and distress continued unabated.

As public and medical opinion in Britain began to solidify against the practice of treating shell-shocked soldiers as either lunatics or malingerers, the Army Council issued a directive that shell-shock cases due to enemy action should have 'W', for Wounded, stamped on their reports, and that they were now entitled to wear a special wound stripe on their tunics. The letter S was affixed to all uncertain cases, and NYDN for Not Yet Diagnosed (Nervous) for those falling into neither category.

The theories of what caused shell shock continued. Major Frederick Mott, who was considered an expert on the subject of neurological disorders, gave a lecture in London on the effects of explosives, in which he argued that even a good, sound soldier could find his nerves shattered after prolonged combat exposure. The evidence seemed to back his hypothesis. Between the outbreak of war and April 1916, a total of 11,300 men – comprising 1,300 officers and 10,000 other ranks – had been admitted into UK hospitals for shell shock. Countless others remained in clearing stations or at the front, unable to escape their living hell. And the worst was yet to come.

The Germans attacked Verdun in February 1916, raining 100,000 shells an hour down on the war-weary French before fierce fighting left nearly a million men dead and the area pounded to dust. Augustus Couchin, one French captain who was later killed, wrote of the battle: 'I came here with one hundred and seventy five men; I leave with thirty four, several of them half mad.'

As a counter-measure General Haig launched a massive attack along a fifteen-mile front on the Somme river on 1 July 1916. At what was to become known as the battle of the Somme, thousands of men from Kitchener's New Army were sent to the front. Their commanders hoped that what they lacked in experience, they made up for in fighting spirit. Because they had no training, they were ordered to make their initial assault in straight lines, rather than perform complicated manoeuvres. Soldiers carrying seventy-pound packs of ammunition, rations and digging equipment, were ordered to walk the five to eight hundred yards of no man's land and take the German trenches. A week-long Allied bombardment used 1,537 guns firing a million and a half shells to destroy the enemy trenches and cut the ubiquitous barbed wire. But an estimated third of all the shells fired were dud, and most were of far too small calibre to achieve their aim. The German defences remained remarkably intact and their subsequent use of machine-guns, mortar bombs and shells easily mowed down the British 'Tommies' when they emerged from the trenches to go over the top.

There were 54,470 casualties on the first day, including 19,000 dead – the biggest losses ever sustained by an army in one day. It was arguably the most ghastly few hours in the history of warfare: men shredded by machine-gun fire, dying agonizing deaths racked on the barbed wire; blown to pieces by shells or driven over by their own tanks – used for the first time by the British, but plagued with mechanical and manoeuvrability difficulties. By the time the battle finished five months later, there were 415,000 British casualties, 195,000 French and around 600,000 Germans were dead.

Not surprisingly, the bloodletting brought an orgy of breakdowns, particularly among the new recruits who had seen huge swathes cut through their 'Pals Regiments', wiping out the men they had known or worked with all their lives. With an estimated thirty thousand cases of shell shock now recorded, it was becoming increasingly difficult for the military to maintain that the condition was either lunacy or cowardice. The statistics presented a serious crisis. Individual stories told of broken men, the spirit sucked out of them.

Captain L. Gameson, one front-line MO, reported an incident following a shelling raid in which one man died and his best friend, although physically unharmed, went to pieces. Asked to examine him in his battery, the doctor wrote:

> The scene is still most vivid to me: the deep, German dugout, the usual passage running from end to end, the usual tiers of bunks. The place was dimly lit by a few candles. My patient was sitting up in his cramped bunk, leaning forward, gripping hard to an upright with both hands. In most bunks were men who stirred as they slept. Some woke, but did not complain of the boy's shouting. I spent the better part of the night with him but completely failed to comfort him. Finally, I gave him an injection of morphine and waited until this rather handsome, undoubtedly intelligent child, had dropped into a restful sleep.

In another much more serious incident, several members of the 11th Border Regiment 97th Infantry Brigade 32nd Division, which had suffered terrible losses, were affected. All their officers and half their men had been killed in a single week, five hundred souls in all. Of the remaining two hundred and fifty survivors, a hundred were then ordered to take two hundred yards of the enemy's front trench under continual heavy shelling. As many as two dozen men refused, claiming they were shell-shocked, sick with nerves and couldn't go over the top. It was the Army's worst nightmare: mass hysteria leading a whole group of men to insubordination. It flew in the face of the concepts such as honour and unquestioning obedience that had been instilled in them for generations. The men were told to pull themselves together and get some rest.

Faced with their continued resistance, the captain in charge sent for the doctor to examine them and say whether he thought the men were in a fit state to fight. Lieutenant George Kirkwood, the medical officer, pronounced them unfit at 11.45 p.m. He wrote in his report, later to form part of an RAMC Court of Enquiry Report:

> I gave my opinion that they were unfit based on the following: the attack on 1 July when the battalion lost all its officers and more than half its men had a most demoralizing effect and the men had not recovered their mental equilibrium. The few days' rest sorting deceased comrades' kit did not improve their mental state. Carrying up rations under heavy and incessant shell fire, digging out the dead in the trenches and carrying them down as well as living in an atmosphere of decomposed bodies, exposure in open trenches under continual fire and without sleep.
>
> Twenty men that day had been sent to the Advanced Dressing Station suffering from shell shock. In view of the bombing attack to be carried out by 11th Border Regiment, I must hereby testify to their unfitness for such an operation as few, if any, are not suffering from some small degree of shell shock.

Lieutenant Kirkwood signed a certificate agreeing to their unfitness for battle, but the acting brigadier-general, J. B. Jardine, ignored it. He said later that he did not 'attach much importance to the MO's ideas' and blamed the insubordination on 'not physical disability but mental – caused by the failure of the NCOs to preserve the right spirit, to encourage the men and set a good example in the absence of officers'.

On his orders, a lieutenant was deputized to lead the attack, but he reported a 'great lack of offensive spirit' with men making slow progress, lagging behind and losing their way. Barely half-way to the attack point, and several hours late, the officer was forced to abandon the raid and turn back.

A court of enquiry was set up into the incident under Major General W. H. Rycroft, commander 32nd Division. In his concluding report, Rycroft lamented that the NCOs had 'tarnished the reputation' of the battalion. He added:

> Sympathy for sick men under his treatment is a good attribute for an doctor. But it is not for an MO to inform his CO that the men are not in a fit state to carry out military operations. The men being in the front line should be proof that they are fit for any duty called for. Evidently the MO, who has been with the battalion during the winter, showed undue sympathy with the men on the occasion. The MO was to blame and he has been relieved.

Lieutenant Kirkwood was later recommended to be dismissed from the Army.

A memo on the incident, from Major General Sir H. de la Gough KCB to the corps commander, commented: 'The facts disclose a deplorable state of discipline and an entire absence of courage and of any soldierly qualities amongst the non-commissioned officers (NCOs) and men of the battalion. The conduct on the part of Lt Kirkwood shows him to be totally unfit to hold a commission in the Army or to exercise any military responsibility.' He ordered that the men be assembled in the presence of the remainder of the brigade and publicly castigated for bringing disgrace on the battalion, adding: 'It is inconceivable how men who pledged themselves to fight and uphold the honour of the country could degrade themselves in such a manner and show an utter want of manly spirit and courage which at least is expected of every soldier and every Britisher.'

Elsewhere, a similarly Victorian attitude prevailed in the belief that such a huge citizen force would crack unless strict discipline was imposed. The CO of the 1/5th Royal Warwick Regiment reported to his brigadier that he had about a hundred 'utterly useless wasters' in his battalion, who were 'petrified with fear' at the sight of the Germans. He said they were of miserable physique, lacked intelligence and had a 'hang-dog, vacant look'. His brigadier agreed. He described the men as: 'degenerates, a source of danger to their comrades, their battalion and the brigade'. He ordered that they be dispatched to labouring duties at home ports.

Much to the consternation of the hierarchy, officers too were increasingly reporting unfit for duty, with no physical injury. The problem became so acute that the High Command issued a general order under the heading 'Officers – Fitness for Duty', which required all officers to justify their alleged ill-health. It read:

> *Instances have recently come to notice where an officer without definite manifestation of a physical disability or injury has asserted his inability to perform military duty on the ground that he is the subject of defects in health or temperament. In future, where the assessment of an officer's fitness for duty or disposal depends wholly or in part on his own statement, the officer will be required to sign a written statement clearly setting forth the history and present particulars of the condition which brings his capacity, physically or temperamentally, into question.*

Charles Moran, who eventually became Winston Churchill's personal physician, served with the First Battalion of the Royal Fusiliers. The first case of shell-shock he saw was a trembling sergeant who had lost the ability to speak. Moran commented in his notes: 'It was plain to me the game was up and he was done. When this sort of thing happens to a good fellow it is final.' Much later, when he had seen his fill of shell shock cases and came across one of his junior officers cowering, head in hands in a trench, he had hardened his opinion, describing him as 'a worthless chap', Moran came to believe that you could divide men neatly into three categories: the brave, those who disliked the war but did their duty, and cowards. He sneered that the latter were 'misshapen creatures from the towns'.

Several years after the war, his attitude softened again and he wrote movingly of the conditions British servicemen faced, in his book *The Anatomy of Courage*.

> *There were men in France who were prepared for [death] if it came swiftly and decently. But that shattering, crude, bloody end by a big shell was too much for them. It was something more than death, all their plans for meeting it with decency and credit were suddenly battered down; it was not so much that their lives were in danger as that their self-respect had gone out of their hands. They were at the crisis of their lives, dishevelled, plastered with mud and blood, their actions at the mercy of others. They were no longer certain of what they might do.'*

Shell shock was a great leveller. All ranks were exposed to the extreme conditions that brought it on, and both officers and men capitulated under the strain. Not only junior officers broke down. On the first day of a battle, one sergeant found his brigadier slumped in a chair staring at a hanging lamp like a man in a dream. 'He was broken. He made no objection to coming with me. He just got up very slowly and, during a break in the shelling, we went out.'

Captain Leland, still writing home to his wife almost daily but obviously unwell, eventually succumbed to the mental pressure in spring 1917 when he was invalided home with shell shock. Just prior to his collapse, he wrote, after one battle:

I feel a bit depressed over the day's happenings, so many good fellows gone, but it is a war and we must go on smiling to the end. When will it end? A tremendous strafing has been going on, and I suppose it is going to be a question of get out or go under, and very soon too. I should love to get some leave, but I don't like to ask. It was suggested to me by the GSO the other day, but in such a way that if I had risen to it I should have felt that I was shirking, for I know what a lot there is on hand just at present.

In March, he wrote of coming across a clump of snowdrops in the midst of the desolation of a recent battle. He and a fellow soldier fell to their knees and wept at the sight, before discovering five dead British soldiers nearby, one still clutching his Bible in his hand. Captain Leland wrote:

For the first time in my life I think I am suffering the torments of hell with neuralgia. I have had it for three nights and days now and sometimes I don't know what I'm doing or saying. I hinted the question of leave this morning, but was advised to wait. I think I will take the first opportunity and ask right out. I don't want to appear as if I wanted to shirk my work. If this neuralgia would quit I should feel as right as rain. I sleep in spasms and have some hideous dreams.

In April, he was stretchered to a base hospital for rest.

I had been feeling seedy for some time, but stuck it out as long as I could, not wanting to go sick, but after five nights of absolute sleeplessness I had to give in as I found that I could not carry on my work to my own satisfaction, so I went to see the Medical Officer who told me I had foolishly left the thing too long, and promptly ordered me into hospital and away from the sounds and medley of war. I went the same night. I think I must have had a collapse or something, for I do not remember much of the journey. I remember when I arrived they gave me a draught and some hot milk and I slept for the first time, waking in the morning. Oh, so wonderfully better, and ate a hearty breakfast. The rest has done me a world of good. Evidently I was in need of it.

Returned, without respite, to the front lines and appalling conditions he started to suffer again with his nerves and wrote to his wife of 'this Land of Hell'. In October 1917, he told her: 'I am afraid that I have been out here long enough. I am not so young as I was. I try to do as these "children" do, but I shall have to give it up. I am terrified that my nerve will go – I don't really mean this – but the strain is intense at times. I am so horribly war worn.'

His letters became shorter and shorter, monosyllabic almost, and spoke of his head 'bursting', his double vision and his total exhaustion. A bitter tone entered the letters for the first time:

Death and Glory I suppose they call it. All my friends gone, not a soul to go to even for a chat. I have lost all I knew and have become absolutely callous. All I want now is to return home. I feel too rotten for words. I wish my head did not ache so much, and that I had less of a quiver on. I think I have run my length, but shall stick it as long as I can.

SHELL SHOCK

Captain Leland's grandson said: 'You can see from his letters that he was crying out to be given a rest, given a break. Had he been, he probably would have been able to continue indefinitely, but without that break you see it getting worse and worse, getting through to him.

'There was one occasion when they'd been heavily shelled and a number of the shells had got into the stables and decimated a large number of the horses. Most of their horses were either killed or wounded and he said it was terrible and really affected him. He got used to his best friend being blown up alongside him and losing so many men and seeing the wounded coming back. But those helpless horses, putting their trust in humans, looking up to him for help and all he could do was put a bullet through their heads. He found this really very difficult. It was something he could express in the letters whereas the carnage amongst the humans was something he had to repress or he'd go mad. He denies it more and more in his letters but obviously the stress just built up too much and eventually he had a full breakdown.'

Struck by the symptoms of complete physical exhaustion, Captain Leland was eventually sent to the officers' hospital for a rest. After a good night's sleep, he asked to be returned to the front, but was refused, despite expressing his theory that he was only suffering from 'delayed action shock', coupled with a chill.

On 28 November he wrote:

> I have had quite enough rest and am quite fit. The doctors insist on giving me complete rest away from the sound of the guns and I am to go home, for at least a month. One of those blooming specialists who haunt these hospitals, together with the ordinary MO, came to me at 11am and overhauled me, asking me all sorts of questions. 'Had I had a recent shock? How did I sleep?' etc, etc. Then the great man said: 'Undoubtedly you have been going through a very trying time and there is only one thing for it – rest and no worry.' I assured him that I never felt fitter in my life, but it was no use. I was then informed that I had no reason to imagine that there was anything seriously wrong, and that after the rest I should be able to return to France, strengthened in mind and body, and able to tackle the Winter campaign.

Ashamed of himself, Captain Leland added:

> Don't worry. It is not my fault. I have fought against it for a long time, and my doctor was kind enough to say that if I had given in a bit sooner it would have been better for me. I am so sorry that this has happened, for your sake. But I stuck it as long as I could.

His final letter was accompanied by one from a major at the Special Hospital for Officers, Palace Green, Kensington, which told Mrs Leland her husband had been admitted for treatment for 'stress of overwork'. He added: 'For a few days there was slight mental confusion and profound exhaustion. He is now doing quite well with us, resting quietly and mentally quite himself. We are in no way anxious about him and feel that he will improve steadily, but he is certain to require some weeks' further hospital treatment.'

The battles raged on with horrors anew. Thousands died horrible deaths as thousands more looked on. The stresses and strains of war continued to take their toll. At the towering white stone memorial at Thiepval on the Somme in France, the name of Private Harry Farr, a twenty-six-year-old Londoner serving with the 1st Battalion West Yorkshire Regiment, is among hundreds of others.

'I always thought my father had been killed in action, shot by the Germans, until one day when I was in my forties a relative let something slip,' said Gertrude Harris, Farr's daughter. 'Then the real story came out and I was terribly upset. He hadn't been shot by the Germans at all, he'd been shot by his own people. The first my mother knew that anything was wrong was when she had a letter from my father saying he was in hospital with shell shock. It was written by the nurse because his hands were shaking too much to hold a pen.'

After five months' treatment for shell shock in hospital in Boulogne, Farr – who had previously had an exemplary military record – was returned to his regiment and the front line. Six months later, at the battle of the Somme, Farr felt his nerves give way again and he was hospitalized once more for two weeks. Three months on, he reported sick for a third time. In September, when asked to go with a ration party up to the front lines, Private Farr refused, claiming that he was simply unable to face the gunfire. 'I cannot stand it,' he repeated to his senior officer. 'I cannot go.' He tried to report himself to the dressing station but they wouldn't take him because he was not wounded. When ordered to be taken to the trenches under escort, he screamed and struggled and refused to go. This time the soldier who had first enlisted in 1908 – not during the rush to arms of 1914 – found himself under arrest and facing a court-martial for cowardice.

The trial was held in the town of Ville-sur-Ancre on 2 October 1915. Farr and his fellow 'cowards' shared the cellar of a local guesthouse before appearing in front of a panel of senior military men. In his evidence, Farr told the court: 'I reported to the sergeant major and told him I was sick and could not stand it. He then said: "You are a fucking coward and you will go to the trenches. I give fuck all for my life and I give fuck all for guns and I'll get you fucking well shot." The Sergeant Major then grabbed my rifle and said: "I'll blow your fucking brains out if you don't go." '

A second witness, Lieutenant L. P. Marshall, told the court: 'I have known the accused for the last six weeks. On working parties he has three times asked for leave to fall out and return to camp as he could not stand the noise of the artillery. He was trembling and did not appear in a fit state.'

Farr's commanding officer, Captain A. Wilson, told the court: 'I cannot say what has destroyed this man's nerves, but he has proved himself on many occasions incapable of keeping his head in action and likely to cause a panic. Apart from his behaviour under fire, his conduct and character are very good.'

W. Williams, MO, said in a written statement, 'I examined No. 8871 Pte Farr. His general physical and mental condition were good.' Williams then crossed out the word 'good' and replaced it with 'satisfactory'. The MO who examined Farr during his first bout of shell shock was unable to give evidence personally on his behalf because he was wounded, and Farr was expected to conduct his own defence.

Janet Booth, Farr's granddaughter, who has read the trial transcripts, said her grandfather was court-martialled because he refused to fight that day, not because he refused to fight the war. 'He'd been out in France two years and just couldn't face the gunfire, he felt so traumatized by it all, but he said himself in his own defence that when he was away from the gunfire he felt all right.'

Like so many court-martials at the time, the trial of Private Harry Farr lasted just twenty minutes. A man of limited education, suffering from acute stress, he was pitted against the wits of Oxbridge-educated senior officers, who had probably already decided his fate. 'It must have been a terribly frightening experience. These soldiers were so stressed out in their mind that even if they hadn't got a problem they just couldn't think straight,' said Mrs Booth.

Lieutenant General Cavan, the 10th Earl of Cavan, commanding the 14th Corps, pronounced his verdict on Private Farr four days after the trial. 'The charge of cowardice seems to be clearly proved and the sergeant major's opinion of the man is definitely bad to say the least of it. The GOC 6th Division informs me that the men know the man is no good. I therefore recommend that the sentence be carried out.' The court found Farr guilty of 'misbehaving before the enemy in such a manner as to show cowardice'. The sentence was death.

'My grandfather was probably like all the other soldiers that were executed, plied with brandy so he didn't know what state he was in,' said Mrs Booth. 'They were normally dragged to the firing post and a card or piece of flannel pinned to their hearts. I'm proud to say that in my grandfather's case he refused the blindfold and he stood there, open-eyed, facing the firing squad. Not only must have it been awful for him – although I think by this time he was probably thinking it would be a release from the terrible noises going on in his head – but for the firing squad, men who had been fighting with him a month before, and they had to stand there and shoot him and watch him die.'

Farr was executed at 6 a.m. on 18 October 1915 by a firing squad made up of members of his own regiment. He was tied to a stake at Carnoy, like so many others marched out for that grisly dawn ritual. A doctor who witnessed the shooting described the death as instantaneous. Farr was one of more than three hundred British soldiers executed for cowardice, desertion or other 'crimes' during the First World War, some aged just seventeen. Those shot were among 3,080 charged and sentenced to death (the remaining sentences were commuted); many of these were men whose actions might now be better understood in the light of modern medical and psychiatric experience. Only three of the three thousand were officers. Later research claimed that as few as 5 per cent of those who said they had shell shock may have been genuine malingerers and yet the dead were stripped of their war medals, their names left off memorials and their widows refused a pension.

The next letter Private Farr's wife received was from the War Office. The brutal wording said: 'Dear Madam, We regret to inform you that your husband has died. He was sentenced for cowardice and was shot at dawn on 18 October.'

Mrs Harris said her mother was devastated by the letter. 'That was all it said, no apology, no nothing. After we had that, our war pension was stopped and the landlady threw my mother and me out of our house. We were homeless for a while and they tried to put me in a home. My mother eventually went into domestic service and took me with her, but was so ashamed of what had happened to my father and the stigma of it, that she never mentioned it to anyone for years.

'She never believed he'd been a coward, and some time later the local vicar came round with a letter he'd got from the army chaplain, asking him to go and see my mother and explain how he died. The letter said: "And tell Mrs Farr that her husband was no coward. He wouldn't even have a blindfold on."'

The only recognition the family have of Private Farr's war service is at the Thiepval Memorial where his name is engraved along with 75,000 servicemen with unknown graves. Mrs Booth said she had heard of flowers placed at the memorial after the war being kicked away by an officer who said: 'These men don't deserve flowers.'

The gruelling nature of trench warfare reduced many men to gibbering wrecks, but sometimes it had the opposite effect. Richard Trafford, the boy of fifteen who saw so much action, believed that those in the trenches were placed in a no-win situation. If they stayed, they would most likely be killed, injured or go mad. If they ran, they'd be executed as cowards. For some, the only option left was to do something heroic. 'In my opinion, many of those who got medals for heroic actions – like the chap in our regiment who captured a German machine-gun on his own – were shell-shocked. Otherwise they just wouldn't undertake such an action. The likes of me wouldn't have dreamed of it.'

Siegfried Sassoon said as much in his book *Memoirs of an Infantry Officer*. Desperate men trapped in the trenches suddenly did something uncharacteristically heroic, filled with 'invincible resistance', and ran towards the enemy lines, guns blazing, either to get a 'Blighty wound' – one that would see them sent home – or to have a hand in ending their own misery. If they happened to survive the attempt and receive a medal in the process, then at least they had done something to break the relentless monotony.

Describing his own actions in frightening off a German advance, for which he received a bullet in the shoulder and was awarded the Military Cross, Sassoon wrote:

My overstrained nerves had wrought me to such a pitch of excitement that I was ready for any suicidal exploit. This convulsive energy might have been of some immediate value had there been any objective in it, but there was none . . . After a short spell of being deflated and sorry for myself, I began to feel rabidly heroical again, but in a slightly different style, since I was now a wounded hero, with my arm in a superfluous sling.

He later threw his MC ribbon into the river Mersey in disgust.

Others, unable to endure another day in the trenches but afraid of being branded a coward by running away feigning shell shock, would shoot themselves in the foot, leg or hand to qualify for a spell away from the front lines, or possibly a permanent discharge on medical grounds if the wound was debilitating enough. The letters 'SIW', for Self Inflicted Wound, were a common sight on many medical reports. For those who confessed to their crimes it often meant dispatch to a lunatic asylum as soon as the physical injury had been treated.

By the end of 1916 the fortunes of the Allies were at their lowest ebb. The Somme had been a disaster in terms of loss of life, the Anzac battle for the Gallipoli peninsula a shambles, and the French and Russian armies were on the point of collapse. The winter ahead was expected to be cold and bleak. Army statistics for the year indicated that an estimated 40 per cent of the year's casualties had been shell-shock cases, far surpassing anything expected before the war. Medical science had progressed to such an extent that the physically wounded were receiving better treatment than ever before, while the treatment for the mentally wounded was still unsystematic. One of Haig's commanders warned him: 'No one who has not visited the front can really know the state of exhaustion to which our men are reduced.'

And still the war continued, well into its third year, with a few battles won but the shell-shock casualties mounting. At the joint Canadian and British assault on Vimy Ridge, to the south of Ypres, seven thousand yards of territory were gained at the cost of 160,000 lives in April 1917. At the Messines ridge, twenty-one mines containing over a million pounds of explosives – and secretly buried in five miles of tunnels dug by British miners under German lines – were set off. The shock wave was so enormous it was felt across southern England and in Downing Street, London, 130 miles away. The explosion wiped out the German positions, killing 10,000 outright. Troops moved in and took a further 7,000 prisoners, at the relatively low cost of 16,000 casualties.

Passchendaele was next – more than four million shells poured down on the German lines in fourteen days in July 1917, with the result that the local dikes were destroyed. The heaviest rains in decades added to the problem and the battle area soon became a swamp. British tanks were unable to get through, the Germans used mustard gas for the first time and utilized their planes to strafe Allied infantry positions – the first time that air support had been used for ground troops.

The cost of the attack was 370,000 casualties. More than 42,000 British casualties listed as missing in action were never found; many had simply disappeared into the mud. Allied gains were made but this battle, more than many, came to symbolize gross military incompetence and senseless loss of life. It was also one of the most unpleasant in terms of fighting conditions, resulting in a new whole flood of shell-shock cases into the casualty clearing stations.

Back home, the government and the military were facing a mounting dilemma. Public opinion was against them; letters and articles critical of the war and the treatment of shell-shock victims started appearing in the press. It was impossible to conceal how many officers were affected by the condition and it would have been political suicide to maintain that so many members of the upper classes were insane.

Attempts were made to suppress some of the worst details coming out of the lines. Shell-shock cases were not listed as casualties, to keep the numbers down. Media representatives were urged to write upbeat reports to boost public morale and letters from the front, which had always been censored for sensitive material, were now even more thoroughly scrutinized.

Guy Botwright, whose job it was to read and censor the letters sent home by his men, suddenly found it all too much for him. 'I had to read every one of those letters to make sure that the men weren't conveying information which the enemy could make use of if he got hold of them. It became obvious that I couldn't concentrate on what I was doing. You still did your job but you were living on the other side of the fence, so to speak.

'When resting I presume I slept, when the meals came along I presume I ate them, but it got to the stage where it was just impossible to do anything. It was a horrible period, looking back. One day I was doing the letters and I dropped the pencil, I dropped the letters and that was it. I don't remember going back, I woke up in a hospital in England. I wasn't sick, I had no diarrhoea or anything like that. There was nothing. It was the brain; what was left of it had gone. It was quite a common thing, this shell-shock business. I have no idea what the doctors gave me for it. I couldn't tell you because the world had ceased to exist. There was this terrible shivering business, not with cold. The body shivered but it didn't seem to vibrate.'

Botwright was treated for shell shock at a Brighton hospital. 'It was horrible. I made up my mind I would never write a word about it or discuss it; it was so shameful. I tried to live it down. A lot of men were shot for being unable to face the music. It wasn't until long after that I realized what had caused me to break down.'

By this stage of the war there was a turning point in official attitudes to shell shock. Up to now the authorities had paid lip service to the physical-effect theory. But the military began to see it as Myers and more enlightened medical men had seen it for the last year – as a temporary psychological breakdown brought on by the strains of war.

In recognition of his work, Myers's title was changed to consulting psychologist and his demands for proper organization and resources finally listened to. The military realized that its manpower problem was made worse by the lack of proper medical organization to deal with shell-shock cases. It was now the considered view that men should be examined near the battle-field and only evacuated when necessary. A return to England, away from fellow soldiers, was often found to precipitate an attack of shell shock, as in the case of one non-commissioned officer reported by Professor G. Elliot Smith, in the *Lancet* in April 1916. He wrote:

This man went through the first eleven months of the war in France and in Flanders, was subjected to every kind of strain – physical, mental and moral – was wounded twice, gassed twice, and buried under a house. On all five occasions being treated in a field ambulance and then returning to the trenches. After all this experience he was granted five days' leave to return home, apparently in a good state of health. After reaching the homeland, and while waiting for a train in the railway station, he suddenly collapsed, became unconscious and for months afterwards was the subject of severe neurasthenia.

Apparently at the front the excitement and his sense of responsibility, and especially the example that he felt he should set his men, seemed to have kept him right. This stimulus removed, he broke down. There was nothing of malingering or shirking in his case; there was no fear of physical injuries or of returning to the front – on the contrary, he was anxious to go back. His fear lest . . . his failure be bad for the platoon was wholly due to that remarkable emotion of regimental loyalty.

Thus came about the birth of what the military call 'forward psychiatry', the principle of which was that those affected must be kept within earshot of the guns and close to the physical presence of their men. The aim was still to return as many as possible to the front lines without allowing them the time and space to dwell too deeply on what they had been through and what they were yet to face.

Myers proposed forward 'sorting areas' to be set up behind the front, each with a maximum of 250 cases received from field ambulances, with a specialist assisted by an MO in charge of each one. 'In these centres, the strictest adherence should be paid to military discipline, to which the patients should be returned to as soon as possible. No cases should be retained except those which were likely to be cured within two or three days and to be fit for the front lines after a further few days re-education.'

Myers had reached the conclusion that nervous disorders among soldiers were caused either by shells bursting nearby or long-standing fear, horror, fatigue and insomnia. He petitioned for the abolition of the term 'shell shock' and announced that he planned to write his findings in a book, something he didn't do for many years for fear its publication might lower public morale.

Despite Myers's best efforts, thousands of men were still being admitted to military hospitals in Britain as insane. The court-martials continued unabated and the MOs weren't helping. One, Dr Harold Dearden, admitted that most were out to prove there was nothing wrong with the men in their care. Dearden was called by one man to give evidence on his behalf at his court-martial, but was far from helpful. 'I went to the trial determined to give him no help of any sort, for I detest his type,' he wrote. 'I really hoped that he would be shot, as indeed was anticipated by all of us.'

Details of the individual cases highlighted the unfairness of war: a lance corporal was executed for cowardice although no medical officer was available to report in his case and colleagues had said that he had been spattered by the brains of his friends and fellow soldiers during a vicious bombing attack. And of a private from the Hampshire Regiment, the corps commander wrote: 'Cowards of this sort are a serious danger to the Army. The death penalty is instituted to make such men fear running away more than they fear the enemy.' Rejecting an appeal for mercy in the case of a young private of previous exemplary character who has deserted his trench during a heavy bombardment, General Haig scrawled a note on his decision: 'How can we ever win if this plea is allowed?'

In the trial of Private Bertie McCubbin, a twenty-two-year-old member of the Sherwood Foresters Regiment whose nerve went after enduring twenty-six days of continual shellfire, the young soldier himself appealed for mercy in a note to the court. He wrote: 'During my stay in the trenches, I had my nerves shattered by a shell. I have never been up before my company officer before and I have always tried to play my part while in the Army. If you deal with me leniently in this case, I will try and do my bit and keep up a good reputation.' His company commander recommended mercy on account of the private's previous good character and condition of health. But the Army commander, General Sir Charles Munro, rejected the appeal, writing: 'If toleration be shown to private soldiers who deliberately decline to face danger, all the qualities which we desire will become debased and degraded.' Private McCubbin was shot at dawn. Death was not instantaneous and the sergeant commanding the firing squad took out his revolver and finished him off.

Myers knew that he had to do something positive to help those who suffered mental and moral breakdown, and did all he possibly could to implement proper medical care for them. He considered himself very much at the forefront of the new psychiatry and wrote that he wanted each patient to 'face without undue emotion the experiences which have troubled him, clearly comprehending the chain of mental processes responsible for his condition'. It was truly pioneering work.

'He felt the coward or deserter label was very wrong, and was greatly concerned for these young men,' his daughter recalls. 'He felt that he was the pioneer in this thought that so many of the problems were due to psychological factors – mental history, family background and the traumatic situations they were in. The shell-shocked were bunched together and my father felt very strongly that they were not cowards and they were not deserters through any fault of their own. They were just inadequate in neurological or psychological conditions.

'He felt that he could help them initially with psychological treatment by getting them to recount their own memories, memories which had often receded into the background, under mild hypnosis or just through talking. He felt this would benefit the men, providing they could be treated early enough after a so-called incident. He wanted to treat them immediately.'

Thanks largely to doctors like Myers, the principles by which military psychiatrists still work were laid down in the First World War: the PIE model of Proximity, Immediacy and Expectation. The theory is that if you treat men near the front, you treat them straight away and you treat them like soldiers, not like patients, they have a much greater chance of recovery. It was the start of a marriage between psychiatrists and the military that endures today.

In England where the shell-shocked patients who had slipped through the net were still guinea-pigs for new treatment, groups of psychotherapeutically minded RAMC-enlisted doctors continued to throw themselves whole-heartedly into the higher principles of research. At establishments such as the Red Cross Military Hospital (later the Moss Side Hospital) in Maghull, near Liverpool, and the Royal Victoria Hospital in Netley, Hampshire, devotees of psychotherapy – previously ignored or marginalized – could meet to discuss theories and develop their technique.

For Myers, the lonely pioneer in the godforsaken war zones of France, there was no such kudos or shared pioneering spirit. Frustrated and exhausted by day-to-day struggles with prejudice and ignorance, drained by the terrors of war that haunted his patients, he feared he himself might be on the point of mental breakdown. On the verge of collapse, he took two months' sick leave, before giving up his job and asking for a prolonged period of leave. He returned to England in November 1917, feeling unable to offer anything more after two and a half years in France, and worked at the War Office before taking on a training and consultancy role. His departure marked the end of an era for the men at the front, who had lost not only an ally but a man of tremendous compassion, who had fought his own battles in the face of complacency and military hostility.

Chapter Three

No doubt they'll soon get well; the shock and strain
Have caused their stammering, disconnected talk.
Of course they're longing to go out again –
These boys with old, scared faces, learning to walk.
They'll soon forget their haunted nights; their cowed
Subjection to the ghosts of friends who died –
Their dreams drip with murder; and they'll be proud
Of glorious war that shattered all their pride.
Men who went out to battle, grim and glad;
Children, with eyes that hate you, broken and mad.
                        'Survivors' Siegfried Sassoon

The First World War was fast becoming a watershed in the acceptance of invisible injury. Everyone wanted to be part of the psychiatric revolution, it seemed, and post-war careers were already being mapped out. To the great consternation of the War Office, there was much more emphasis on the theory and treatment of shell shock and far less on the cure. Private nursing homes opened across the country, offering restful havens for those afflicted. Academics keen to be at the forefront of the great debate produced lengthy papers, lectures and books on the subject, all of which served only to highlight the lack of a clear consensus of opinion.

On one side of the argument, 'tainted heredity' was blamed, while others still clung to the belief that the cause was somehow organic. Were the horrors of war solely responsible or could shell shock be traced to childhood fixations and other Freudian concepts? There was growing popularity for the 'flight into illness' concept, between fear and duty, and the previously highly controversial Freudian theories started to get a foothold for the first time within the Royal Army Medical Corps. Hypnosis became increasingly popular as a method of taking victims through their traumatic experiences and talking about them, and dreams were studied in earnest.

Treatment for the condition became as varied as the theories behind it, ranging from periods of absolute peace and quiet and 'cheery chap' therapy, to intensive bouts of electric-shock treatment amounting to little less than torture. The shortage of hospital beds created by the unexpected influx of mental casualties led to a national emergency, and county lunatic asylums, private mental institutions and disused spas were taken over and hastily adapted. Some officer patients were even sent to private country houses under the 'country host' scheme, which urged the landed gentry to pull off the dust sheets and open their spare bedrooms to the less seriously ill. Others were sent to hospitals in London, Scotland, Merseyside or the Home Counties, depending on their condition and the availability of beds. Where patients were sent and whether they received the pampering treatment or discipline was down to pot luck.

Those fortunate enough to be sent to D Block of the Royal Victoria Hospital in Netley, Hampshire, on the banks of the Solent, were generally well looked after, despite the indignities of being recorded on film. Netley was the established institution for the treatment of mental patients in the service of the Army and it offered a hundred beds to shell-shock cases. When those filled, the men were set up in tents in the grounds and in adjacent fields, overlooking the harbour where the hospital ships came in.

Arthur Houghton, who as a boy visited a sick relative there, recalled the scene: 'When I was about three, Mum used to take me down to Netley Hospital and we used to get out of the train at Hamble Halt station and then walk across the fields to the back entrance. In so doing we had to pass all through the tents and it's quite a big field and quite a long walk and there were these hundreds, it seemed to me to be hundreds of these tents.

'And Mum used to keep on saying to me, "Shush. Shush. Don't touch those [guy] ropes. Shush." And I used to ask why and she'd say, "Well, they're shell-shocked soldiers in there and they can't stand the slightest noise, so please be quiet and don't talk and don't touch any of those ropes." And this is how we would eventually get across to the back entrance to the hospital. It was thought they needed complete peace and quiet.'

Theresa Hoare was a young child when her father used to take her for walks in the grounds of Netley, and she would see the shell-shocked cases sitting in their basket chairs. 'When I first saw them I was absolutely terrified. They looked so dreadfully vacant and had strange gaits when they walked. They would twitch and some of them would fall over where they were, they couldn't walk properly. The poor souls, there was just no recognition in their eyes. It was their eyes that frightened me – staring. They didn't know where they were or why they were there or what they were doing.'

She remembered hearing of a number of suicides at the hospital, men who stood in front of trains on a nearby railway track or who took more direct measures. 'They must have been absolutely desperate. They used to go into the bushes. One had a knife and cut his throat right across and others used to go to this ditch with just a few inches of water in it and they'd lie down and submerge their faces until they drowned. Others strangled themselves with a belt or piece of rope, or hung themselves. People knew about it but it wasn't publicized a lot then.'

Netley was not the only refuge: in London, the neurological sections of the 4th London Territorial General Hospital, including the Maudsley wing, a new specialist psychiatric hospital, taken over by the military before it became world-famous as a civilian psychiatric hospital, offered four hundred beds to

French soldiers in trenches on the Northern Front, circa 1915.
(*AKG London*)

A First World War firing squad takes aim.
(*Ron Wilkinson/Pen & Sword Books Ltd*)

Moss Side Military
Hospital at Maghull,
near Liverpool.
(*Dr. J. Rowlands*)

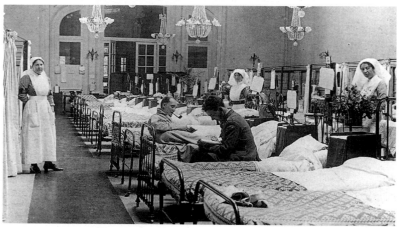

The Duchess of Westminster hospital at Le Touquet where pioneering
Doctor Charles Myers first worked. (*Imperial War Museum*)

The Royal Victoria Hospital at Netley in Hampshire. (*Patrick Kirkby/Hampshire County Council*)

2

SCHEDULE.

Date. 2nd October 916.   No. Cm/330

Name of Alleged Offender (a)	Offence charged	Plea	Finding, and if Convicted, Sentence (b)	How dealt with by Confirming Officer
No. 8871. Private Harry FARR, 1st. Battalion West Yorkshire Regiment.	Section 4.(7) AA. Misbehaving before the enemy in such a manner as to show cowardice.	Not Guilty	GUILTY. DEATH.	Minhford Reserved Br Cmo/318 58 Confirmed Ottaviani 14 Oct. 16

(a) If the name of the person charged is unknown, he may be described as unknown, with such addition as will identify him.

(b) Recommendation to mercy to be inserted in this column.

Minhford   Brig Genl.   F. _____ Lt Col.
            Convening Officer.   President.

The official schedule giving the guilty verdict and death sentence for
Private Harry Farr, a 26-year-old infantryman with the 1st Battalion West
Yorkshire Regiment who was convicted of cowardice and shot at dawn.
(Public Record Office)

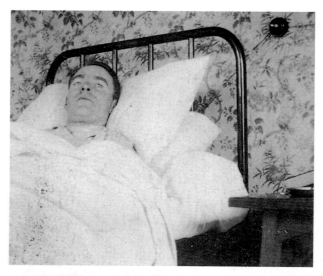

An unknown shell shock patient in bed at Craiglockhart Hospital, Edinburgh, Scotland.
(*Maureen Huws*)

Craiglockhart Hospital – 'Dottyville' to First World War poets Siegfried Sassoon and Wilfred Owen, who were both treated there.
(*Maureen Huws*)

Gertrude Farr in 1910, aged sixteen, six years before her husband's execution.
(*Gertrude Harris, daughter of Gertrude Farr*)

William H. Rivers, Craiglockhart Hospital's most famous doctor of neurasthenic officers. (*Royal Society*)

An official portrait of Lieutenant John Harry Burns of the 6th Northamptonshire Regiment, before shell shock rendered him unfit for duty. (*Maureen Huws*)

A First World War advanced dressing station near Yprès, September 1917. (*Imperial War Museum*)

Injured US assault troops take time out for a cigarette break after storming a beach-head in the Second World War.
(*Topham*)

William Sargant, pioneer of deep sleep treatment for shell shock sufferers at Sutton Hospital, Surrey.
(*Guys & St. Thomas' Hospital*)

Vernon Scannell, who was jailed for his so-called desertion in the face of the enemy during the Second World War's desert campaign. *(Vernon Scannell)*

Northfield Military Hospital, Birmingham, where group therapy was born. *(Mrs Simmons)*

A Royal Marine Commando stands guard over three captured Argentinians who await questioning. (*Holdgate/ Photo Press*)

Iraqi troops surrendering to US troops during the Gulf War in February 1991. (*AKG London*)

Bosnia, 1995: a man whose family were executed by Serbian forces weeps for their loss as a colleague looks on. (*Magnum Photos Inc/ Gilles Peress*)

those suffering from the milder symptoms of shell shock. With its treatment programme of rest and feeding up, along with gentle psychotherapy, an estimated 40 per cent of patients were returned to the front. Elsewhere, four private hospitals for officers suffering from war neuroses were set up as charitable trusts by Lord Knutsford, including the Special Hospital (later known as Hospital I) at Palace Green, near Kensington Gardens, the hospital to which Captain Leland was eventually moved. The *Lancet* reported at the time:

> The house looks out on to the Palace Gardens across a quiet roadway, where the din of traffic and motor-horn is almost inaudible. The spacious reception rooms give the feeling of a well-ordered private house and in no wise that of an institution. There are thirty-three bedrooms, each with one bed – 'austere little rooms', as the medical officer called them – with plain grey walls with no pictures or ornaments or anything else to attract or distract the attention of the tired men, to whom complete and absolute rest of the body and mind was the first essential to recovery.

The men were ordered to remain in their rooms and take all their meals alone with the exception of afternoon tea. They were allowed out only for a short walk once a day in Kensington Gardens towards the end of their stay. There was little or no active treatment apart from suggestive therapy which took the form of 'explaining to the patient the mechanism of his retarded mental processes'.

On average the officers stayed there three to four weeks before being moved to Hospital II in Campden Hill, a sort of half-way house – 'as quiet and secluded a haven as could be found anywhere in the Home Counties'. The *Lancet* reported: 'The note of austerity is no longer present, the reception rooms are used for meals and recreations, and the reviving brain can refresh itself with the sight of beautiful pictures hung in beautiful rooms.' Billiards and croquet were allowed, massage and mild electric shock treatment employed. After six weeks an inmate was deemed fit and returned to the front.

Not all the therapy on offer was quite so pleasant. Given a free hand by the War Office and vying with rival doctors for a greater success rate of returns to the front, some budding therapists felt it was within their remit to use force on particularly stubborn cases. After all, these patients had let the side down and needed to be cured quickly before they set a bad example to others. At the National Hospital for the Paralysed and Epileptic in Queen Square, Bloomsbury, one of those at the forefront of such new methods of treatments was Canadian-born Lewis Yealland.

Yealland advocated his own special brand of therapy using the German-inspired electric-shock method and the power of personality in autosuggestion propounded by Dr Kauffman. He used a technique called 'faradization' after the farad, a unit of electrical capacity named after Michael Faraday, the chemist who discovered it.

He was sent the most recalcitrant cases of hysteria, and quickly gained the reputation of being a miracle worker, able to send a man back to the front within days of seeing him. His electric-shock treatment to stimulate the nerve endings was developed specifically to cure hysteria, and also claimed to weed out the malingerers. Some of the case histories are quite horrific in their detail.

In his memoirs, Yealland recalled the case of 'A1', a private aged twenty-four who had fought and survived successive battles at Mons, the Marne, Ypres, Neuve Chapelle, Loos and Armentières, some of the worst fighting of the war. He was then sent on to the Balkans to help repel the Bulgarian offensive, and at Salonika, he fell from his horse, remaining unconscious for five hours. From the moment of waking he shook all over and was unable to speak. In the nine months that followed before he was sent to Queen Square, he had not uttered a word, despite various quite brutal efforts to force him. Yealland wrote: 'Many attempts had been made to cure him. He had been strapped down in a chair for twenty minutes at a time, when strong electricity was applied to his neck and throat; lighted cigarette ends had been applied to the tip of his tongue and hot plates had been placed in the back of his mouth. Hypnotism had been tried, but all these methods proved unsuccessful in restoring his voice.'

Yealland said the man appeared indifferent as to whether or not he was cured. The doctor told him he owed it to his wife and children to speak and ordered him to recover his speech at once.

In the evening he was taken to the electrical room, the blinds drawn, the lights turned out, the doors leading to the room were locked and the keys removed. The only light perceptible was that from the resistance bulbs of the battery. Placing the pad electrode on the lumbar spines and attaching the long pharyngeal electrode, I said to him: 'You will not leave this room until you are talking as well as you ever did, no not before.' The mouth was kept open by means of a tongue depressor; a strong faradic current was applied to the posterior wall of the pharynx, and with this stimulus he jumped backwards, detaching the wires from the battery. 'Remember, you must behave as becomes the hero I expect you to be,' I said. 'A man who has gone through so many battles should have better control of himself.' Then I placed him in a position from which he could not release himself, and repeated: 'You must talk before you leave me.' A weaker faradic current was then applied more or less continuously, during which time I kept repeating: 'Nod to me when you are ready to attempt to speak.' This current was persevered with for one hour with as few intervals as were necessary, and at the end of the time he could whisper: 'Aah.'

Yealland continued with the treatment for thirty minutes longer, constantly persuading his patient to try to repeat the letters of the alphabet, and commanding the man to keep awake, for he was exhausted from his ordeal. He made him walk up and down for some time, and blocked his attempts to escape from the room. The man could only repeat a letter with considerable effort. 'Each explosion of the whispered "ah" was accompanied by an almost superhuman effort, manifested by spasmodic contraction of the muscles of the neck, the head being raised in jerks,' Yealland wrote. Strapping his patient into the chair once more he applied electrical currents to the outside of the neck this time, using a key electrode on the larynx, urging him to repeat the letters of the alphabet.

'It was not long before he began to whisper the vowels with hesitation . . . then he began to cry and whispered in a stammer: "I want a drink of water."' Yealland refused any refreshment until the man could speak in more than a whisper. He said he applied 'shock after shock' for some considerable time, until the man could not only speak but could repeat whole sentences without even a stammer. The hysterical paralysis of his throat was then seen to pass to the soldier's left arm, which was twitching and to which Yealland also applied the electrode; then to the right arm, left leg and right leg, as Yealland 'chased' the hysteria from the soldier's body. The entire process took four hours, at the end of which the doctor pronounced his patient cured.

Yealland effectively engaged in a battle of wills with his patients, isolating them in a room with him, refusing to let them go until they were cured. For him, shell shock was all about a lack of discipline and sense of duty. But all his treatment did was remove the hysterical symptom, it did little for the cause. His success rate was almost 100 per cent, but nobody kept any record of the relapse rate.

To illustrate that his treatment was also effective in identifying malingerers, Yealland cited the case of a twenty-two-year-old man, who was feigning paralysis of the hand. 'He was taken to the electrical room where a strong faradic current was applied by means of a wire brush to the elbow . . . he instantly shouted, "you've beaten me, you have beaten me," and admitted he had been shamming.' Yealland's treatments were described graphically in Pat Barker's *Regeneration* trilogy, including one incident in which, having cured a man, Yealland took offence at his ironic smile and proceeded literally to wipe it off his face, applying repeated doses of electricity, until the corners of the man's mouth had turned down again.

Dr Michael Yealland, the son of the late doctor, and a retired neurologist himself, believes that much of his father's work has been taken out of context. 'Some people reading my father's accounts of his patients who were suffering from shell shock might think that he was cruel. Rereading his case notes, I don't think he was. He was using as little force as possible to effect a cure. The alternative was that if these people didn't get better they might spend the rest of their lives as invalids. Quite a lot of his patients recovered without any electrical stimulus at all, just with suggestion and persuasion.'

Dr Yealland said that his father was a young and relatively inexperienced doctor fresh to Britain from Canada when the First World War started. 'Beastly as it was, the war was really responsible for my father's career – it gave him this great chance to fulfil his potential.' The patients sent to his hospital were suffering from gross physical disorders caused by hysteria, such as mutism, deafness and paralysis. Yealland did not make any special study of the causes of their problem, or try to distinguish between malingerers and genuine cases. His sole interest was in curing the patient and getting him fit for duty.

'His first step was to make quite certain that there was not any physical disease because the treatment which was used for those who were thought to be shell-shocked would be really quite inappropriate,' said his son. 'One way of making sure there was no organic disease was with a small electric current to stimulate a nerve to see if the muscles were working. I think, following on from that, he realized that this was a good way of convincing a patient that really the arms, legs or whatever it might be did indeed work. That, coupled with persuasion, was I think the basis of his treatment.'

Dr Yealland likens his father's work to that of a dentist who hurts his patient briefly for the greater good. In some instances no pain was involved, just 'trickery', as in the soldier who could not speak, but who blurted out a defence of his mother when Yealland accused her of wearing a wig. Other, more serious, cases required faradism. 'I think my father was unique in that he used the technique with a great deal more enthusiasm and much more success than others had done. One of the things that stands out is his persistence. He was prepared to go on and on and not give up until he'd achieved the desired effect, when other doctors might well have thrown in the sponge very much earlier. He wouldn't be defeated. It was a question of chasing out demons.'

Dr Yealland claims that, generally speaking, his father was a kind man who used faradism as infrequently as possible and in the smallest doses. 'On occasion, the strength of the current was what might be regarded as excessive at the present time,' he admitted, but added that eighty years ago, his father would have been regarded very much as the commanding officer, with a specific role to fill. 'The aim of the treatment was to get patients better as quickly as possible in the hope that some would be able to return to duty,' said Dr Yealland. 'I don't think he was punishing them in any way.'

Yealland was not alone in his belief that what his patients needed was a short, sharp shock. Similar treatment was already widely used in Germany, where Julius Wagner-Jauregg, the only psychiatrist to win the Nobel Prize, in the 1920s, is reported to have killed a number of patients. In France, doctors, called the system *torpillage*, which consisted of 'the brusque application of galvanic currents, strong enough to be extremely painful, in hysterical conditions, and the continuance of the procedure to the point at which the deaf hear and the dumb speak'. Such treatments soon gave rise to accusations of cruelty and torture.

Sigmund Freud, asked to report to an Austrian War Ministry inquiry into the use of electric shocks on war neurotics, declared that medicine was 'serving purposes foreign to its essence'. He described the doctors using it as 'the machine-guns behind the front', but reminded the inquiry that any doctor who carried out such procedures was under military command and feared the loss of his job if he did not achieve results.

'The insoluble conflict between the claims of humanity – which normally carry decisive weight for a physician – and the demands of a national war was bound to confuse,' he said. 'The successes of treatment by a strong electric current, which were brilliant to begin with, turned out to be not so lasting. A patient who, having been restored to health by it, was sent back to the front, could repeat the business afresh and have a relapse . . . In these circumstances some of the Army doctors gave way to the inclination . . . to carry through their intentions regardless of all else, which should never have happened.

'The strength of the current, as well as the severity of the treatment, were increased to an unbearable point in order to deprive war neurotics of the advantage they gained from their illness. The fact has never been contradicted that in German hospitals there were deaths . . . during treatment, and suicides as a result of it.'

Fortunately for the shell-shocked, there were many more enlightened doctors. The Red Cross Military Hospital, at Maghull near Liverpool, later known as the Moss Side Hospital, was one of the most radical and innovative of the era. With its villa-pattern layout, Maghull was built in 1912 as a colony for epileptics, and requisitioned by the War Office for the more serious cases of shell shock. One in every fifty affected ordinary soldiers was treated there, nearly four thousand men, all wearing the distinctive blue uniforms that identified them as wounded in some way and stood them apart from other servicemen.

A band of brilliant young doctors gathered there under the tutelage of Richard Rows (pronounced Rowse), a former asylum supervisor with an interest in Freud, Jung and psychoanalysis. His most celebrated member of staff, neurologist and anthropologist William H. R. Rivers from Cambridge University, worked briefly at Maghull before transferring to Craiglockhart in Edinburgh. Other staff members included Tom Pear, a brilliant academic and professor of psychology, Grafton Elliot Smith, a lively professor of anatomy, William Brown, reader in psychology at London University, and Millais Culpin, an Army surgeon sent from France to study shell-shocked cases.

Their mission was to use psychotherapy to analyse servicemen back to the front, an incredible idea for its time. Maghull became a seedbed of British psychology: before the war only a handful of people had even read Freud and now they were practising techniques never tried before. It was a mark of how troubled the military and the government were by shell shock that they were prepared to fund and endorse this pioneering new work.

Rows had hitherto supported the establishment belief that all mental patients should be kept in bed unless they became so agitated that prolonged bath treatment was called for. Bath treatment involved locking patients into wood-encased hot and cold baths designed to calm them down. But he described the effect of reading Freud and Jung as 'like a tornado' in his mind, and became an ardent campaigner for the early treatment of mental disorders with a more humanitarian approach, which he was able to practise freely at Maghull.

Rivers described Maghull as 'a running symposium of the mind, a society in which the interpretation of dreams and the discussion of mental conflicts formed the staple subjects of conversation'. Elliot Smith wrote to a friend: 'I am doing real psychology here. The work is extraordinarily interesting and instructive.' A *British Medical Journal* report described the treatment used at Maghull: 'It embraces suggestion, persuasion, therapeutic conversions, re-education and exercise of the functionally paralysed limbs. The physician masters the patient, gains his confidence and analyses his troubles and morbid ideas, and sets his mind at rest.' Utilizing Freudian theory, the doctors at Maghull concluded that the root cause of the symptoms of shell shock was a traumatic event that had been repressed and which, they believed, would reveal itself in dreams.

The atmosphere at the five-hundred-bed hospital was generally relaxed. Patients lived either in red-brick, two-storey mock-Georgian villas or makeshift huts set up in the grounds. Occupational therapy, dabbled with elsewhere, became a way of life at Maghull: patients were encouraged to play games such as cards or billiards, or to work on the hospital farm to provide food for the hard-pressed kitchens that turned out several hundred meals a day on scant provisions. When not keeping busy, the patients were psychoanalysed, the aim being to unearth hidden anxieties by simply talking sympathetically to each patient for at least an hour at a time about their fears, hopes and dreams, without pandering to them. But even among the lower ranks the stiff-upper-lip mentality prevailed and the idea that one could talk openly with a stranger about matters of the heart was new. It was the birth of the talking cure.

Not only did the War Office take the unprecedented step of funding Maghull, which had previously been a civilian hospital, but from 1917 it dispatched small groups of doctors there for training courses. These men were to learn the techniques and transfer them to the new hospitals being opened in France and England, or bring their newly learned expertise to post-war tribunals to deal with claims for pensions. The message the Army sent to the Maghull practitioners was clear: do your job well and we'll back you all the way. Little wonder that so many doctors wanted to jump on the shell-shock bandwagon.

Marjorie Beadle, Tom Pear's daughter, recalled her father's good fortune at being sent to Maghull: 'He was the first full professor, the first chair in psychology in the country. When war broke out, somebody – and I'm pretty sure it must have been Myers – suggested that my father would be wasted being sent to the trenches. Anybody could go to the front and get killed, but there weren't many psychologists, and they were needed. Myers arranged for him to go to Maghull and work with shell-shocked patients there.'

Mrs Beadle has fond childhood memories of life at Maghull and of 'the blues' – the name they gave to the patients because of their distinctive uniforms. 'We had very friendly feelings towards these men in their lovely blue uniforms – bright blue uniforms with white shirts and red ties – much prettier than all the men in khaki,' she said. 'They were people apart and my father's policy was to treat each patient as a person and not just somebody who had to be cured and sent out again. He was very kind and humane and there was a great deal of ignorance at the time about madness. People were frightened of it. Madness was a very useful word to put on anything you didn't understand or which frightened you. But shell shock was something which happened to perfectly ordinary young men, the man in the village, the man in the shop, men whom you knew were not mad before they went to war.

'My father believed that the young men who suffered shell shock would not necessarily have had mental illness in ordinary life. It required this frightful thing of being blown up or buried for thirty-six hours or whatever, a real shock, to produce some sort of mental imbalance. He talked to the patients about their dreams and nightmares because he believed that things happen in dreams that people don't allow to happen in their waking life.'

Pear's subjects were largely working class men with little education, traumatized by what they had been through, said his daughter. He talked them through their problems, and tried to instil confidence in them. It distressed her father greatly that his treatment often only helped them be returned to the traumatic situation that had caused their breakdown in the first place. 'Maghull was run as a military hospital, he was under military discipline and was unable to query the instructions that the soldiers had to be sent back to the trenches. But he personally thought it was quite dreadful to cure them in order to send them back to the war to be killed. He was deeply resentful of it, and became very anti-war.'

Mrs Beadle remembers seeing shell-shocked servicemen selling street wares during and after the war, and said her father would always give them money. 'These men would stand in the street with a tray suspended from their necks with a string, selling boxes of matches or bootlaces or small articles. There would be a placard round their neck saying "Ex-soldier" or "Three years in the war, suffering from neurasthenia", and I remember my father always gave them money but never took the matchbox or the boot lace. He felt very sorry for them, and particularly that nobody in the outside world would ever understand what these men had been through.'

Her father, she said, was sympathetic and loving, and it was because of people like him that the stigma of being 'a loony' was removed. 'He would tell people, "This is an illness. It's called mental illness. They're not lunatic and they're in a mental hospital and there are all sorts of treatments that can help people with mental difficulties." Psychology became much more popular and people started taking a real interest in it, and began to understand the mental troubles that ordinary people might have. He was a tremendous popularist.'

Andrew Goodwin was sent to Maghull after being hit in the head by a spent mortar shell at Passchendaele. His son Ken Goodwin, recalled: 'He was a stretcher bearer in the 9th Battalion Liverpool Kings Regiment and it was a pretty grim job because he had to go out to collect the bodies from no man's land between the lines at night and bring them back in. After he got hit in the head he suffered from depression and violent headaches and had the occasional fit. He was sent to Maghull to recover from his wound and for treatment for his mental condition.

'He used to say that if you had all your marbles when you went in there, you certainly wouldn't have them when you came out. It was seen very much as a mental hospital and anybody coming out of it was not regarded the same way as somebody on crutches. You were a mental case and regarded as such.' Private Goodwin was so traumatized by his experiences at Passchendaele that he vowed he would never go back to France again. 'He said he'd rather be shot than go back there,' recalled his son. He was eventually discharged from Maghull and the Army in 1918, and spent the rest of his life struggling to come to terms with what he had seen.

Betty Leyland's father, Samuel Pickstock, joined the King's (Liverpool) Regiment when he was seventeen and was another patient who passed through Maghull. Having been shot through the leg, treated and returned to the front in time for the battle of the Somme, he was in an observation hut when it received a direct hit from a German mortar shell. 'Everyone in the hut was killed but him, but it was also assumed that he was killed. They found him four days later, the only one alive, lying there, drifting in and out of consciousness. He didn't know where he was, he didn't know what his name was, he didn't know anything, so they shipped him back to England and he was sent to the military hospital at Maghull,' said his daughter. 'It was a long time before they discovered that in his mind he kept going through the fighting as if he were still there. His legs would just collapse under him and he'd go hysterical and didn't know what time of day it was. People used to have to hold him down and sometimes they had to put him in padded cells so that he wouldn't hurt himself. It was for his own good.'

Betty's mother Emily Webb worked as the head laundress and part-time nurse at Maghull and met Private Pickstock there. 'A lot of the men were really ill, but they were ill in their minds. I think they must have been quite frightening for the nurses. They were doing funny things you wouldn't really see anybody doing unless they were mentally disturbed. But the nurses just used to take it in their stride. They were fantastic with them.

'My father was one of the patients and at first my mother wasn't all that keen, even though he chased her. They used to have dances at the hospital and he'd never let up, he'd try and dance with her. But he was younger than her and she just thought he was a lonely soldier away from home. But they grew quite fond of each other as time went by and then when the war was over they got married.'

The inmates at Maghull were not all soldiers. Several naval and merchant seamen, affected by their experiences of the dreadful sea battles such as those at the Dardanelles, Jutland and the Falklands, joined those in the rows of metal beds. New technology in naval strategy had brought torpedoes, mines, radar and submarines into the equation, adding to the stresses and strains of warfare for men who had previously been merchant seamen. By the end of the war a quarter of all British ships leaving home ports never returned, thanks to the deadly accuracy of the German U-boats. The convoy system of protecting vulnerable ships, which eventually led to the failure of the U-boat campaign, also placed intolerable strain on the minds of the men acting as 'sitting ducks', and many cracked under the pressure.

In the Royal Flying Corps, too, the technological advances often only added to the psychological burden of the pilots and crews. Flying aircraft such as Sopwith Camels, Dolphins and Pups, or DH2s – known as 'spinning incinerators' – to altitudes of 24,000 feet, pilots experienced intense cold, a dangerous increase in blood pressure, G-forces that burst blood vessels in the eyes and ruptured ear drums, and lack of oxygen, which combined to make twenty-four-year-old men look forty. A First World War pilot had to experience, almost daily, the same physical strains as an Edwardian mountaineer in the Himalayas in terms of height, unsuitable clothing and lack of oxygen, but with the ascent from base camp to summit and the return compressed into two hours the discomfort increased accordingly.

During 1916 the average pilot had a life expectancy on the western front of three weeks, which reduced to two during the early months of 1917. A lucky pilot might last three months, and an exceptionally fortunate one, six. This waiting for death took its toll on sleep patterns, increased irritability levels and heavy drinking sessions. Many pilots became unable to fly because of severe hand tremors. By the end of the war some nine thousand had lost their lives – a mere bagatelle compared to the losses of the ground forces – but when there was only a tiny strike force of some five thousand men in the air at any one time, the losses are seen in their true perspective.

Initially, senior officers believed that incidents of mental breakdown were caused by the physical effects of flight, but it was soon realized that psychological factors were more important. J. L. Birley, who was put in charge of investigations into what was called 'flying fatigue', described the development of 'wind-up'. He said that, if unrecognized, this condition led to the affected individual becoming 'irritable, unsociable, morose, losing his inspiring personality and adopting a black outlook on things in general. Although he feels tired, he is excitable and restless; unable to sit down to read or write, he must always be pottering about the aerodrome looking at the weather. Sooner or later, he must give in.' Wind-up was recognized as an anxiety disorder particular to pilots, along with 'aeroneurosis' and 'effort syndrome'. Once fully developed, the individual's career as a war pilot was irrevocably finished. Treatment consisted of rest and recuperation. One study found that 10 per cent of six hundred pilots had developed the psychological disorder and urged that sufferers should be discharged from the air station as unfit for flying before the condition 'infected' any other airmen and 'marred' a squadron.

The analysis of dreams continued to play a key role in the treatment work at Maghull, and was followed closely by other doctors elsewhere. Rows and his colleagues were invited to write up their findings in the medical journals. A wave of published work followed including the book *Shell Shock and Its Lessons*, written in 1917 by Pear and Elliot Smith, who dedicated it to Rows. It was the first readable account of the subject, written in terms the lay person could understand, and it created a furore. The medical establishment hated it because of its reformist attitude, which had made such a big impression on the general public. After all the hype and all the conflicting theories, here at last was a book that allowed ordinary people to understand what shell shock was and how it could best be treated.

Pear and Elliot Smith argued that the lesson of the conflict was the importance of early treatment, that a nervous breakdown should be treated quickly, with common sense and sympathy, before it developed into something much more serious. 'The war has shown us one indisputable fact,' they wrote, 'that a psychoneurosis may be produced in almost anyone if only his environment be made difficult enough for him. It has warned us that the pessimistic, helpless appeal to heredity, so common in the case of insanity, is no longer adequate.'

The doctors found that a large number of their patients had had an unhappy childhood and had enlisted in the armed forces as a means of escape. Many had hoped that military life would provide a 'haven of rest' where they would be taken care of, have little responsibility and not be called upon to exercise much initiative. They had not banked on the horrors that awaited them.

The published case histories of the Maghull patients fascinated doctors throughout the country and abroad. In the relaxed climate of the hospital, it was noted, the men 'raved and sleepwalked at night, giving the intelligent nurse the opportunity for revealing reports'. A patient who had shot a fellow soldier by mistake was heard to shout in his dreams: 'It was an accidental shot, Ma'or, it was not my fault.' Another patient's dream recalled terrible experiences in the trenches but ended with him having sex with his wife. In another case written up by Rows, a man was tormented by the memory of an experience he had had during the first winter campaign. 'He and a comrade were carrying a pail of water to the trenches. It was very cold and they set down the pail to warm their hands. The comrade placed his hand against the cheek of the patient and said, "This hand is cold." At that moment he was shot dead. The incident was revived not only in dreams at night but if during the day he were quiet and closed his eyes, he could feel the cold hand against his face.'

Not all the patients at Maghull were so accommodating in sharing their dreams with the doctors. Many were deeply alarmed by what they were experiencing and asked if they were going mad. Others were less than enthusiastic about all the mental probing and suspicious of it. They never forgot Maghull's role in the military apparatus of the war. Rivers complained: 'The idea had got around that dreams were being used by medical officers as a means of testing whether their patients were to be sent back to France, and it was only rarely that one was able to obtain more than the merest fragment of a dream.'

This was the contradiction at the heart of the doctors' work, as they quickly discovered. Having crossed the Channel, the shell-shocked soldier felt such a sense of relief, of safety, at having escaped the terrible conditions on the other side, that he was overwhelmed with a desire not to return. In other words, there was no earthly incentive to get better and a great many to remain ill.

'The further the invalid soldier went from the front line, the more difficult it was to get him back to it . . . They were terrified at the thought of going back but they loathed the idea that they might be considered cowards,' wrote Rows in the *Lancet*. 'If, however, their confidence was gained and they saw the doctor did not think anything derogatory of them, and if he assured them that as soon as they got better he would do his best to get them out of the Army and into civilian life, their improvement was often rapid or striking.'

The treatment at Maghull was almost unique among British hospitals at the time in showing sympathy and understanding towards the men. Through long, persuasive talks, the patient was encouraged to face up to his memories and live with them. Millais Culpin tried to take the lessons learned at Maghull to a London hospital and was treated as a 'credulous fool' for taking the rantings of the shell-shock cases so seriously. Fortunately for Maghull, its recovery rate remained high, or it might have been dismissed in much the same way. The majority of patients were persuaded back to the trenches, and squads of RAMC doctors continued to come for three months' training in psychotherapy and dream analysis.

The Army's sudden interest in the new methods was not entirely altruistic. With no armistice yet in sight and conscription bringing fresh blood for the war machine, a new concern was looming: the government was panicking over how much money it was going to have to pay out in pensions after the war if these men didn't get better. Doctors whose wages were being paid by the military and who were already under pressure to get the men back to the front were made aware that they now had an additional function: to cure those with no hope of going back or to organize their discharge so that they would no longer be a burden on government resources.

At Craiglockhart Military Hospital at Slateford, two miles from Edinburgh in Scotland, only 'neurasthenic' officers were allowed entry into what was to become one of the most famous treatment centres of the First World War. Formerly a dilapidated Victorian hydropathic hotel 'for convalescence, health and recreation', it was built in the Italianate style in the grounds of the ruined thirteenth-century Craiglockhart Castle, with commanding views over the surrounding countryside. The bedrooms were small and accommodated two or three patients, but the sporting facilities included golf, cricket, boxing, swimming, bowling, billiards and tennis.

There was a small agricultural quarter, which grew vegetables and raised chickens, and the picturesque surroundings and good walking country more than made up for the 'gloomy, cavernous' architecture. The camera and field clubs, and the making of model yachts for a regatta on the pond, were specifically designed to occupy and distract the minds of the residents and a brisk, cheerful atmosphere was maintained throughout the day, to counteract the terrifying dreams and depression of the night.

SHELL SHOCK

Dr William H. R. Rivers, the fifty-two-year-old Cambridge anthropologist, budding psychologist and neurologist, former tutor of Charles Myers and previously under Rows at Maghull, was promoted to chief psychologist and placed in overall charge of approximately a hundred and fifty officers. Fascinated by dreams, Rivers had found the patients at Maghull frustrating: even if they opened up to him, the dreams of working-class men were too simple to be worth analysing, he claimed. That was not to be the case at Craiglockhart, where he was truly to find his métier, not least among the most problematic of his new charges, Second Lieutenant Siegfried Sassoon of the 3rd Battalion Royal Welsh Fusiliers, who arrived in July 1917.

Sassoon, in exile and discredited by the authorities as neurasthenic after writing a letter to *The Times* denouncing the war, was sent to Craiglockhart for treatment in lieu of being court-martialled. In his semi-autobiographical novel *Sherston's Progress*, he wrote vividly of Craiglockhart as 'this live museum of war neuroses'. He nicknamed the hospital 'Dottyville' and added: 'The doctors did everything possible to counteract gloom, and the wrecked faces were outnumbered by those who were emerging from their nervous disorders. But the War Office had wasted no money on interior decoration; consequently the place had an atmosphere of a decayed hydro, redeemed only by its healthy situation and pleasant view.'

Sassoon became friendly with the shy twenty-five-year-old Wilfred Owen, a second lieutenant in the Artists' Rifles and later the 5th Battalion Manchester Regiment, who had been concussed by a shell and forced to lie out in no man's land for several hours beside the mutilated body of one of his compatriots. Plucking up the courage to talk to Sassoon, who was already a published poet, Owen – who edited the hospital magazine called the *Hydra* in which many of the two men's poems were first published – described the hospital as 'an excellent concentration camp' where men could recover from the shock of coming to England.

Despite its atmosphere of recreation and relaxation many seriously ill patients walked its corridors, and at night, the fears repressed during the day could no longer be contained. Sassoon wrote:

> By night . . . the hospital became sepulchral and oppressive with saturations of war experience. One lay awake and listened to feet padding along passages which smelt of stale cigarette smoke . . . One became conscious that the place was full of men whose slumbers were morbid and terrifying – men muttering uneasily or suddenly crying out in their sleep. Around me was that underworld of dreams haunted by submerged memories of warfare and its intolerable shocks and self-lacerating failures to achieve the impossible.

Betty Stein, whose mother Mary McGregor was a nurse at Craiglockhart, remembers being frightened by the austere building: 'It was dark, like a mausoleum,' she said. Her father, Captain Harold Stevens, was a Craiglockhart inmate suffering from neurasthenia, who had volunteered from Edinburgh University for the 12th Battalion the Royal Scots in 1915 as one of 'The First Hundred Thousand' to enlist, and saw service throughout the war. He was seriously wounded for the first time at the battle of Loos in September 1915. In March 1916, when he had recovered, he was posted to the 13th Battalion where, two months later, he assumed command after the CO and most of his staff were killed. He was awarded the Military Cross for rallying the men and taking control of the situation at a critical moment. In July 1916, the first day of the battle of the Somme, he was wounded again and rejoined his battalion ten months later. Six months after that he was sent to Craiglockhart, suffering from neurasthenia, and was returned as a major, 'only fit for light duty', for the final year of the war.

'I think he must have been pretty badly traumatized but he never spoke to anyone about his experiences in the war, not even his own father or sister,' recalled his daughter. 'He was a very private person. I remember my mother telling me that his best friend took a direct hit and was destroyed, blown up on to him. The greatcoat that my father was wearing at the time was bespattered with this poor man's remains and he refused to have it cleaned in any way. It went into a tin trunk and he wanted it kept, like a sort of gravestone. She used to say to me, "Don't ask your father about the war – he doesn't want to talk about it."

'My mother and he met and fell in love at Craiglockhart. He was eventually returned to the trenches, and was later awarded the MC for conspicuous gallantry, so whatever the doctors did must have worked,' she added.

Rivers, working from Freudian concepts, believed that officers such as Captain Stevens who suffered mental collapse would respond in a different way from their men because of their additional guilt: they were in command and meant to be responsible. The prevalent theory was that the ordinary soldier exhibited gross hysterical conditions such as paralysis and deafness, while the preferred symptom of an officer was a gentle stammer. It was a bit like the old adage 'Horses sweat, men perspire, ladies merely glow.' The evidence did not always back up the theory, but many of the officers at Craiglockhart indeed suffered from chronic and debilitating stammers.

Rivers believed that what he called 'anxiety neurosis' came about because in battle servicemen were torn between the desire to run away and the obligation to stay and fight. Worn down with the mental struggle between those two conflicting instincts, a soldier's body found a clever way out in exhibiting signs of serious physical illness, thus giving him an escape route without capitulating to either side. The trigger event for this physical collapse was always something traumatic, usually involving a corpse. Rivers found that the sight of corpses, above all other horrific sights, broke a soldier's self-control more than anything else. Persuading his patients to remember that incident, confront it and find something positive about it, Rivers started them on the road to recovery.

A classic example was the patient who had seen lengthy active service at the front, which included being buried alive after a shell blast. Returning to duty, he went to look for a friend and fellow officer who had not yet returned from 'no man's land'. He came across his friend's dismembered body scattered across the battlefield, his head and limbs lying separated from the trunk. After this experience, the young officer broke down completely and was sent to Craiglockhart, suffering from terrifying nightmares every night, in which the mutilated and rotting corpse of his friend stalked him. His days were spent awaiting the torture of the nights. Rivers found a way of making the memory 'tolerable': he pointed out that if the friend had died in a shell explosion, his death had been instantaneous and painless. Rivers records that 'the patient brightened at once', and his dreams changed immediately to more positive ones, like lying beside his friend's body, weeping gently as he carefully removed any objects his family would value, a task he had actually carried out.

Rivers acquired something of the reputation of a miracle worker. The recipients of his 'miracles' included a soldier who had been paralysed and wheelchair-bound for six months who was walking within a month of arriving at Craiglockhart. Like Yealland, Rivers believed in the power of personality, but the only sparks that flew in his case were from his eyes. A cartoon in the *Hydra* even showed him dressed as a wizard, standing on a pile of books, a snake winding round his legs, wand in hand and a box emitting smoke in the other. Sitting before him was a group of five hypnotized officers repeating a Latin incantation.

With his gentle, patient approach, Rivers gained the complete trust of the officers in his care, who spoke to him, and him alone, of their fears and dreadful experiences, some of which were too terrible even for him to find an answer to and he could only listen and offer advice. 'Sometimes the experience which a patient is striving to forget is so utterly horrible or disgusting, so wholly free from any redeeming feature which can be used as a means of readjusting attention, that it is difficult or impossible to find an aspect which will make its contemplation endurable,' he wrote. To illustrate his point, he reported in the *Lancet* on one case in which a soldier was flung by a shell explosion, head first into the distended belly of a German corpse, several days dead; the impact of the fall ruptured the belly. 'Before he lost consciousness the patient had clearly realized his situation and knew that the substance which filled his mouth and produced the most horrible sensations of taste and smell was derived from the decomposed entrails of an enemy,' Rivers wrote. The soldier relived the experience night after night for several months and was barely able to eat or drink for profuse vomiting. Realizing that, in this instance, there were no redeeming features and the memory would be better repressed, Rivers abandoned his usual technique and recommended that the patient be discharged from the Army to move away to the country, where he might find respite from all that could remind him of the war.

Maureen Huws, whose father Captain John 'Harry' Burns was a Craiglockhart patient and a friend of Siegfried Sassoon, believes that he was the unfortunate soldier referred to. Her mother told her that after several months' treatment at the hospital, the doctors took her to one side and told her that there was nothing more they could do for him. 'I think he experienced such terrible things through those months and the awful, awful things he saw, that his mind was unable to cope with the horrors and it snapped. He wasn't wounded and he wasn't gassed. Something was still locked away and they couldn't help any further. They couldn't unlock his mind,' said Mrs Huws.

Captain Burns had been a successful businessman in the Mersey cargo business when war broke out and he joined the Cheshire Greys Regiment in 1914. 'My mother always said my father went away a lovely laughing boy and came back a broken old man,' said Mrs Huws. 'He had the most appalling time of it and he was terribly shell-shocked. He had nightmares every night and my mother used to say, "He has neurasthenia." I thought neurasthenia meant that you couldn't sleep. I will always remember his horrific shouting and screaming in the night and my mother trying to calm him down. It went on every night and it was almost too much for her to bear. It didn't bother me in the least at first, I didn't think there was anything unusual about it, but as I grew up I realized that there was something very wrong with him.'

Her father suffered from a terrible tremble, which was so pronounced that he couldn't carry a cup of tea across a room, and would go berserk if he heard a loud noise. 'They had a maroon in our town called the one o'clock gun which went off every day at one o'clock to tell people the time, and he never got used to it. He would run around the house calling for my mother and me. He had only to see a cap or a military badge and he was off, it was absolutely dreadful. If a motorbike or motor car went past the house at night, he let out the most terrible howls and dived under the bed and lay cowering and gibbering, because it was like machine-gun fire. And that went on for years. I thought that was what everybody's daddy did.'

She said her mother had always believed that Craiglockhart had been her father's salvation; that they had done all they could for him at a time when psychiatry was still in its infancy. She used to visit him there once a month, taking him out boating or for a walk, before finally being allowed to bring him home. 'Craiglockhart was a household name in our home. My mother called the nurses angels fallen from heaven. But for the rest of her life, she never dared take her eyes off him, in case he did something peculiar or responded in a strange way. Going to the cinema or theatre was almost always out of the question,' she added. 'Sometimes when we were having dinner he would lower his knife and fork and gaze off into the middle distance and would stare and stare. I'd open my mouth to say something and my mother would hush me and we would just sit and wait, perhaps as long as twenty minutes, and then he'd suddenly come to and he'd say, "You know, Gladys, my dinner seems to have gone cold." And she'd quickly produce another plate from behind the scenes.'

Not all the men in Rivers's care discussed their anxieties freely with him. Some were suicidal, many were angry and anxious at being sent to 'a lunatic asylum', and begged their families in pitiful telegrams and letters to come and free them. Many were manic, paranoiac, delusional and heard voices. The nursing staff were instructed to prevent them from leaving the hospital grounds and several were kept heavily sedated.

Among the hospital records is a letter from one young officer to his sister, in which he explained why he attempted suicide by taking an overdose of sleeping draught.

> I feel that I could not for one hour longer bear the mental tortures of hell I was experiencing and have been for some time past. I was dreading what I had to suffer in the future as much as I suffered recently. I was not insane, far from it, because I did it in a most deliberate way. I would willingly die fighting, but to be tied in my condition is too terrible to contemplate. I only wish I had never woken up. PS. I lie on the bed all night in all my clothes, afraid to leave myself alone with my thoughts.

Left to their own company, the officers fastidiously sidestepped the issue of war, feeling guilty and self-conscious in their blue armbands, which branded them neurasthenic to the outside world. Sassoon wrote:

> With my fellow 'breakdowns' I avoided war-talk as far as was possible. Most of them had excellent reasons for disliking that theme; others talked about it because they couldn't get it off their minds, or else spoke of it facetiously in an effort to suppress their real feelings. Sometimes I had an uncomfortable notion that none of them respected one another; it was as though there was a tacit understanding that we were all failures.

In an article in the *Hydra*, a young officer visiting the zoo in Edinburgh was reported as being convinced that a monkey was staring at his armband. 'It brought out its six babies to see the phenomenon. The officer could not cope with all these pairs of simian eyes staring at him,' the article stated. It was obvious that the monkeys represented the Edinburgh public, who often regarded the men as objects of scorn or pity.

Rivers had not only to contend with the officers and their many problems, but with the military authorities, who disapproved of his gentle and consequently slow methods. Some considered Craiglockhart a disgrace to the military, and an example of what happened when civilians in uniform were allowed to run a war hospital on their own terms. Following one 'fishy-eyed' inspection by the top brass, there were complaints that Rivers wore carpet slippers, the inspector could not see his face reflected in a single frying pan, and that the ubiquitous Sam Browne belts were conspicuous by their absence. It was widely believed that the avuncular chief doctor at Craiglockhart was far too familiar with his charges, on first-name terms with them and allowing casual consultations.

It was certain that many of the patients held Rivers in the greatest esteem and with much affection. Sassoon liked him the minute he met him, describing him as his 'father-confessor', and the pair remained friends for years. The two men interested one another: Rivers even pondered what would happen if Sassoon converted him to his pacifist views, instead of the reverse. Sassoon recalled with undisguised fondness his long conversations with Rivers in the late summer of 1917. Over tea, he wrote, Dr Rivers would sit with his spectacles pushed up on his forehead, his hands clasped in front of one knee, always ready to listen in spite of his weariness after long days with patients whose ills took so much out of him. Sassoon said Rivers regarded each mind as 'a sort of aquarium to study'.

He added:

> . . . sitting in a sunny room, a man could discuss his symptoms with his doctor, who could diagnose phobias and conflicts and formulate them in scientific terminology . . . But by night each man was back in his doomed sector of horror-stricken front line where the panic and stampede of some ghastly experience was re-enacted among the living faces of the dead. No doctor could save him then, when he became the lonely victim of his dream disasters and delusions.

Pat Barker, who made the relationship between Rivers and Sassoon the basis of some of her novels, put the following thought in the young poet's mind: '[Rivers's silences] are not to try to make you say more than you want; he's trying to create a safe space around what you've said already, so you can think of it without shitting yourself'.

Sassoon was sympathetic to Rivers's plight at being so in tune with his patients when he was also allied to the military. He wrote:

> A handful of highly qualified civilians in uniform were up against the usual red-tape ideas . . . the military authorities regarded war hospitals for nervous disorders as experiments which needed careful watching and firm handling . . . Rivers told me that the local director of Medical Services nourished a deep-rooted prejudice against Craiglockhart, and asserted that he 'never had and never would recognize the existence of such a thing as shell shock'.

Fortunately for Rivers and the other staff at Craiglockhart, who included the kindly Scot Major William Bryce, the effusive American Major Ruggles and Captain Arthur Brock, their methods proved effective, and many men were genuinely helped to recover from their terrible experiences. Had it not been so, Craiglockhart and its relaxed treatment might not have survived. Of the 1,801 officers treated there between 1915 and 1918, 735 were discharged as medically unfit, 167 were given home service of light duties, but 758 were returned to the front on active service; 141 needed specialist medical treatment at other hospitals.

Several years later a volunteer at Craiglockhart, who had worked alongside Rivers, wrote to *The Times* about his work: 'He gave, indeed, his whole soul and fine mind to this most trying work, I fear often to utter exhaustion . . . nearly all these heroic soldiers recovered their serenity and peace of mind under his care, and so were able to take up their life's work again.'

The First World War ended at 11 a.m. on 11 November 1918, three days after the last British soldier was executed for cowardice in the face of the enemy. Confronted with a revolt on the German home front, with servicemen instigating mutiny and revolutionists whipping up anti-war fury, the German High Command signed the terms of surrender in Marshal Foch's railway carriage in the Forest of Compiegne, France. The cost of the war had been catastrophic: nearly nine million men from all nations had been killed or wounded. In the cold light of peace it was hard to justify, for although the war had brought much-wanted changes, they could not reasonably be held to balance the losses. Moreover, far from making the world safe for democracy, the resentment of the defeated powers against the terms of the treaties imposed upon them sowed the seed of future conflict and went some way towards encouraging the growth of barbaric totalitarianism, which was to become such a marked feature of twentieth-century politics.

The cost in terms of mental strain was incalculable. The fate of most of those who suffered from their experiences during the four-year war can only be guessed at. Sassoon, the most famous inmate of any of the military hospitals, lived to the age of eighty-one and enjoyed a popular status for much of his life. He was created CBE in 1951 and became a devout Roman Catholic in 1957, ten years before his death.

Wilfred Owen, perhaps the most deeply missed voice of the First World War, was sent back to France as a company commander, but was killed a week before the armistice trying to lead his company across the Sambre canal as the German Army retreated. He was posthumously awarded the Military Cross for gallantry. Due largely to the encouragement of Sassoon, his family agreed to publish his letters and poems, which have provided a window on the human experience of war and bear legendary testimony to the pity of it.

Captain Harold Stevens, MC, returned to the front categorized as 'fit only for light duties'. In July 1918 at Berzy-le-Sec, now Major Stevens, he earned a Croix de Guerre with Palme for once again taking command after a shell hit the battalion HQ shelter, killing the CO and other staff, and rendering his captain shell-shocked. He was awarded a Légion d'Honneur in August. Despite suffering from hand tremors for the rest of his life, he joined the Indian civil service in Bengal and became district magistrate of Midnapore, then described as the most dangerous job in the world – three predecessors had been assassinated. He was knighted for his contribution to ending the Bengal famine. He retired to Bexhill-on-Sea in 1947 and died in 1969, aged seventy-seven.

Captain Leland, whose poignant letters to his wife vividly evoke the horrors of the battlefield, was sent to a nursing home after his stay at the Special Hospital for Officers and was ill for some time. He eventually rejoined the South Staffordshire Regiment and saw duty in Singapore, before being invalided out of the Army aged forty-seven due to ill-health. His daughter, Jean Robertson, said: 'My father was never really the same after the war and if you read his letters and know what he went through it wasn't very surprising. He stayed a captain and put all his energy into the British Legion, but it just shattered him.'

She remembers her father as 'an absolute angel' most of the time, until someone gave him a drink, when he became irrational and argumentative. 'He was on medication and he couldn't drink, and people very stupidly would give him a drink and then he was pretty awful. My parents had dreadful rows, which frightened the daylights out of me. One time he disappeared and they said he was going to France. How he got down to Harwich, I'll never know. But the doctor contacted the police at Harwich and told them he was a sick man and that his papers weren't correct. They sent him home. He just went to bed and slept.' Captain Leland died of cancer of the pharynx in 1931, aged fifty-four. Doctors told his family that the illness was probably caused by the gassing he received in the trenches.

Long after Samuel Pickstock was discharged from the Army and got a job with the post office, his daughter said he was still badly affected by his experiences, suffering from tremors and violent mood swings. 'He wasn't a handyman around the house, he had no co-ordination because he'd start shaking, and even at meals he used to get the shakes and we used to just live with it because he would lose his temper if he thought you were noticing him too much.

'He never really talked about what happened during the war, Mum told us, but he did say that the Germans were in the same boat as them – up to their chests in rats and mud. One Christmas in the trenches he could hear the German soldiers singing German carols, and he and his mates were singing English carols and they all joined in the same tune.' Her father used to get upset, she said, at the sight of wounded servicemen selling on the street because they could have been him. 'Whenever the radio had military music on, or it was Armistice Day, we used to have to hold him down on the floor because he would just think he was back in the firing line on the front. Mum used to have to sit on his arms and we would try and keep his legs down and this went on until the radio would go off. This happened for years and years. He'd have these fits and collapse on the floor, and we'd have to throw water around his face to cool him off.'

Years later, when the Second World War broke out her father was 'petrified' and still suffered badly with his nerves. He became the air-raid warden for their local community and was always first in the shelter during an attack. 'He was a very nervous man and some of the neighbours would say, "Oh, your father's always first in the shelter and he cracks on that he's getting everything ship-shape for everyone else to be there." They never said it to his face, but they did appreciate him because when they got to the shelter it was always spotlessly clean – he'd clean it out with disinfectant till it literally shone and make beds out of fallen leaves packed into sacks – and he'd make sure everyone was in, children, everyone.'

Gertrude Farr, the widow of Private Harry Farr, shot at dawn at Carnoy in 1915, later married Harry's friend and companion-in-arms William Batstone, who had been gassed and developed emphysema. Gertrude went into service, had two more children, and nursed her second husband until his death at forty-nine. She lived on until her hundredth year, dying in July 1993, after recording her memories of her First World War experiences for the Imperial War Museum. In her family, Harry's name was never mentioned again. Her daughter, Janet Booth, said: 'It was like having a murderer in the family – no one ever talked about him again. It was a big stain in the family. The curtains were drawn and that was that.'

SHELL SHOCK

Captain Harry Burns, the soldier Rivers couldn't help, returned to France after the war and visited the battlefields of Arras, scene of some of the fiercest and most futile battles of the First World War. It was there that he met officials from the Canadian War Graves Commission and spent several months with them, helping to exhume and identify many of those who had been killed. He returned to his job on the Mersey as a wharfinger, but suffered all his life from the effects of his terrible experiences. He had difficulty eating, could not bear noise and shook almost permanently. 'He used to burst into tears at the slightest thing, and his trembling was terrible. It never left him, what lived in his memory never died,' said his daughter, Maureen Huws. Her father suffered a series of strokes and finally died, aged fifty-two. 'Even at the end, before he lapsed into a coma and died, he grabbed my hand, pushed the bedclothes off and shouted, "Come on, we've got to get out of here." It was with him to the end.'

Guy Botwright, who suffered a complete breakdown while reading his troops' letters in the trenches, left the Army and got a clerical job in the financial world. He never married but became one of Britain's leading entomologists. His butterfly collection is housed in the Booth Museum in Brighton.

William H. R. Rivers went on to become the first psychologist to the Royal Flying Corps in 1917, where he did original research into the stress of flying, becoming a regular passenger in the accident-prone Sopwith Camel warplanes to understand what the pilots went through. He wrote a book, *Conflict and Dreams*, set at Craiglockhart, which gave considerable insight into the way he worked at the hospital and which gave him entrée into the world of the fashionable intellectual set. He returned to his beloved Cambridge after the war, and was persuaded by his friends George Bernard Shaw and H. G. Wells to stand as a Labour candidate in the 1922 general election, giving up his earlier membership of the Conservative Club. But he died suddenly, a few months before, of a strangulated hernia on 4 June 1922, aged fifty-eight.

Sassoon wrote of his death: 'It is difficult to believe such a man as he could be extinguished.' In his poem 'Revisitation', he wrote: 'What voice revisits me this night?/What face to my heart's room returns?' He said Rivers had helped and understood him more than anyone he had ever known.

In the library of St John's College, Cambridge, where a portrait of Rivers hangs, staff still remember the pilgrimages by a man called William Arnold Middlebrook, who came annually to Cambridge for several years during the 1950s. Malcolm Pratt, of the library staff, said: 'He would come and politely ask if he could view the portrait of W. H. R. Rivers that we held. He would gaze at it for several minutes, then take a pace backwards and give a smart military salute. He very rarely entered into conversation with the staff, but he did on one occasion state that Rivers had saved his sanity. On another visit, which turned out to be his last, he again saluted the portrait and said, "Goodbye, my friend, we shall not meet again." We were sorry not to have seen him again. His affection and reverence for Dr Rivers was most sincere, of that there is no doubt.'

CHAPTER THREE

Little is known of William Middlebrook, except that he was a company commander in the East Yorkshire Regiment, who was treated by Rivers for shell shock in 1917. After the war, he was offered a commission overseas, but he left the Army to work in the family firm of Wood's gentlemen's outfitters in Hull. He lived in Kirk Ella in East Yorkshire with his wife and two sons, and became a pillar of the local community. During the Second World War, he was a captain in the Home Guard and a keen member of the local church. He died in 1972, at eighty-nine.

Lewis Yealland, who went on to specialize in epilepsy and cerebral tumours, became a zealous teetotaller and non-smoker. He had an undistinguished post-war career and specialized in 'persuading' epileptics that their fits were hysterical. He died in 1954, aged sixty-nine. His obituary in the *Lancet* said: 'In his early days he was a witty companion, fond of harmless practical jokes, but in later years he became very serious, devoting his time to alcoholics whom he tried to reform by their acceptance of his evangelical religious beliefs.'

Charles Myers went on to work for the Royal Navy for a time, developing psychiatric screening techniques for candidates. After the war, he became director of the Institute of Industrial Psychology, which examined the relationship between psychology and the workplace. He was made a fellow of the Royal Society, president of the British Psychological Society and was awarded the CBE for his services to shell shock victims, an honour he at first refused. 'He was so upset and concerned that so many of his young colleagues who'd worked as he had done himself had been given no recognition that he refused it,' said his daughter, Mrs Rumens. 'But soon after that he had to accept it because he was summoned to an investiture by George V and he couldn't refuse.' Myers finally published a book of his experiences *Shell Shock in France 1914-1918* in 1940, fearing that the lessons of the First World War would be lost and that neurology might again defeat psychology.

Tom Pear became one of Britain's most distinguished psychologists, and also a pacifist. Under his influence, his son became the first boy to refuse to join the officer corps at Eton. Rows, the pioneer of Maghull, took up an appointment with the Ministry of Pensions at their London hospitals and acted as a consultant to the ministry. He was awarded the CBE and an honorary degree, by Manchester University, and went on a speaking tour of America. But after his own health collapsed he ended up back at his old job as pathologist to the county mental hospital in Manchester. Years of living with war neurotics had burned him out. Rivers could only take a year of it at Craiglockhart; Rows had four. His mental powers began to fade and he was unable to write up his experiences lucidly. He died suddenly in 1925, aged fifty-eight.

Official British figures claimed that, by the end of the war, 80,000 cases of shell shock had passed through military medical facilities, but this was later considered a gross underestimate: the true scale of the problem was covered up and a large number of the psychiatric patients were sent to regular hospitals. A closer figure, many have suggested, would be 200,000. By comparison, the German Army figures registered 613,047 cases of 'disorders of the nerves' between 1913 and 1918.

Two years after the armistice, some 65,000 ex-servicemen were drawing disability pensions for neurasthenia; of these 9,000 were still undergoing hospital treatment. The goal of wartime psychiatry had been to keep men fighting and many had failed to get a discharge from the Army when they should have done. By the end of the hostilities, they were past cure, and those fortunate enough to be drawing pensions for their disabilities were costing the government £10 million per year. The less fortunate ones, those who were never officially certified or whose MOs refused to diagnose them as unfit for service, were driven to beg in the streets or sell door to door, sporting their war medals and cardboard labels reading: 'Shell Shocked'.

On 28 April 1920, Lord Southborough addressed the House of Lords on his motion to establish a committee to investigate the nature and treatment of shell shock. 'The subject of shell shock cannot be referred to with any pleasure,' he said. 'All would desire to forget it – to forget . . . the roll of insanity, suicide and death; to bury our recollections of the horrible disorder, and to keep on the surface nothing but the cherished memory of those who were the victims of this malignity. But, my lords, we cannot do this, because a great number of cases of those who suffer from shell shock and its allied disorders are still upon our hands and they deserve our sympathy and care.'

By the time the Southborough Inquiry ended in 1922, after a full two years spent deliberating the issues, the view was that the term shell shock was too generalized. The Army was advised to distinguish between those brave men who had been 'knocked silly' by the effects of bombardment, and those for whom fear, or some personal defect, had overcome an ability to fight.

William Rivers, giving evidence, told the committee that he objected to the term shell shock and that as far as he could see, the main factor had been stress, with shock in most cases being the last straw. He separated cases into two categories: the officer who broke down soon after going to the front because he was unsuited to the position in which he finds himself, and he who broke down after long and continued strain.

When asked about morale, Rivers said: 'My experience is that the whole object of military training is to produce *esprit de corps* and other factors which give good morale, and that the lack of them is a very strong factor in the production of war neurosis of certain kinds. Man's normal reaction to danger is manipulative activity. If he cannot have that, or if it is restricted in some way, you have a prominent condition for the occurrence of neurosis on one form or another. That only confirmed my experiences in the Army – that the trying time was the period in the trenches when there was nothing to be done.'

The inquiry recommendations were predictable and conservative. It rejected the 'mental' origins of neuroses but was forced to admit that neither the medical profession nor the military authorities had been able to cure the problem. Its recommendations were:

1. No soldier should be allowed to think that loss of nerve provided an escape from duty.
2. Minor cases should be prevented from leaving the front.
3. The simplest form of psychotherapy was adequate for the majority of cases.
4. Proper medical screening of recruits was vital.
5. Concussed victims to be listed as battle casualties/not other types of mental illness.
6. Officers to study the psychology of the soldier.
7. Unit morale and discipline of utmost importance in preventing neurosis.
8. Short tours of duty and frequent home leave.
9. Physical comfort and rest for those under strain.

Trying to put the report's findings to some practical use for the civilian population, the 1930 Mental Treatment Act promoted outpatient clinics and voluntary treatment, sounding the death knell for the old Victorian asylums. In the new spirit of public sympathy for the victims of shell shock and all they had been through, it was recognized that many had scars on their minds that would never heal.

Within the military, the inquiry's recommendation that more RAMC officers be trained in psychology was not received with much enthusiasm and little was done. The war experiences of doctors and servicemen might have jolted the powers-that-be into the twentieth century, but then they stalled: in peacetime, the issue once again lay dormant. As before the First World War, it was felt that there was no need to debate the matter when there was not a war on. It had, after all, been the 'war to end all wars' and the prevailing thought was that after such a mass bloodletting it could not possibly happen again.

Chapter Four

More life may trickle out of men through thought than through a gaping wound.

Thomas Hardy

Most of the psychological lessons learned from the dreadful experiences of the First World War and acted upon in the following years were in the civilian field. Out of kindness to those still suffering from shell shock, 'lunatic asylums' were renamed 'mental hospitals' and the term 'lunacy' was replaced with 'mental illness'. Previously dismissed as 'aliens', a species apart from the rest of society, those who were mentally ill were now looked upon more kindly. The psychologists or neurologists who treated them were no longer referred to by their early title of 'alienists'; they were now called psychiatrists. For the first time, it was appreciated that fit young men could become seriously mentally disturbed. The therapeutic optimism engendered by the shell-shock experience was to become one of the early strands of the community-care movement.

New treatments were experimented with for those still affected by the war, including malaria therapy, in which patients were injected with malaria-infected blood, forced into the potentially fatal shivering agues and hallucinations that accompanied it, and found to be mentally cleansed afterwards. Lectures on 'mental hygiene' attracted students and doctors alike, as the public interest in all things psychiatric showed no sign of abating.

With so much of the nation grieving for lost loved ones or still reeling from the horrors of the battlefields, a period of mental numbness lasted for about a decade, before erupting in an explosion of anti-war sentiment expressed in books, plays and films. In the 1920s opposition to rearmament grew, culminating in the publication of several harrowing literary works, including the poems of Wilfred Owen and Siegfried Sassoon, on what trench warfare was really like. Linked to the Labour movement in Britain, the 'No More War' campaign thrived on the depressed and disillusioned climate of the 1930s, in which the conflict was viewed as senseless slaughter, leaving a 'butcher's bill' of killed and wounded.

In response to public feeling, the Army and Air Force Act of 1930 abolished the death penalty in the armed forces, except for the offences of mutiny and treason. The secretary of state for war had told the House of

Commons that the Army Council argued against abolition, claiming that the death penalty was still a necessary deterrent that would prevent many men becoming cowards, and similarly for desertion. Their advice was taken initially in the case of desertion, but a substantial majority in the Commons carried an amendment to the Act, substituting imprisonment as the maximum penalty for desertion. No trembling teenagers would ever again be shot at dawn for being unable to contain their terror.

The ghosts of the Somme were still casting their shadow over the next generation. Never before had it been so widely felt that some form of therapy would be helpful to those who had survived the war and yet were still suffering from its effects. The Tavistock Clinic, set up in 1920, became the first outpatient clinic in Britain to provide therapy for ordinary people unable to afford the expensive private fees of the new psychiatrists who had made their names – and fortunes – during the war. The clinic's founding medical director, Hugh Crichton-Miller, had worked with shell-shocked sufferers sent home from France and was keen to continue all that had been achieved. A psychoanalyst at heart, Crichton-Miller wanted to offer a refuge for those dismissed as the 'dregs of society', or said to be suffering from imaginary illnesses, under-employed or lacking in purpose.

His general aim was to try to understand each patient as the product of his environment and personal history. He undertook some of the first psychiatric work with children – many of them rendered fatherless by the war – and introduced social workers and speech therapists to the treatment as part of a holistic, ideologically free approach. Nearly 60 per cent of all the patients seen were reported to have been the product of 'an adverse early environment', much of which had been caused by the hardships of war.

Thanks largely to the integrity of the Tavistock's work, the new psychology gained credibility and respect within medical circles, with the clinic receiving the patronage of the Duke of Kent and the support of the British Medical Association. By 1931, the Tavistock had treated more than 11,000 people, although when Crichton-Miller resigned he cited as his reasons for doing so the arrogance and independence of its new staff.

Under the influence of J. R. Rees, the new medical director who joined in 1933, the clinic experimented with the recently discovered intravenous barbiturates for what was called 'chemical' analysis. As biochemical knowledge increased, the use of drugs to treat mental illness and neuroses gained in popularity in private clinics and mental hospitals across the country. Bromides had long been dispensed to relieve the tension of unresolved nervous states and milder depressions, but now everything from cocaine, hashish and mescaline to insulin, alcohol and paraldehyde was employed. Electro-convulsive therapy (ECT) came into fashion, putting faradism in the shade, along with the controversial use of surgery to remove the frontal lobes of the brain in the most severe cases of mental illness.

The years between 1918 and 1939 were ones of experimentation and progress. The new psychiatrists began to divide themselves into two clear groups: those who favoured the analytical psychological therapy advocated by Freud, and their counterparts who favoured the physical approach, dabbling with the many new tools at their disposal. The military, thankful to be free of the doctors who had so infuriated them during the war, watched their puffing and postulating from afar with the usual mix of scepticism and disdain. They might never have felt the need to approach them again, had not world events forced their hand.

On 1 September 1939, Germany invaded Poland, primarily in an attempt to reverse the result of the First World War and to undo the settlement that followed it. This aggressive action by the ambitious Nazi leader Adolf Hitler set up a chain of events that led to the first truly global conflict just twenty years after the war that it had been thought would end all wars. Prime Minister Neville Chamberlain, who had entered into a formal military alliance with Poland in an attempt to put a stop to Hitler's plan to overrun Europe, declared war on Germany on 3 September 1939. The announcement was not unexpected in the light of previous events, but it still caused considerable shock, especially to those who remembered the carnage of the last war.

Few realized what lay ahead. If they had, the psychological consequences could have caused mass mental breakdown. The new war was to entail the mobilization of armies on a vaster scale than ever before, the introduction of fearful new weapons of destruction and the involvement of civilian populations, which hitherto had been largely spared the full horrors of war. By the time it drew to an end, the dreadful cost in human suffering could only be speculated about. An estimated fifty million people were to lose their lives, of whom the majority were civilian victims of genocide, aerial bombardment, mass starvation and, finally, atomic warfare. And the toll on the minds of those employed to defend and attack them was to be almost as monstrous.

At the time of the invasion of Poland, 120,000 pensioners had received or were still receiving money from the War Office for psychiatric disability dating from the First World War. The Royal Army Medical Corps had just two psychiatric consultants, one for Britain and one for those troops abroad, and the Ministry of Pensions announced that while it would treat any servicemen found to be suffering from war neurosis, it would not give pensions except in special circumstances.

There was nothing like the eager rush to the colours that there had been in 1914, but none the less a steady stream of men had volunteered for the Territorials in the run-up to the war, willing to do all they could to prevent Hitler's advance across Europe. With a new wave of nostalgia for the Old Comrades, the veterans of the First World War, who spoke movingly of their experiences in a way that inspired the younger generation to take up arms on their behalf, young men offered their services. Although less trusting and respectful of their superiors than their predecessors had been, the servicemen of the Second World War hoped that as their superior officers had been young men during the First World War they would not risk the same heavy casualties or repeat its fatal mistakes.

In the strange, static climate of the conflict's first few months – known in Britain as the 'Phoney War' because of its lack of action or direct contact with the Germans – the feeling grew that no matter how much the new recruits were going to suffer, their predecessors had undoubtedly suffered more. In effect, the First World War became a touchstone of horror by which all later experiences were compared. Servicemen were said to be 'less scared of being afraid' than their forebears because they believed that it could never be that bad. But the Phoney War ended quickly and real conflict began. After the *blitzkrieg* [lightning war] of Poland, in which superior German ground–air attackers overwhelmed the ill-equipped and outnumbered Polish army, Hitler turned his attention to Holland and Belgium, invading in May 1940 as part of his master plan to capture France then England. British troops were sent in their droves to fend him off. Thereafter there was nothing phoney about what the young men sent to battle had to face.

What the servicemen of the 1940s failed to realize was that all wars are terrible for those who have to fight them, and each new experience has its own and entirely personal level of horror. In many cases, the physical conditions endured twenty years later were as gruelling, if not more so, than those of the trenches, and there was little or no preparation for the ordeal ahead.

The writer and poet Vernon Scannell, who was eighteen when he joined 'The Young Soldiers', the 70th Battalion of the Argylls with his brother, signed up because of an idealized view of what war would be like. Rejected by the RAF because of his short-sightedness, he was 'cold and broke' and joined the Army by default. 'I knew a lot about the First World War because I read everything I could lay my hands on, writers like Siegfried Sassoon and Owen. I thought that going into the Army would be pretty well what my father had done,' he said. 'The poetry and the books I'd read created within my mind a kind of romantic warscape of barbed wire and dugouts and sand-bags and so on, but the actual reality of the mud and the filth and the decaying corpses and the rats and the terror, of course, hadn't really sunk into my consciousness.' He was sent for training to become a 'machine for destruction', stabbing straw figures with bayonets after being told to think of them as Hun soldiers out to rape his sister and mother. 'The whole purpose of military training seemed to me that you would do things that the alter ego, the civilian self, would not even dream of doing. I don't think one made the connection with reality. It wasn't proper preparation for the real thing. That was a total shock to my entire being.'

The technological advances that had made the industrial use of weaponry so formidable in the First World War had been taken to new heights by the time the Allies were squaring up to Hitler. Soldiers now faced attack from every possible killing machine, and the air bombardments and those of the formidable German Panzer tanks brought a new meaning to the word terror.

Vernon Scannell described hearing his first full barrage. 'I had never heard that before and it really is a terrifying noise, a tremendous din. The kind of noise you would never, ever hear in another context. To be under a barrage, you feel that you are the personal target, that all this red hot, white hot metal that is screaming through the air and landing around you with extraordinary force is actually out to get you. When one is crouching in one's slit trench, one has one's hands down protecting one's genitalia because that is what you're most afraid of losing. It is absolutely instinctive.

'One recollection that stays very vivid in my mind is the voices of the wounded shouting. If they were making sense and shouting, "Stretcher bearer" and so on, they sounded pathetic enough, but I remember one very tough sergeant and he was hit very badly and was in great pain, and he was wailing and crying for his mother. This absolutely shook me, to hear this man who I'd always regarded as a hard case, wailing and moaning for his mummy. That was one of the things that no amount of preparation and training prepares you for.'

He said that nobody seemed to know what they were doing. 'It seemed to me utter, insane, mad confusion. Nobody had the foggiest idea. Believe it or not, they actually had a starting line for an attack, with white tape laid down like a school sports day. The whole thing was total chaos and confusion. The Germans were the baddies, as they had been in the First World War, and the Nazis were wicked and we didn't know a great deal more than that.

'What protected me was a curious kind of sense of unreality, which cocooned me against the reality of what was happening. When I look back it is really like a dream, and I think it was dreamlike even while it was happening. Everyone finds their own way of having to get through it, I suppose.'

By late spring 1940, the German Army had the Allies on the run. In six weeks, by effective operational planning backed by more than 4,000 dive-bombing aircraft and 141 divisions, Hitler had conquered the Netherlands, Belgium and Luxembourg and forced the French to capitulate. Spurred on by the German success, Italy declared war on Britain and France, and after a disastrous two-week campaign the British Army was pushed back to the beaches of Dunkirk. Many of its soldiers were raw recruits, and they were helpless in the face of the far better equipped and trained German military.

What followed was a chaotic evacuation, exposing many soldiers to constant bombardment for ten days, without food or sleep. Their units had been split up and their officers lost. They had seen French civilians killed and had not been able to retaliate. Men were trapped, waiting on the smoke-clouded beaches, expecting to be captured or injured or killed as the German planes dive-bombed them overhead. The military had expected to rescue a hundred thousand of them at most. Thanks to the legendary assistance of eight hundred volunteer civilians in charge of a motley array of pleasure boats, fishing skips and other assorted vessels, however, more than 340,00 rag-tag French and British troops were saved, a further 190,000 men from Normandy and Bordeaux.

Of those who arrived in Dover, having been forced to destroy almost all of their equipment, and watch helplessly as thousands of their comrades died, many crumbled mentally on reaching British soil. This demoralizing episode marked the end of the first phase of the war, and was a rapid, harsh induction into the horrors of warfare for those who had never before seen active service. Military commanders had thought that mass psychiatric breakdown was something that happened in the past and wouldn't happen again under the sort of leadership and training of which they had been in charge. This war was to be the most technologically advanced ever fought, they argued. It was not just a question of sending men over to the trenches armed with bayonets. But the stresses and strains of retreat and defeat, being sniped at and outgunned, and watching so many French civilians killed, produced wave after wave of shell-shocked cases. Four thousand had been killed on the beaches or at sea, thirteen thousand needed immediate medical attention and between 10 and 15 per cent of those were psychiatric cases, much to the horrified surprise of the administration.

In a 1940 memorandum for the medical profession from the Ministry of Pensions, anxious not to have to spend the next fifty years paying out vast sums to those affected by war, doctors were warned: 'The term shell shock has been a gross and costly misnomer and should be eliminated from our nomenclature . . . such terms must be rigidly avoided . . . The war produced no new nervous disorders and those which occurred had previously been recognized in civilian medical practice. No cases of psycho-neurosis or of mental breakdown, even when attributed to shell explosion or the effects thereof, should be classified as a battle casualty.'

Philip Gee, who was conscripted into the infantry battalion of the 5th Queen's Royal Regiment at the age of twenty-one, had been a pacifist in his youth. After five months of inactivity during the Phoney War and several days without food and water, he and his company were sent to hold back the German advance on Dunkirk while unarmed civilian refugees made their way to the coast for evacuation. Depleted of ammunition and mortar bombs, his unit came under heavy bombardment for twenty-four hours. 'It was literally a *blitzkrieg*. At least half of my company were either killed or badly wounded, I saw my own pals – lads from my own village – being blown to bits. I came across my best friend lying on the ground dead, half his head gone, and our driver with both legs blown off, shouting for water. It was terrible, really terrible, something I'd never seen before and never wanted to again. I changed from a teenager to a man overnight just because of that experience. We were building up to a situation which was becoming more terrible almost by the minute.'

On the retreat, he and the civilians he was protecting were repeatedly strafed by German machine-gun fire from the air, and he watched women and children killed in the ditches. 'I will never forget it. Even sixty years on I can wake up and still see it vividly in my mind, I can relive every single moment and always will.' By the time he and his fellow soldiers got to Dunkirk, they were shattered. 'We were so tired and fatigued that just keeping going took all the time and mental energy we had. We saw all the devastation all around and the distress amongst the civilians, but we didn't really take it all in. We just had to get to the beaches, that was all we knew.'

Dr Patrick de Mare, who worked in a field dressing station in Normandy, ten miles from the front at Caen, said: 'It was called the planned evacuation, but it was a whole army collapsed, really. It was around that time that they decided not to shoot deserters – well, they couldn't shoot the whole Army, could they?' Dr de Mare said that shell-shocked soldiers could hear the battle in the distance and had to be constantly reassured that the canvas of the tents was thick enough to prevent shrapnel getting through. 'It was gruesome work, some of them were in a terrible state – shaking like a leaf, blackouts, loss of memory, heart pains – and when you think of it, how could they stand it all? One person's comrade had his head blown off, others stood up to their necks in water in a slit trench and began to hallucinate, hear voices. One man behaved like an ape. It affected his posture and he was suddenly mentally defective. One of my jobs was to send people back if they recovered sufficiently but I must say I didn't find many were fit to go back.'

He ordered that the men be washed, fed, given a clean pair of pyjamas and put to bed. Using treatments based on rest and quiet, gentle hypnosis and occasionally Pentothal, it took him ten days on average to decide who was fit to return to duty, who required a further period of convalescence, and who needed to be sent back to Britain for more specialized treatment. 'Those who had "deserted" were sent to the glasshouse, a military prison, where they gave them an awful tough time. About a hundred of them who were in the glasshouse agreed to come back and face the battle again, and they were sent forward as a group to go back to their units. I was the last stepping-stone and was asked to screen them to decide which were too psychologically disturbed to go back. I failed all of them. They were all unfit, many were hallucinating and having panic attacks, they had no co-ordination and would have been very demoralizing to the forward areas because they were all shaking. The command psychiatrist was furious, but after he had seen them all too he agreed with me, and back they went.'

Dr de Mare said it was difficult to differentiate between those who were well enough to go back to fighting and those who weren't. 'I had one man who thought he could face it again and so did I. Suddenly there was a bit of strafing by a plane overhead and he was absolutely shaking like an infant, a frightened baby. He just switched from being a perfectly strong, confident-looking man to becoming a terrified baby and looking up at the sky with eyes of terror.'

The sheer numbers of those affected swept away any lingering notions that breakdown was only something that happened in the First World War trenches. Faced with the unpalatable statistics of psychiatric casualties they had never fully envisaged, the powers-that-be realized that there would have to be a major rethink. However much it went against the grain, they came to the conclusion that the war against Hitler would almost certainly have to be fought with the help of psychiatrists, although world events were not giving them much time.

Two months after Dunkirk, Britain found herself suddenly alone against an Axis-dominated Europe. The devastating ease with which Hitler had achieved his aims had staggered everyone and made him overconfident. With the fall of France, Germany had, for all practical purposes, won the war, and Hitler offered a dubious olive branch to Britain, which was not taken seriously by the government.

Hitler had no particular wish to invade Britain – his heart was set on the Soviet Union – but he knew he had to neutralize her, and that meant more than conquering her small and ill-equipped Army which was no match for the highly trained German forces. Fortunately for Britain, she was protected by a much larger Navy and the most advanced air-defence system in the world, built up in the 1930s to counter the German air threat.

Germany had to achieve air superiority to win, a fact recognized with some discomfort by the Führer's military chiefs. When Hitler decided to invade Britain on 16 July 1940, Hermann Goering, First World War fighter ace, air minister and chief of the Luftwaffe, promised to defeat the Royal Air Force in a couple of weeks as a prelude to the invasion of the English south coast. He told his generals: 'The Führer has ordered me to crush Britain with my Luftwaffe. By means of hard blows I plan to have this enemy, who has already suffered a crushing moral defeat, down on his knees in the nearest future, so that an occupation of the island by our troops can proceed without any risk.' His colleagues in the German High Command were not so sure.

None the less, from July to September 1940, the German Air Force mounted a relentless attack on British airfields, radar installations, ports and military bases. On 13 August, codenamed the 'Day of the Eagle' by the Luftwaffe pilots, 1,458 German aircraft attacked England and continued to do so for five days. Despite the heavy losses incurred by both sides, the campaign failed. British Spitfires and Hurricanes took on the German Stukas, Heinkels and Messerschmitts and won. German aircraft casualties totalled 1,733 against the British 915, and by the end of the battle the Germans had only 275 serviceable fighter aircraft against Britain's 732. Frustrated, Hitler switched to a strategy of mass bombing of British cities, a change of tactic that most historians since have regarded as a mistake. The subsequent Blitz took the pressure off the RAF and brought the Battle of Britain to an end.

British military hospitals were suddenly overrun with psychiatric casualties, and the continued bombing of London and other cities compounded the problem. Many of the major receiving centres for shell shock cases, including the Maudsley Hospital in London, had to be evacuated for fear of bombing, and the staff divided between the hastily converted Mill Hill School in north London and the Belmont Emergency Hospital in Sutton, Surrey, a former Victorian workhouse, commandeered by the Army and on the railway line between Epsom and London. Sutton soon became one of the chief centres for neurosis patients in south-east England, with more than two hundred transferred there after Dunkirk and the Battle of Britain, and many thousands passing through over the next few years.

In overall charge of Sutton was William Sargant, a civilian psychiatrist, a tall, immaculately dressed man with an imposing personality and an evangelical zeal who, in the course of his work with servicemen during the war, was to become one of the most controversial medical scientists in Britain. Fresh from working in America, Sargant knew only too well that the intense competition between the various hospitals recruited by the military would result in early comparisons between the methods of treatment and their successes, and he was determined to achieve results.

He knew, from those he had treated after the evacuation of Dunkirk, that the task facing him would be enormous and the numbers made effective treatment impossible. He wrote in his book *The Unquiet Mind*: 'I shall never forget the arrival of these Dunkirk soldiers in their tin hats and filthy uniforms, some of them wounded, many in a state of total and abject neurotic collapse, slouching along. What the papers termed a great British achievement seemed to us nothing better than a rout. Men swarmed into the hospital, some raging mutinously against their officers for having deserted them in a panic, and others swearing that they would never fight again. So complete a loss of morale was frightening to witness. Many were suffering from acute hysteria, reactive depression, functional loss of memory or of the use of their limbs, and a variety of other psychiatric symptoms which one would see in such abundance only during a war or after an earthquake or railroad accident, when even perfectly normal people are apt to break.'

Sargant had vivid childhood memories of mentally impaired veterans of the First World War begging on the streets of London. He blamed the lamentable existence of 'these utterly unemployable human derelicts' on a lack of early and proper psychiatric treatment by his predecessors. 'The most important lesson taught to us by Dunkirk and the Battle of Britain,' he wrote, 'was never to let a neurotic pattern of thought or behaviour remain fixed in the patient's brain for a minute longer than necessary. It is like the surgical rule which requires that a fractured leg must immediately be put into a splint.'

Sargant considered himself a saver of lives and of money. He claimed after the war to have saved millions of pounds in war pensions by curing men who might otherwise have been a burden on the tax-payer for the rest of their natural lives. He was fortunate that, in his friend Dr Eliot Slater and in Dr Louis Minski, his clinical director and medical superintendent, he was allowed to experiment on his new patients as much as he liked, with little or no supervision. As in the previous war, doctors like William Sargant, an ardent anti-Freudian, were given free rein by the military to experiment on the men in their care, as the race to prevent a mass epidemic of hysteria began. With his colleague Dr Nellie Craske and others, he tried and tested some mould-breaking techniques, in particular using recently discovered barbiturate drugs. 'They never once put an obstacle in my way when I wanted to try new treatments on our patients,' he wrote later. 'We were not subject to some of the irksome restraints imposed on our younger colleagues at Mill Hill. We generally got our own way in the end.'

Most servicemen who arrived at Sutton were suffering from the type of mental and physical exhaustion, a state of constant fatigue, that could not be relieved by normal rest. They were thin and pale, with listless apathy and permanent tremors of their head or hands. Many suffered from terrifying dreams, became easily startled or confused, and were tense and lacking in confidence. Some had lost their memories, others their speech or the use of their limbs – the classic acute hysterical reaction to the terrors they had undergone. Sargant quickly snapped into action.

With rest and proper food, occupational therapy and quiet, the majority improved rapidly and were allowed to return to their units. Those who couldn't sleep voluntarily were given drugs to help them sleep, eat and remember. Hypnosis was used to encourage patients to recall their experiences, along with sedatives to dampen down the waves of emotion that often engulfed the patient when a memory returned. In overall charge of treatment, William Sargant's imposing character dominated all.

Dr Ann Dally, a former student of the psychiatrist, described him as 'egocentric, powerful, very ambitious and more than a little scary'. She recalled: 'He liked dramatic treatments and situations and he worked very hard on that. The war offered him a lot of severely psychologically damaged patients and he had a lot of power over them because he wasn't supervised. One patient he showed to us over and over again, who never seemed to get better, had been trapped in a sea of boiling oil at Dunkirk and Sargant used to give him carbon dioxide or something to release his memories and he would then act as if he was in a sea of boiling oil, shouting and screaming and leaping all about the place. The medical students loved it.'

Dr Dally said that Sargant gave his patients drugs that would 'blow them out of their mind' and make them do things they thought they couldn't do, like walk or speak or move a previously paralysed limb. In some cases, he gave them such huge doses that they slept almost continuously for three weeks at a time. He called it 'first aid for the brain' and believed this enforced deep-sleep treatment broke up the 'vicious circle' of the panic state and stopped anxieties spreading.

'He liked using drugs, he was always experimenting with new drugs, always excited when he found something new that he thought worked better,' she said. 'He was very fond of sodium amytal and amphetamines and the various forms of anaesthesia. He used to do this continuous narcosis treatment, keeping people asleep for weeks on end, only waking them up to be fed or washed. He had a whole ward of them which I found quite creepy, all these people sound asleep in darkness, a bit like the nocturnal house in the zoo.'

Dr Peter Dally, Sargant's senior registrar after the war, described the treatments as 'speeded-up psychotherapy'. He added: 'When Sargant started doing psychiatry he nearly despaired and went into general practice. It was all psychotherapy and hours and hours of talking and it was very dull. But the arrival of the war gave him a freer hand. He was really inspired and felt that he could really effect cures. It was like a religious conversion.'

Sargant quickly dismissed psychotherapy as 'useless talk' when fast action was needed. He considered it a waste of time and maintained that it had not fulfilled the promise held out for it by its exponents after the First World War.

Instead, he wholeheartedly embraced the technological advances made in chemical research and modern machines, which provided a quick remedy for any soldier needed back in the theatre of war.

'He found that drugs could effect a change even if it was only very temporary and short-lived. He felt that if he could experiment with combinations of drugs and huge doses of them, he might achieve some good results,' explained Dr Dally.

In the course of his work, Sargant discovered that sodium amytal often made his patients relive their most horrific battlefield experiences. Having spoken of it and gone through a catharsis, they generally made a full recovery. The drug encouraged them to talk and talk, so much so that a separate drug would have to be given to make them stop. It was the birth of the truth drug. He called his technique 'abreaction', or the release of buried emotions. Inducing a semi-hypnotic state with drugs, Sargant encouraged the release of the rage and agony of a terrible event, he laid the patient in a darkened room and prompted the memories with suggestions of what it must have been like. When it came to the crucial moment in the event, such as the death of a close friend, Sargant would ask the patient to focus all his anger and grief on the German machine-gunner who had done it, or the man who fired the mortar, thus channelling all the suppressed fear and anger at the enemy. The patient would often become very distressed, screaming and shouting his rage at the imagined gunman. Only when all the rage was spent would Sargant interject and tell the patient he had overcome the enemy and confronted his own fears.

His most celebrated case of abreaction, which he wrote up in the *Lancet*, concerned a soldier, retreating to Dunkirk, who came across his own brother lying by the roadside with a severe abdominal wound. At his brother's earnest plea, the soldier dragged him into a field and hastened his end with a rifle shot. Thereafter, the soldier's right hand, the one he used to pull the trigger, became paralysed. With the use of the drug and hypnotism, Sargant claimed he was able to rid the soldier of his guilt and grief, and thus restore his mobility.

The following week, the *Daily Mail* picked up on the case history under the headline: 'Hypnotized Soldier Tells of Secret Grief: He Shot Brother'. The patient was desperately upset – the other men in the ward had quickly worked out it was him – and he relapsed to such a degree that Sargant had to arrange his immediate discharge from the Army. Medical ethics, not truth, were the first casualty of William Sargant's war, although he later expressed his remorse over the incident.

Sargant believed that many of his patients' neuroses could be attributed to what he described as 'personality deviations, constitutional instability and lack of stamina'. The most serious cases that emerged from Dunkirk, he said, suffered an accumulation of strains: 'bodily danger, continuous physical exertion, loss of sleep . . . intermittent but perpetually recurrent bombardment . . . the sight of comrades and civilian refugees being killed round them . . . and continual withdrawal from the enemy; the impossibility of striking back produced a sense of frustration that contributed to the disastrous effect on the mind'.

One of his patients, who lost two thirds of his unit before being captured by the Germans on the retreat to Dunkirk, suffered from extreme hysterical symptoms, including fainting, vomiting and severe headaches. Sargant wrote in his notes: 'Escaped after bayoneting guards and appears to have wandered about in captured territory . . . appears to have had some terrible experiences, including seeing four hundred Guards massacred after surrendering, and tanks running backwards and forwards over civilians in a town square.'

Another man, a driver in the Royal Artillery who had lost his memory so completely that he did not know his own wife, was given sodium amytal and recalled the events of a particularly nasty bombardment. 'He saw people with heads blown off and holes blown in their sides. He was saved by being behind a tree.' Sargant wrote. 'He saw horses and cows in the field next to the wood all wounded and struggling. He got a revolver and shot some of the animals dead.'

Sargant went on to develop his deep-sleep treatment still further for his most severely depressed patients, giving them huge doses of insulin – enough to bring down their blood-sugar levels and put them into a coma – before feeding them large quantities of sugar through a stomach tube. There were incredible risks with the treatment – irreversible brain damage or death could easily have occurred in patients forced into such a coma – and there was no scientific basis for it, other than the idea of giving the system a total shock. Sargant based his claims for its success largely on the healthier-looking men who emerged physically heavier from the treatment, believing that the weight increase 'greatly speeded recovery and armed them against further stresses'. Faced with the problem of acquiring sugar in wartime, he switched to potatoes, mashed into a fluid at first and then fed orally to semiconscious men. The treatment was so different from anything tried before that it soon caught on, and within a few months other hospitals were trying it.

But Sargant's favourite treatment was electro-convulsive therapy (ECT), which was brand new and a significant advance on the First World War's faradism technique. It was developed after doctors treating mentally ill epileptics noticed that their patients' psychiatric symptoms improved after a fit. The idea was that if enough electricity was passed through a patient's brain for long enough and at sufficient strength, it would induce a seizure or fit that would clear the mind of the problem. Treated with great suspicion by the British medical establishment, ECT could only be used in extreme cases, but Sargant used it on hundreds of patients believed to be suffering from severe depression.

'He gave people enormous numbers of shocks, more than anyone else dared to,' said Dr Ann Dally. 'He took great risks with his patients and he boasted a lot about what he had done. His patients either absolutely adored him or saw him as the devil incarnate.' She admitted that Sargant could be considered fanatical. Several patients, arching their backs during the course of the fits the electrical current induced, fractured their vertebrae. 'He might give some patients twenty shocks at a time, usually twice a week. It was fairly horrifying in those days because you didn't use anaesthetics or muscle relaxants and the patient was held down by a sheet while they had a fit. It appeared terribly brutal – I didn't like it – and I think the reputation spread that here was this monster who was handing out electric shocks to everyone, and the stories spread that people's backs were being broken. He became the prototype of the wicked person using ECT.'

Philip Gee, the young pacifist who saw so much horror at Dunkirk, and who had to resign his Army commission on medical grounds, was given the insulin-coma treatment and then ECT when he suffered a breakdown. 'That was a terrible, terrible experience,' he said. 'You had no breakfast and you were wheeled up on a trolley and laid on a bed. You had no idea what was going to happen. Nobody told you anything at all, and then all these figures came out of the darkness of this room towards you. And that was it. I remembered no more at all because an electric pulse was sent through all the things they put on your head and knocked you out and induced an epileptic fit. I shall never forget those figures coming towards you, ready to grab you. All of us had a great deal of dislike for it because it made you much less than you were. It put you into a state of convulsion which was totally alien to your personality and it was imposed on you without you knowing.'

John Hanstock, a Yorkshire-born sailor on the battleship *Warspite* in the Mediterranean Sea and the Indian Ocean, suffered a complete mental breakdown when his best friend was killed after being transferred to another ship. 'He came to see me the night before and I said cheerio and he said, "I've got a bad feeling about this." I promised to write and he turned round and said it again. About two days later it was broadcast on the ship's Tannoy that the ship had been sunk with all hands. I was very unhappy about this. I can't describe it. He knew that was going to happen. It happens to everyone in the Navy in wartime. At one time your luck's going to run out and that was it.'

He had previously found the experience of being on a warship during a battle quite terrifying, and developed chronic claustrophobia at being stuck in a room ten feet by seven feet with six other men. The death of his friend made matters worse. 'That really started to increase the effect, I was getting worse and worse,' he said. 'The thing I feared more than anything was when the orders were passed out over the Tannoy to prepare for sea, duty men close up, close X and Y doors, close daylights and scuttle, and believe me, I was bloody terrified. Nobody knew I was terrified. You don't allow yourself to complain in the Navy.'

He bottled up his feelings successfully until he was knocked out by the explosion of an ammunition dump and felt himself losing control. 'The anxiety was a gnawing thing. It gnaws at you, so you have to make more of an effort to hide it. I thought I was very successful, I thought no one else knew. I convinced myself that I was not showing the staring look that was one of the symptoms of the First World War. But things seemed to be coming to a head. I was feeling I couldn't go on. We got back to Portsmouth and I did what I usually did. I was on the guard-rail looking into the water, trying to get a bit of order into my thinking. I felt a hand on my shoulder and it was this tall chap from Newcastle, a medical chap and he said he'd been ordered to take me to the sick bay. I told him there was nowt wrong with me, but I knew instinctively that someone must have been watching me, keeping his eye open. He took me by the shoulders and led me down.' In the sick bay he met a sub-lieutenant from his home area. 'He just came up to me and looked in my eyes and he said, "Now then, lad." He spoke Yorkshire just like I did. A kind word. I'd not had a kind word. Nobody does in the forces. I couldn't bear to talk. I just let go. The floodgates opened and I cried and cried, as my mother would have seen me cry as a child. I was broken-hearted. I had no way of controlling it. I thought I'd let the side down really badly, I felt I had tried so hard up until then. I couldn't speak, I couldn't say thank you. I couldn't say anything. I've got parents who can't speak, and whether I were frightened to speak I don't know to this day. And that was the end of my life in the Navy on board ship. I couldn't have given anything more to the Navy then. I was empty.'

He was sent to the Knowle Naval Hospital in Manchester where he was shocked to find men in white coats, locked doors and windows too small to escape from. He felt as if he were in a prison and realized that he had become a mental patient virtually overnight. All his preconceived ideas about life in an asylum were confirmed: the sounds and sights terrified him. Being on the receiving end of the new treatments was equally bewildering. He soon became a recipient of early narcotherapy, hypnosis and insulin treatment, as well as ECT.

'There was a little lady, a cleaner on the ward, and she used to take a great deal of pleasure in saying "Treatment day today," ' he recalled. 'And they'd bring all the twelve beds together, cheek by jowl, moved up till we were touching each other with the head to the centre. And then came the brilliant big blue capsules, about two of them. "Take these," they'd say, and it made all your flesh creep and go prickly. And then you heard the people coming along, the doctor, sister and nurses. They came along the line, one by one. I always seemed to be the last to go. Out of the corner of my eye I could see them coming, but I couldn't really see what was going on.

'And then the nurse comes along with the sponge and they put the saline solution on the head, then the earphone things, and you're thrashing about and someone holds you by each arm and the treatment comes closer and closer to you. Things start feeling a little wobbly then because you do not know what the treatment is doing. You think it's going to produce pain because it's electrical – I mean, when you think of saline and electricity, it's the perfect carrier of voltage, isn't it? And then they say, "Now then, Mr Hanstock, just lay back gently," and you feel the damp of the thing. And then nothing. The next thing you know you'd be saying to the nurse, "When am I going to have the treatment?" and they'd say, "You've had it." There was something about the words ECT, it sounded medieval, it sounded painful. No matter how many times you had it you always thought it was going to be painful. I can't say that it ever made me feel better.'

Given sodium amytal, however, John Hanstock said he felt 'cleansed' after reliving his wartime experiences. 'You've got no control, your mind's up in the air, you've no control over the power of the drug and you just talk and talk and talk. You're asked a question and you answer the question. There's no dodging it. You can't fight against it and if you've got a skeleton in the cupboard, believe you me, they'll find it,' he said.

Margaret Boger, a nurse at Sutton, has vivid memories of the ECT treatments in which she said she could hear bones cracking like pistol shots. 'I never liked it,' she said. 'It was really unpleasant. Even worse was the cardiazol injection. With cardiazol, the worst thing was you couldn't talk, you couldn't cry out. They would struggle and writhe about. It was horrible, and without the muscle relaxant you got broken bones. It was like going back to primitive medicine. We had a lot of fractures to begin with. My job was to put the gag in their mouth. You just opened the mouth and said, "Bite, please," otherwise they would bite their tongues in half. In some cases the treatment helped but I'm not sure, really, that all that stress and strain was worth it.'

Nurse Boger remembers the convoys of men arriving at the hospital. 'Some arrived on stretchers, they arrived clad in whatever they could find. Some of them had semi-uniforms on, anything that people had given them. Some of their uniforms were all in tatters. They were grimy, dirty, wounded and shell-shocked, shaking, unable to speak – rambling, some of them. I did see that and I shan't forget it,' she said. She and the other nurses administered hot drinks to the servicemen and put them to bed. Later, they were given a cocktail of drugs, under what one of the doctors referred to as the 'Brave New World' regime. The drugs she gave out included 'Blue Bombers' and something they called 'Jungle Juice', which was paraldehyde. 'You mixed it with water and swallowed it. We used to dispense it out at night. The men liked it, it was all they had.'

Another nurse, Anna Maria Donegan, said some of the patients became hooked on the drugs they were given. 'People got dreadfully attached to it, it was very addictive,' she said. There were several suicides, men who would take sleeping tablets and cross the Downs and be found dead. 'I remember one chap who cut his wrists with a razor blade. There was blood all over the toilet floor. And another man, a captain in the Navy, a very nice man with lovely children, who had been bombed and sunk at sea. We thought he was all right and then one evening he was missing and didn't come back, and the next morning we found he had killed himself. That was such a shock, he didn't tell anybody. The worst was a medical orderly who seemed to be better and we let him home for Christmas. First he killed his two daughters, then his wife and finally himself. It was terrible.'

One of the Sutton inmates was Bert Woolhouse, one of six bomb-disposal experts who had been buried alive after a German bomb exploded and killed five of his colleagues. In bomb disposal, casualty rates were as high as in any war zone, and fatalities were double. Before the experts went in, soldiers had to spend hours or even days uncovering the bomb buried in the ground beneath them, knowing that death could be just seconds away.

'You always think that you're not the one going to get blown up, it's going to be other people,' said Bert. 'When it happens your world collapses around you. They had to sweep up the pieces of the other people that were there. Pinky's arm came flying by and all they found of my dear friend Jacky was his leg in a wellington boot, which was all they were able to bury. Me and my mate Swanee were the only ones who survived and he was very badly hurt mentally and he ended up in a mental asylum.'

Bert can hardly remember arriving at Sutton, where he was sent a few days after walking out of hospital. 'I was shell-shocked and I kept shaking and things weren't right with me. My senses weren't there. I was like a zombie. When I saw these nurses, I thought I was in heaven. My whole world had collapsed around me, I'd lost all my friends. They put me in bed and gave me some tablets and I slept. They tried to give me some sort of meal, it was always macaroni cheese and mashed potatoes, but I couldn't eat. They would give you some sort of pill, and you'd go and lie on your bed and sleep there till the next day. And the next day they'd ask you all the most intimate questions about your life, all sorts of things about your sex life. There was a thing going backwards and forwards, a graph of some sort, which I'd only ever seen on films since, but which I now know was for the truth drug. The next thing they give you is another tablet of some sort, magic pills they called them, and after you'd had several other things done to you, you laid on your bed and you didn't wake up until another day.'

It was at Sutton that Bert Woolhouse encountered another weapon in the armoury against war neurosis, Sargant's right-hand woman, Dr Nellie Craske. 'I was frightened out of my life by Dr Craske,' he said. 'I was frightened to look at her because she could do things with her eyes. She had greyish blue eyes and you seemed to look right through them. She got me all wired up, asking me questions and touching different parts of my body. She asked me all sorts of questions about sex – I couldn't believe it, I'd never heard anything like it. She'd sit in front of you and she used to wear stockings with suspenders and she used to pull her skirt up and put your hand on the top of her thigh and make you look into her eyes.' Dr Craske also asked Bert's wife Jane several deeply probing questions about their sex life, which came as a great shock to a woman who had never before come into contact with the enquiring spirit of psychiatric science. 'I couldn't believe what I was being asked,' she remembered.

Bert was given an assortment of drugs, but often pretended to take his pills because he didn't want to sleep all the time. 'One fellow, it was horrible, he was on paraldehyde which is a very powerful drug, and when you take someone off it, they crave for it. I've seen this particular fellow claw at the drug cabinet with his fingers, until his nails were bleeding, to try and get the drug. They used to have to give him some other injections to quieten him down so as we'd all get some sleep.

'The nurses knew about paraldehyde and some of them used to get it as well and they became addicted to it. Some of the capers they got up to was no one's business. We had a staff dance each week when the nurses and the patients used to go together and we used to get up to some capers. They'd been at the paraldehyde and they'd say, "Well, I had a tiny little drop," and it made them potty as a pancake, that was our expression. It was a bloody madhouse.'

Sargant had a still more experimental way of mending the defective human computer. Using a legal loophole, he managed to perform the ultimate operation on several of his patients: leucotomy – a surgical procedure to cut away the nervous pathways connecting different parts of the brain believed to affect emotions. A similar operation called lobotomy had been widely practised in the USA from the late 1930s, but the operation was frowned upon in the UK. Sargant, unsupervised and unafraid to experiment, would discharge a patient into the care of a friend at a teaching hospital – which was not subject to the same regulations and allowed more experimentation as many patients were volunteers – and carry out the operation there. The patient could not be readmitted to Sutton as people would start to suspect, and had to be sent instead to 'understanding friends'. The psychiatrist described the subterfuge in his autobiography as 'doing good by stealth – it had to be done somehow'.

Largely because of the success of Sargant's experiments and those of doctors elsewhere, narcotherapy – the use of sodium amytal, sodium pentathol and new short-acting barbiturates to produce an emotional crisis – became a standard element of military psychiatry in the Allied armies. A patient fresh from the battlefield would immediately be put to sleep for a day or two. It was believed that such front-line sedation prevented irreparable damage. By triggering the release of pent-up emotions quickly, Sargant claimed, few nervous cases would go beyond cure or reach the point of complete mental disintegration.

Set against the time-consuming methods of the Freudian analysts, who believed it took years of intensive therapy to cure a neurotic, Sargant's pioneering ideas held immediate appeal to the military. Quicker, easier and cheaper to carry out – like Lewis Yealland before him – his treatment could almost guarantee to get a soldiers back to the front line with a few weeks.

Dr Peter Dally insisted that despite some of the more unusual and experimental aspects of life at Sutton, Sargant – who himself suffered from depression – did mould-breaking work that was ultimately for the greater good of his patients. 'He benefited from the war in the sense that he had a purpose. There was so much chaos going on and he had a free hand to experiment and do what he felt might do good. He liked being misunderstood and the object of controversy to a certain extent, and he was prepared to take great risks for the sake of his patients. He had tremendous enthusiasm and understanding of psychiatric form, but Belmont (Sutton) was a tight little unit and he ran his own empire, really. That was why he experimented so dramatically, to get bigger and better results.'

Despite his apparently draconian methods, there was a genuinely altruistic side to William Sargant, who was not afraid of the military men who gave him orders. He wrote angrily of the 'folly' of patching up servicemen only to return them to the same kind of stress that had caused their break-down. Wherever possible, in severe cases, he arranged for the patient to be discharged from the Army, 'hoping that they would make some sort of success in civil life'. He dismissed the First World War practice of shooting men for cowardice as an example to others, claiming 'mere will-power cannot control the failing functions of a broken-down brain. Under strong or continuous stresses, no threats or exemplary punishment can prevent breakdowns.'

He cited the case of one tough sergeant major ordered by his senior officer to encourage his men during the Battle of Britain to stand to attention in the middle of the square at an airfield in Kent, which was subject to repeated daylight bombing attacks. He collapsed and was sent to Sutton. Sargant commented that the only treatment he needed was a change of unit and a new commanding officer. Sargant was also instrumental in the campaign to obtain pensions for war neurotics in defiance of the government decree that it would not provide them. One of his patients, later immortalized in the popular wartime film *The Foreman Went to France*, was a soldier who rescued some special machinery from a French factory for making guns synchronized to fire bullets through revolving aeroplane propellers. Against all odds, and with the Germans at his heels, the man managed to get the consignment out of France and away from enemy hands, before collapsing with a nervous depression so severe that even Sargant couldn't cure him.

Discharged from the Army, the soldier found that the only job he could hold down was making cups of tea at the air ministry. He was denied a pension, although he had been in perfect health before the war and had perhaps done more to win the Battle of Britain than anyone else in his building. Sargant wrote: 'We could do nothing more for him except protest and nobody much listened to us. We were learning to get round by guile. Some of us had friends in high places.' Eventually, those friends blew up such a storm in the House of Commons that the government capitulated and neurosis was recognized as a disorder 'attributable to or aggravated by war service'.

Because of its proximity to a railway line, Sutton was repeatedly bombed during the war, including one raid in which sixteen patients were killed and many more injured. 'As soon as the sirens sounded,' Sargant wrote, 'soldiers and civil-defence patients would rush madly out to some supposedly safer place. Those whose nerves had originally broken down while they were sheltered by a house would make for the open and often stay out all night, returning almost frozen in the morning. Those, on the other hand, who had been bombed and broken down in the open would take cover in buildings. It was complete chaos.' After a brief period of evacuation to Sussex, Sargant and his staff returned to find every window-pane shattered.

For the final years of the war, they lived in near darkness inside, behind boarded-up windows, continuing their research, while those in the medical profession who favoured the physical methods lapped up every report they produced.

'To the young psychiatrists, Sargant's work was very uplifting,' explained Dr Wilfrid Jones, a doctor in the RAMC. 'He was showing us all these treatments that could be done, that it wasn't necessary to embark on long-term psychotherapy. There were short-cuts to improving the anxious and tense patient by abreaction, ECT and insulin coma. The results were immediate.'

By the time the war had advanced into its third year with no sign of abating, many doctors began to realize that the real issue was not which type of treatments were used and to what effect, but that many of the servicemen arriving in their care through conscription should never have been sent to war in the first place. They referred to what the Army called 'the dull and backward, the feeble-minded, imbeciles or idiots', who were wholly unsuited to the business of war.

The warnings that echoed through the centuries, from the American Civil War and beyond, of the importance of proper screening at recruitment level, had been ignored yet again, mainly because of the threat such interference imposed on the military commanders. Less than twenty years had passed since the Southborough Inquiry made it clear that to prevent such a mass psychological crisis happening again, military recruits should be properly screened and unstable men turned down. But at the outbreak of war, no system was in place: the military was recruiting anyone it could get its hands on, including the 'dullards', mental defectives and even those still suffering from shell shock incurred during the First World and Boer Wars.

Vernon Scannell, the teenage poet and idealist who joined up with his brother, said there was no attempt to screen recruits in any way. 'They would have taken anyone who had two more or less workable eyes, arms and legs,' he said. 'There was a man in my platoon who was retarded. He was a simpleton and he certainly had no imagination. He didn't have much sense, poor chap, and he couldn't stand it in Normandy at all. And somehow he managed to get his rifle muzzle into his mouth and blow his own head off. He shot himself because he couldn't stand the strain, simply that. He was like a desperately terrified animal and he couldn't bear it any longer.'

In a mood of public gloom following the Dunkirk débâcle and the influx of the first wave of psychiatric casualties, the Army Council was divided. Some generals insisted that dull men made the best servicemen; others claimed that modern warfare no longer required sheer weight of numbers or cannon fodder, but demanded skilled personnel. Faced with the prospect of another hysteria epidemic among its troops and with front line doctors pressing for change, the modernizers finally won, and turned to the Tavistock Clinic to help them solve their manpower problems.

CHAPTER FOUR

An eclectic mix of Freudian psychoanalysts and radical psychologists, thirty-three Tavistock psychiatrists took the King's oath, a uniform, and the instant rank of major. Thirty were employed by the Army, where the bulk of the neurosis problems had traditionally been; the remainder served with the RAF and the Royal Navy. Collectively they were known as the 'Tavi Brigadiers'. J. R. Rees, still director of the clinic, was appointed consulting psychiatrist to the RAMC, with his assistant Henry Yellowlees as consultant to the British Expeditionary Forces in France.

For the first time in history, psychiatrists put on uniforms and were drafted into the heart of the military. Within six months, an Army psychiatric service was established, with a psychiatrist attached to the medical headquarters of each command in the UK. These specialist doctors acted as advisers to MOs and consultants for outpatients. Teams of between three and ten area psychiatrists were drafted in to work under the command psychiatrists, running outpatient centres and travelling to India, North Africa and Italy with the troops, to act as filters for the British hospitals.

The primary focus of their early work was prevention, not cure. The doctors were ordered to concentrate on morale-building, man-management and screening techniques for officers and recruits. Systems were set in place for dealing with traumatized men, but their main work was in forming a sort of psychological blueprint for action, based on previous experiences. A battery of new drugs and treatments, already unleashed in the war against neurosis, was given full military backing, paving the way for even more servicemen to become test material for new methods of unlocking the secrets of the mind, even if the public still had no idea what was going on.

David Stafford-Clark, a young medical officer with the RAF who worked at Bomber Command, said: 'Psychiatry in those days was still regarded as an extremely cranky operation. The public didn't understand why doctors should listen to patients and not just prescribe pills. They thought that psychiatrists deserved to be called "trick cyclists", a common term. The whole thing was a joke if you'd not suffered or been treated.'

The Tavistock doctors took themselves seriously. They had a lot of fashionable and rather radical ideas but little real experience, and were reluctant to call upon the expertise of doctors who had worked at Craiglockhart, Netley and Maghull, whom they considered as coming from the Dark Ages of psychiatry. Dr Jones, medical officer to an infantry battalion, explained: 'The doctors at the Tavistock were a different breed. They were concerned about the unconscious mind and psychotherapy, whereas the mental-hospital psychiatrists were more concerned with looking after patients rather than treating them.' He said there was a growing gulf between the two.

Encouraged by their newly acquired status, the Tavistock doctors allowed their imaginations free rein. One Freudian psychoanalyst declared that the Germans, as an essentially homosexual race, should be attacked only from the rear. They demanded that images of large guns be banned from newsreels on the grounds that they caused soldiers' castration complexes. The War Office – already struggling to defend its new psychiatrists against the stiff-lipped generals who dismissed them as 'fifth army columnists' – instructed the doctors to concentrate on the screening and recruitment training instead.

With government support, however, the new psychiatrists gradually began to infiltrate Army recruitment, training and morale. They invented something called 'battle inoculation' in which recruits were subjected to explosions, noise and had to take cover from live ammunition. The result of these extraordinary tests was the discovery that if the size and proximity of controlled explosions near recruits was gradually increased their anxiety was minimized. They also experimented with 'hate training', in which recruits were brutalized, shown atrocity photographs, taken to slaughterhouses and had animal blood thrown on them during exercises, all in an attempt to harden them to the experiences ahead. It was eventually banned as too sadistic.

The psychiatrists put the media to good use. Morale-boosting films were commissioned and scripted, with a Utopian message of creating a New Model Army of psychologically motivated citizens. Using intelligence and personality tests, the psychiatrists believed that they could weed out those men most likely to crack up under the strain of warfare, and make sure that the remainder fitted neatly into their new military roles – in effect, to make sure that a lot of square pegs didn't get put into round holes.

The selection of officers came under scrutiny for the first time in the history of the British military. The Germans had been using psychological tests on officers since 1926, but in Britain, the right school or good family connections had sufficed in an interview process that usually took no more than fifteen minutes and made some disastrous mistakes. The problem was that the Army wasn't getting the right sort of officers: it needed factory foremen, clerks and school-teachers, ordinary men who would be able to relate to the servicemen in their charge, but the right sort of people either didn't want to be officers, or simply couldn't bypass the old system.

Now, based on the German techniques of temperament, personality and intelligence testing, psychiatrically trained MOs asked candidates questions on anything from sex and religion to political tendencies. For the first time, democratic values and scientific methods were replacing the 'old boy network', much to the increasing consternation of the generals who had perpetuated it. The psychiatrists came up with established War Office selection boards, the forefather of modern psychometric testing, in which candidates were divided into 'leaderless groups' and set practical tasks such as building bridges across imaginary streams, carrying fake bombs away from danger areas and so on, to see who were the natural leaders and who worked best in a team.

Major Wilfred Bion, a decorated First World War veteran and psychiatrist at the Tavistock, who was one of those put in charge of such selection processes, wrote in the *Lancet* of its pioneering nature:

The essence of the technique was to provide a framework in which selecting officers, including a psychiatrist, could observe a man's capacity for maintaining personal relationships in a situation of strain that tempted him to disregard the interests of his fellows for the sake of his own.

Making the most of what Major Bion called the 'existing emotional field' of the candidate's eagerness to get a commission and his fear of failure, the leaderless group project was devised.

It was a method so simple and so obvious that its revolutionary nature can easily be lost sight of [he wrote]. The man found he was not entered in a free-for-all competition with other candidates. Instead he found himself the member of a group and the tests were not of himself but of the group. No lead was given about organization or leadership; these were left to emerge and it was the duty of the observing officer to watch how any given man was reconciling his personal ambitions, hopes and fears, with the requirements exacted by the group for its success.

Philip Gee, the former pacifist whose company was decimated in the retreat to Dunkirk, later applied to become an officer and took part in one of the earliest selection boards. 'It was something that had never happened before. The men who were running it were obviously psychologically trained. You had intelligence tests to do, and the practical as well. We were given these tasks and it was a piece of cake,' he said. 'I never saw anything difficult about it at all, I knew exactly what they wanted me to do. It was all rather interesting and I enjoyed it. We were divided into small groups, about six in each and they were obviously looking for ones displaying leadership and intelligence. There were physical tasks, all of which were not easy but not impossible. Provided you went to it through the only logical way that lay ahead, you passed. So often you saw others going about things in a totally wrong way and you inwardly laughed your head off – they simply weren't practical at all – and you weren't at all surprised when they were told no and you were told yes.'

The new personality and intelligence tests revolutionized the Army; it was said that the leaderless group tests did as much to win the war as anything. The success was viewed as phenomenal, and those in industry, impressed with the way such a vast organization as the Army was coping with the problem of man management in a time of crisis, quickly expressed an interest in applying the same technique to their own recruiting trials. It was thus that psychological tests became normal in industry and administration.

But it was not all plain sailing. In the 1940s there was still considerable opposition to the methods and to what was seen by some as the insidious infiltration of psychiatrists into the armed forces. Within a short period of time, the numbers of psychiatrists in the Army had grown from two to more than 130, with an additional hundred or so medical officers engaged in neuro-psychiatric duties. The antipathy to their presence often came from the highest sources: the top brass simply didn't see the need for such mumbo-jumbo and regarded its exponents as civilian eccentrics.

Major General E. Phillips, director of medical services, condemned psychiatry as 'a new form of witchcraft'. His view was that the science had gone too far. 'There is a definite case of psychiatry getting out of hand,' he wrote in the medical diary to the 21st Army group. 'Too many cases are being evacuated back to the UK. A senior consultant psychiatrist should be sent over to go into the matter with a view to tightening up the serious wastage under this heading.'

J. R. Rees, while writing glowingly of the work of psychiatrists in the *British Medical Journal* in 1943, conceded: 'There has been and will still be in the future, much resistance to be overcome before the principle of selection by scientific procedure is accepted. Selection pays, but it also carries a threat; for the more accurate it becomes the more it explodes the pleasant and universal fantasy that each of us has a Field-Marshal's baton in his knapsack.'

Later, he complained:

Much opprobrium has come to Army psychiatrists because there has necessarily been a high discharge rate from psychiatric causes. We cannot tolerate the retention of sickness and inefficiency just because we wish to avoid tiresome opposition and criticism of ourselves. It is very striking how few of the really intelligent and valuable leaders fail to appreciate the contribution of psychiatry, but we have to beware of those who become 'converts' and thus lose their capacity to help us with real criticism.

A memo from Prime Minister Winston Churchill to the Lord President of the Council, on 19 December 1942, referred to the ministerial committee set up by the war cabinet to supervise the use made of psychologists and psychiatrists. Churchill added:

I am sure it would be sensible to restrict as much as possible the work of these gentlemen, who are capable of doing an immense amount of harm with what may very easily degenerate into charlatanry. The tightest hand should be kept over them and they should not be allowed to quarter themselves in large numbers upon the Fighting Services at public expense. There are no doubt easily recognizable cases which may benefit from treatment of this kind, but it is very wrong to disturb large numbers of healthy normal men and women by asking the kind of odd question in which the psychiatrists specialize. There are quite enough hangers-on and camp-followers already.

Aside from the financial burden they placed on his already overstretched resources, the psychiatrists worried Churchill for another reason. In a memo dated 13 March 1943, he criticized their policy of asking servicemen how willing they had been to join up. 'Anything more subversive to morale could hardly be imagined,' he wrote indignantly, adding that the senior officer who had sanctioned such outrageous questions had 'an altogether abnormal fad for this questionable process', before suggesting he be found 'some other employment'.

CHAPTER FOUR

Despite the incredible progress they had made in being accepted by the establishment, the new psychiatrists weren't getting their way on everything. But in any event, out in the theatres of war, there were far more pressing problems to worry about.

Chapter Five

*Courage is a moral quality; it is not a chance gift of nature like
an aptitude for games. It is a cold choice between two
alternatives, the fixed resolve not to quit; an act of
renunciation which must be made not once but many times
by the power of will.*

Lord Moran

The war was reaching crisis point. To the shock of the entire British
empire, Malaya and Singapore had fallen to the enemy, with thousands
of prisoners-of-war taken into camps, and the conflict in the Mediterranean
was intensifying. British Commonwealth forces, which had initially been
successful in driving back the Italian army, faced a new dilemma with the
arrival of a small German army and air force in Libya, and German troops in
Greece.

The United States' involvement in the Second World War was sealed by
the Japanese attack on the American base of Pearl Harbor in Hawaii on
7 December 1941, killing two thousand people and destroying nineteen
warships and two hundred aircraft. The attack coincided with the Japanese
declaration of war on the Allies and was a total surprise, leaving the US base
little more than a smoking ruin. In the wake of Pearl Harbor, what had thus
far been primarily a European conflict became truly global, encompassing
every continent except South America and nearly every country. The United
States entered the fray, offering everything from their Sherman tanks to the
services of their military psychiatrists, who had been previously champing at
the bit on the fringes of war.

American troops were sent to fight off the German assault on North Africa
led by Field Marshal Erwin Rommel, a tank commander and hero of the First
World War. Rommel's spectacular successes against the Eighth Army with
his Afrika Corps earned him the sobriquet the 'Desert Fox' and the unstinted
admiration of his opponents. The Allied forces, led by Field Marshal Claude
Auchinleck, held Malta and Tobruk, despite almost continuous attack and
launched Crusader, a winter offensive designed to rout the Germans. During
the fighting that followed, the British lost 18,000 men, killed or wounded, and
the German-Italian Army lost 38,000. Nearly eight hundred tanks and six
hundred aircraft were also lost.

While the Allies were recovering their senses and still licking their wounds from the offensive, Rommel launched what became one of the most reckless and costly counter attacks fought during the desert war, making great gains and putting further pressure on the besieged city of Tobruk. On 21 June 1942, Tobruk fell, a humiliating capitulation that came as a grievous blow to Churchill and to President Roosevelt in Washington. After almost a year of siege it was a massive psychological as well as military defeat. In the ensuing collapse of morale, rates of mental breakdown escalated to a worrying degree; a factor for which the Army was still unprepared.

Dr Wilfrid Jones, the RAMC doctor then posted to the Middle East, had little or no psychiatric experience when he arrived in Egypt, although he had treated battle casualties from Dunkirk. 'The Army was very short-sighted because at the start of the North Africa campaign there were no psychiatrists in the medical services to the troops,' he said, 'a fact which was attributed to the opposition of the director of medical services for that campaign, who did not think it would be necessary. After a month or so, two psychiatrists were appointed, but it was not enough for all the work they found. One was working forward in front line areas and one was at base, and the psychiatrist at base was so overwhelmed by the patients being sent back because of the stress of war that he had to get help from the Americans.

'The fighting was very hard. There was fear and exhaustion and the loss of comrades, and there were a large number of troops affected. The same happened during the siege of Malta. The deputy director of medical services would not have a psychiatrist so the general medical officers had to deal with the type of cases for which they were not trained.'

Dr Jones was given the job of psychiatrist unexpectedly on the basis of his enthusiasm for the type of work inspired by William Sargant and some notes he had written up on the treatments: 'I was quite warmly received and they questioned me about what I knew of psychiatric treatment and they seemed impressed with the fact that I did know something about ECT and insulin-coma treatment and abreaction. Being posted to a busy psychiatric hospital was the best training I could ever have. Not only were there plenty of patients but the staff were very good and it was an education. Until then I had been a general duty officer. It was quite an eye-opener.'

Dr Jones said his patients were the psychiatric casualties of 'a very large and neglected Army', with a wide range of symptoms from physical exhaustion to severe anxiety. 'The principle in military psychiatry was, of course, early treatment. But we were in Egypt, the last port of call for patients from a very wide area stretching from Syria to Sudan. We received distressed and disturbed patients who had probably been two or three days or even longer getting to us, who would be confused, restless and dehydrated, which was a very bad thing in the hot climate.

'These men had to contend with the heat and the sand; it's not easy to move in sand. Then there were the emotional factors – the fear occasioned by the enemy action. One particular stress which was found was the dive-bombing by the German Stukas in surprise attacks, which made matters very much worse. And then the normal stresses of being away from home for a year or two. All these were factors in producing a breakdown.'

Dr Jones used ECT extensively and found it effective. 'We found that doing ECT early saved a great deal of trouble and suffering. We'd give distressed and disturbed patients ECT almost on arrival and that would calm them down and make them suitable for proper nursing care. It was a much, much better treatment than trying to fill them up with sedatives and calm them down that way.' The treatment would be given twice a day for two or three days, then reduced to twice a week for the following month. 'There wasn't much persuasion involved. The patients were under military discipline and if they were ordered to have ECT, they had it,' he said.

Despite all that had been achieved in military psychiatry elsewhere, there was still considerable resistance from the generals at the front line of fighting, who believed that if these doctors of the mind were given credibility with an official posting, the ordinary soldier might be tempted into insubordination. The fear of malingering was still strong. After the fall of Tobruk, the alarming rise in cases led General Sir Claude Auchinleck, commander-in-chief in the Middle East, to call for a return of the death penalty for desertion and cowardice, thinking that making an example of a few men might stem the tide of those going AWOL or collapsing under the mental strain.

His replacement, Sir Harold Alexander, was also in favour, but the war cabinet rejected the idea, fearing a public backlash. In a confidential memo in response, the cabinet said:

> The general view was that if at any time the morale of the Army suffered a serious deterioration, there would be no option but to reintroduce the death penalty for these offences. It was clear, however . . . that the state of morale in the Army . . . did not justify this course of action at the present time. Moreover, account must be taken of the fact that the reintroduction of the death penalty would have a most unfortunate political effect, and would give rise to rumours that the morale of the Army had been seriously impaired.

Instead, it set up the Directorate of Army Psychiatry to 'maintain and promote the mental health and efficiency of the Army by every possible means'. It was responsible for co-ordinating and developing all psychiatric services within the Army, giving its new psychiatrists even more powers to deal with everything from morale and training to discipline and equipment. Ever keen to categorize and classify, the Army officially defined a psychiatric casualty as 'a man who becomes ineffective in battle as a direct result of his personality being unable to stand up the stresses of combat'. Doctors were sent to the furthest corners of the battlefields in an attempt to organize the special hospitals and clinics and help the men facing the conditions that had traditionally caused them to crack.

The poet Vernon Scannell experienced some of the worst hardships of the desert campaign: the weather – heat and sandstorms – the flies, the lack of water and being constantly thirsty, the body lice and being so far from home.

Even when he got home, he found it was no longer a place he recognized. Injured on patrol, shot in both legs, he was sent to a Surrey hospital to recover. 'I thought, God, I'm safe at last and then I heard air-raid sirens. I said to a nurse, "What the hell's that?" and she told me they were V1 buzz bombs. I didn't even know of their existence, I'd not heard of them. These things were beginning to crash around and I was absolutely terrified.'

Returned to the desert campaign to fight at El Alamein under Field Marshal Montgomery, he saw several fellow soldiers break down around him and believed the causes were cumulative physical strain and mental pressures. The North Africa campaign produced the highest rates of breakdown and desertion since Dunkirk. The percentage of psychiatric casualties were estimated at between 7 and 30 per cent, many of whom were working in enemy minefields. 'The thing that finally made men break under the strain was living under the unrelenting threat of being either killed or badly mutilated,' said Scannell. 'The longer you were there, the more you saw this happening to others and the more it began to dawn on you that you weren't immortal and these things could happen to you.'

El Alamein was never going to be an easy battle. Designed to be a reprisal attack on Rommel's Panzer Division after Tobruk, the plan was to stage a deliberate infantry-artillery assault, supported by some heavy tanks and 456 guns bombarding the enemy positions. Montgomery predicted a 'dogfight' and had warned in his orders: 'This battle will involved hard and prolonged fighting. Our troops must not think that, because we have a good tank and a very powerful artillery support, the enemy will all surrender. The enemy will NOT surrender and there will be bitter fighting. The infantry must be prepared to fight and kill, and to continue doing so over a prolonged period.'

Troops were constantly on the move, advancing at thirty miles a day across minefields laid by the Germans. Weeding out the vulnerable soldier who was likely to implode mentally was no longer enough: a change in attitude was required. Thus it was, during this campaign particularly – with its uniquely mobile nature across huge distances – that the term 'battle exhaustion' first came into common military parlance. It was a term much derided by the troops for being the understatement of all time, encouraging as it did the idea that the condition was temporary: that if men were exhausted, then rested, they would recover.

The Army recognized the need for more psychiatrists out in the field, to get to the cases faster and before they reached the point of irretrievable breakdown. Commanding officers and their MOs were taught the value of prevention via a batch of informative education films, such as one in which actors playing senior officers discussed over a beer in a bar those most likely to be affected. Vigilance was urged: if senior officers could spot the signs of physical and mental fatigue and offer men a rest, they would not have to be evacuated to field hospitals later, was the message. These men did not have a 'yellow streak', the film insisted and one actor protested defensively: 'It's not psychiatry, it's common sense.'

No matter how many propaganda films were made, life and death in the battlefields of North Africa was still a question of individual survival, and each man got through it any way he could. Outnumbered and out-manoeuvred, the German Army dug in at the Mareth line in Tunisia and a fierce seven-day battle ensued, in which countless men lost their lives or were taken prisoner.

Vernon Scannell believes that it was fear and pride that kept most men going. 'This raw, primitive, atavistic fear comes when people around you are being killed or maimed in very unpleasant ways and the fear that you're likely to be is monstrously engulfing and it's personal and demoralizing and dehumanizing and shameful because you know that you would do anything, really, to escape from this onslaught. It's more powerful than any rational defences that men have against it,' he said.

He doubted that the threat of shooting deserters ever prevented others from following suit. 'I think that the man who is going to desert in action is going to do it anyway because he is not thinking beyond that isolated moment of pure abject terror. It is not a rational act. He's like an animal scuttling for safety; it's almost reflex. I think he just turns and goes and runs or – in my case – walks.'

Vernon Scannell had been under fire almost continuously for six months when he cracked. A group of soldiers who had spent the previous night with them at a place called Wadi Aqarat on the Mareth line on the Libyan-Tunisian border were mown down by the German artillery when they moved forward. 'It was then that I saw my own unit, my own friends, my own comrades, going round looting these bodies. I'd seen them do it umpteen times to dead Germans and Italians and I don't know why it was worse seeing them take things off their own men, but I was morally outraged and somehow thought, I can't take any more of this, and I turned round and walked away. I thought, I've had it. Enough. I don't want any more. I was simply sick of them, of me, of everything, of what people are and what humans can do. They were like vultures.'

Scannell was picked up by a senior officer in a Jeep who gave him a lift back to base, thinking he was a runner with a message. Having been dropped off, he just carried on walking. 'I walked and walked and walked, and covered something like a hundred miles. I eventually got back to Tripoli somehow, which is where I was picked up. It was all so dreamlike and weird and strange. It was like a fugue state, a time of arrested experience. Everything was held in abeyance. I wasn't aware of who I was, what I was or where I was. I seemed to be floating rather than walking. There was no premeditation, it seemed out-side my control. It was partly physical exhaustion and constant strain and it just wears and wears away at you. I think you tend to retreat into an almost zombie-like state. A sort of comatose state descends on you and takes over, and you can scarcely feel or think anything at all. It is an exhaustion of the spirit as well as of the body.

'I suddenly landed back into the real world when I was picked up and taken off and court-martialled and sentenced to fifteen years' hard labour.

CHAPTER FIVE

In peacetime, I would have been dishonourably discharged, sent back to Blighty to a civilian prison, but with all the troop ships and the need for space and so forth I was sent to a military prison in Alexandria.'

Scannell can hardly remember anything of his court-martial, except that he was not defended by anyone and there was no mention of battle exhaustion. He simply told the senior officers trying him that he was sick of the war and didn't want to become one of those bodies being looted by his friends. 'There were no subtleties about such things as desertion or cowardice at the time. It was cut and dried. As far as I was aware, there were no facilities for the mentally afflicted men in North Africa at that time. Psychiatric medicine was, to the average soldier – officer class particularly – a joke. It was regarded as a flunk hole for malingerers. They were frightened of appearing to be soft on desertion, which is why my sentence was so high. They couldn't shoot us any more so they passed these huge deterrent sentences.'

His sentence was eventually reduced to three years on appeal to Field Marshal Montgomery, and he was sent to the Stafford military prison and detention barracks for the next six months, initially stripped naked and forced to sleep on a stone floor. 'The moment you pass through the portals you never move at anything other than a run, double march. The day was spent in PT, which was known as physical torture, an exercise in sadism and pack drill. It was over a hundred and twenty degrees in the shade, with little more than bread and water to live on. It was very hard-going.' He, and many others like him, became the forgotten casualties of the war, while the battles raged on.

In Tunisia, the latest research indicated that it was not cowardice but the particular stresses of the desert war that were causing men to break down – and not all men but mainly those in particularly vulnerable positions: the infantrymen. More than 90 per cent of known cases were among infantrymen. Doctors compiled records of all those passing through their care and found that after thirty continuous days of fighting, a staggering 98 per cent would break down. According to their statistics, any man would break down after six months of combat, as Vernon Scannell had done.

In 1942 the *Journal of Neurology* reported:

Just as the average truck wears out after a certain number of miles, it appears that the infantryman wears out too. Both medical officers and line officers agreed that by the time a man had served two hundred aggregate days of combat in a rifle battalion, he was non-effective. Most men, they stated, were ineffective after one hundred and eighty days, or even one hundred and forty days. The general consensus was that a man reached his peak effectiveness in the first ninety days of combat. After this his efficiency fell away and he became steadily less valuable until finally he was useless.

The impact of the comparison of a man to a piece of machinery was insidiously profound. Armed with the idea that a quick 'pit-stop service' and a few nights' sleep could solve the problem, the British forces were ordered to march on to Italy and the Balkans to fight Mussolini's troops. They were on their way to a campaign that took its toll on them in a whole new way, signalling as it did a return to the grim trench conditions of the First World War.

The bitter and costly Italian winter campaign of 1943–4 provided an extraordinarily high rate of psychiatric disorders. Advances across the mountains were rendered impossible by the snowstorms, so the Allied efforts were confined to short stretches along the coast. As the fighting became bogged down, self-mutilation, desertion and battle-exhaustion figures took on a familiar pattern. During one spell of forty-four days' continuous fighting, 54 per cent of the American Armoured Division casualties were psychiatric. Faced with such numbers, the new psychiatrists were really put to the test, and almost imperceptibly – as they managed to get jittery soldiers out of the lines and into hospitals – their value started to be appreciated by the commanders. The alliance was working.

Appel and Beebe, two American researchers in Italy, found that more and more patients sent back suffering from 'campaign stress' were not young, inexperienced servicemen but veterans with excellent combat records, even medals. The pair concluded that, after a certain length of time, practically all those in rifle battalions who were not otherwise disabled ultimately became psychiatric casualties. 'The average point at which this occurred,' they wrote, 'was between two hundred to two hundred and forty aggregate combat days.'

Elsewhere doctors reported that the largest numbers of those affected by battle exhaustion had been wounded before and had thus lost that rather naïve perception that it couldn't happen to them. Major John Wishart, a corps psychiatrist, wrote:

> Their story was largely the same – wounded in Normandy, evacuated to the UK, three to six weeks in hospital, a month in a convalescent depot, leave, a month's training and out here again; generally it was the first hard battle since their return . . . I took the opportunity of asking numbers of them what their philosophy had been towards being killed or wounded prior to that injury and the answer was nearly always the same: 'Never thought about it.' When asked what their philosophy was now, the general reply was: 'I know what it's like now – I know what can happen.

Having experienced at first hand the pain and shock of being shot or blown up, these men were more likely to crack when faced with the very real chance of it happening again.

At the Benedictine abbey of Monte Cassino, perched high on a mountain top between Rome and Naples, the Germans barricaded themselves in to defend the Gustav line. For centuries the vantage-point had been coveted and fought over by a succession of invaders and the Second World War was no exception. The abbey came to be the linchpin of the German presence in that part of Italy and, during a battle which lasted almost six months, the Allies used wave after wave of Flying Fortress bombers and artillery attacks. The devastation was such that bulldozers had to be brought in to clear away the debris for tanks and vehicles to pass. Monte Cassino was eventually bombed to ruins in May 1944, but over a thousand members of the Polish II Corps were sacrificed in the final battle.

Spike Milligan, the comedian, poet and author, was a bombardier in the Royal Artillery and served in North Africa and Italy. He suffered a complete breakdown at Monte Cassino after a barrage of mortar bombs fell on his unit, killing dozens of soldiers and civilians. He said later: 'From that day I suffered from mental illness.' He wrote in his memoirs of the moment the mortars fell and how he stumbled back down the cliff shaking and in tears, unaware that he had been wounded in the leg.

> The mortars rain down on us . . . I black out and then I see red, I am strangely dazed. I was on my front, now I'm on my back . . . Next I'm sitting in an ambulance and shaking, an orderly puts a blanket around my shoulders, I'm crying again . . . Next I'm in a forward dressing station, labelled 'Battle Fatigue'. An orderly gives me a bowl of hot very sweet tea. 'Swallow these,' he says, two small white pills. I can't hold the bowl for shaking, he takes it from me and helps me drink it.

A week after his initial treatment, Milligan was sent back to his unit, but it was quickly realized that he was of no use. He had developed a severe stammer and was still very emotional. He wrote:

> To add to my misery I am 'court-martialled' by the Major . . . I suppose in World War One he would have had me shot. Mind you, he had had it in for me for a long time. I didn't represent the type of empty-minded soldier he wanted. I had been a morale booster to the boys, organizing dances and concerts, and always trying to keep a happy atmosphere, something he couldn't do . . . I am by now completely demoralized. All the laughing had stopped.

He was sent to a hospital in Caserta and rested before being sent on to a rehabilitation camp north of Naples, where he worked as a reception clerk, taking down the details of all the psycho-neurotic cases or 'P & Ns' as they arrived. In his memoirs, he wrote:

> All day long the battle-weary soldiers filed in. I was asked the same question: 'What are they going to do with me?', and there was a hollow fear in each voice, some cried. God made gentle people as well as strong ones. Alas for the war effort, I was a gentle one.

Of the camp, he wrote:

> It had a turnover of about a thousand men, all in a state of coming and going, unlike me who couldn't tell if I was coming or going . . . Some loonies

tried to climb Vesuvius. God knows how many fell in. A resident
psychiatrist arrived. He immediately dished out drugs that zombified most
of the inmates who walked round the camp starry-eyed, grinning and
saying 'hello' to trees.

Despite Milligan's scepticism, the rehabilitation centres were considered
a great success by the new military psychiatrists, and within a few months of
all the systems falling into place, the front-line doctors felt confident enough
to return between 30 and 60 per cent of all P & N cases to battle: they were
able to distinguish between those constitutionally unsuited to war, and those
who had simply seen or done too much. For the first time also psychiatrists
were permitted to recommend transfers for men to jobs that were better
suited to them.

In the words of Tom Main, a psychiatrist whose work later became pivotal
in the treatment of the shell-shocked: 'The man who has killed too much,
the officer who has lost his men through an error of judgement, the tank
commander who has escaped alone from a burning tank present pictures of
guilt and depression that may be psychotic in depth. Fleeting schizophrenic
screens are drawn down over an anguish too gross to be borne.'

Progress was at last being made, and it seemed that the Army was coming
to terms with the fragility of the human mind. But the advances weren't
across the board. The RAF had different ideas.

With British troops bogged down in every theatre of war, advance was
possible only in the skies. The RAF's commitment to bombing was based on
the conviction that attack was the best form of defence. Strategic bombing
of key German installations, factories, power stations, cities and railways
to cripple Hitler's industrial strength involved sending air crews deep into
enemy territory at night, running the gauntlet of formidable anti-aircraft
weaponry and fighter planes.

The distinctive hum of the massed flying formations as they headed off on
their deadly missions became a nightly lullaby to thousands of beleaguered
Britons. The effectiveness and courage of the RAF supported the Allied
forces on the ground and went a long way towards determining the German
defeat, even though some viewed their attacks on innocent civilians as an
immoral descent to the enemy's level.

The RAF was seen as a breed apart, epitomizing masculine courage and
technical wizardry. If the romanticized public perception was to be believed,
the pilots were all supermen, with nerves of steel, at the forefront of the new
technology. But flying fighter or bomber raids was a terrifying business, and
the death rates were incredibly high. To begin with the technology was
appalling, the Stone Age of bombing. Navigation was such that men couldn't
find their target, let alone their way home.

Every time they went out they had to run the gauntlet of the flak gunners
and the searchlight crews pumping up 88-mm shells in those deadly
beams of light. Apart from the fear and the fatigue, there were the appalling

conditions on board to contend with: extremely low temperatures leading to frostbite and chills; ill-fitting and bulky clothing; lengthy exposure to high altitudes with low pressure and lack of oxygen; multiple G-forces to induce unconsciousness; hearing and vision problems caused by the hostile and unforgiving environment. Those who survived the primitive operations of 1940–41 would look back on them afterwards as almost lunatic in their crudeness compared with what came later: radar, high-performance aircraft and the atomic bomb.

Of the 326,000 British servicemen killed in the Second World War, 112,478 were in the RAF, including an estimated 80,000 front-line air crew from Bomber Command and Fighter Command. The fresh-faced young men who joined up at the beginning of the war, beguiled by the uniform and the urge to fly, quickly realized after the initial euphoria wore off that a large percentage of them would not survive the war unscathed – a salutary thought when flying mission after mission, three nights a week. Thereafter they acquired a 'mask of age' on their faces, sunken eyes and hollow cheeks, with weight loss, excessive drinking, and irritability all part of the package. These exhausted men went out night after night with fear in their hearts to do what they had been ordered to do, even though they knew that hundreds would die.

David Stafford-Clark, RAFVR (RAF Volunteer Reserve), medical parachutist, twice mentioned in dispatches, explained how pivotal the role of a base doctor was. 'The Battle of Britain was what taught everybody that air power means air power and that we needed all the people we could get to stop the Germans. But I soon realized that for people of that age to be doing what they were doing and being killed at the rate they were being killed, they needed a doctor who could very much identify with that. I realized that I could best use my training to help people keep up their morale in the face of appalling odds.'

His primary job was as a doctor for the whole RAF station, with a secondary role to examine morale and the flying experience. He even went on bombing raids with crews to learn about the special stresses they faced. 'Just flying in the dark over enemy territory is terrifying enough. No sane person would be anything but terrified flying an operational aeroplane in war. Flying over foreign territory at night and being shot at and realizing that you might not get back was a raw fear which I kept to myself, stored up for the next time I saw somebody who couldn't do it any more. I wanted to do something absolutely dedicated to helping air crew face the fact that they were in a deadly job. I would be there at the briefings, I would be there when they took off, I would be there when they came back and sometimes I would go with them.'

He was posted to a base in France a few weeks before a pilot called 'Cobber' Cane, a renowned ace, crashed his plane into a tree and killed himself. 'He didn't do it on purpose, but the whole thing had gone to his head. He was a real hero, but he was getting careless and just wasn't thinking. I ought to have realized he'd done enough and that he ought to have been shifted into a teaching job. When I saw him hit the tree I thought, my God, it's my fault. It wasn't my fault, but I learned what I'd not learned before: I realized that an enormous part of a doctor's job in the RAF was morale, flying experience, keeping the people feeling they could come to you and say, "I'm through. I can't do any more." And you would work it out with them.'

Faced with the inescapable fact that their supposedly impervious pilots were cracking under the strain of so many missions, the RAF agreed reluctantly to a limit on the number flown. The Luftwaffe pilots had no limit – they were in for the duration of the war – but the American Brigadier General Ira Eaker, commander of the bomber component in the Eighth Air Force, felt strongly that for a man to stay and fight he needed at least an even chance of survival. After discussions with Sir Arthur 'Bomber' Harris, head of Bomber Command, they tried to work out a formula that balanced operational needs with the crews' chances of survival.

Too short a tour length would badly restrict the available manpower, too long and crew morale would plummet. There was already an overall casualty rate that exceeded 50 per cent of their crew forces. Using the known statistics for survival rates and combining all factors, Eaker's Washington staff worked backwards through the mathematics and came up with a minimum tour of twenty five and a maximum of thirty missions for bomber crews, with 150–200 hours for fighter pilots.

Thereafter in Britain the standard tour for a bomber crew became thirty operations, then a rest for six months, then another tour of twenty. At some periods during the war, there was only a 17 per cent chance of surviving a first tour safely, and an incredibly small 2.5 per cent chance of surviving a second. Dr Stafford-Clark said: 'The losses were awful, really steep. If they survived, they could stop at thirty and have a rest. It was generally understood that they had a one in four chance of surviving until the end of the tour. Obviously the survival rate for the second tour was even less. The odds were heavily stacked against these young men.'

One rear gunner he treated developed severe claustrophobia after weeks of being stuck at the end of the aircraft, able to communicate with the others only via a crackling intercom system that didn't work very well. 'He said he felt as if he would be the first thing targeted by an enemy fighter, and just couldn't go on, so I told him I'd go on a flight, sitting in the rear gunner's position and see what it was like. I realized then that in the rear turret one does feel very isolated. What with the squawking down the earphones and the conversation between the rest of the crew, you are out of it. You can speak up and they'll listen to you, but you're a long way away. So I told him that I understood but that he had only six trips left to go and if he still felt the same after that I'd see what I could do.'

A poem by Dr Stafford-Clark called the '31st Operation' about those occasions when even after a 'final' tour, an extra one was called for because of a vital operation, sums up the feeling of those asked to go that extra mile:

We might have known that there would be a catch
To match the occasion. Thirty ops they said
Completes a 'tour'. Sounds like a picnic
Or a leisurely perambulation around the scenic margins of the coast . . .
'Sorry, chaps,' the Flight Commander droned
'But Group stress maximum effort, every kite to go
It should be quite a show.' He spoke his awkward lines
Without convictions, his words struck like a shower of ice
To freeze our hearts and add a weight of doom to inner thoughts . . .
There was nothing more to say. Tomorrow was a night of fear away
And sure returns were not the order of the day.

Prior to the war, Dr Stafford-Clark had never encountered men breaking down, bursting into tears or becoming emotionally paralysed with fear or grief for lost colleagues. 'I had to get to know what ways desperation shows itself, even in the bravest people. I had to get to know people all over again, really, and every time I went back into the real world outside the station, I realized that nobody understood this at all. Nobody had any idea. They thought that our boys were flying heroes, having a lot of fun and going on leave. Only one thing dominated the minds of the top brass, which was that the Germans had a much better, much bigger, better trained force than we had and that they'd got to catch up. So, as fast as possible, they recruited, trained and got airborne fighters, bombers, the lot. Lots of people joined up not realizing that the odds were so against them, but they got down to it and very few of them faltered. It was part of my job to help them not to.'

He went on to work at Bomber Command, which sustained the heaviest casualties in the RAF. From there, the RAF launched a thousand bomber raids on the German industrial heartland – Cologne, the 1943 Dambusters raid and air attacks on Berlin, Hamburg and Dresden. The Luftwaffe retaliated with devastating raids on Coventry, London during the Blitz and many cities of great artistic and historical importance.

Air crews on both sides were seen as flying export machines, transporting their deadly cargoes abroad. Many cracked under the tremendous pressure of what were often little more than suicide missions, but despite the evidence of death and psychological breakdown, those at the highest levels chose to ignore the findings of their own psychiatrists. Men who broke down under stress were considered feeble. The jokey expression came into common use on the air bases that the choice for airmen was either 'coffins or crackers'.

In April 1940, in response to a growing clamour for recognition for the stresses of the job, an official RAF letter was circulated to set the tone for subsequent policy. It outlined two categories of men 'whose conduct may cause them to forfeit the confidence of their commanding officer'. If a member of an air crew began to show signs of stress, it said, they were to be categorized either as medically ill, or suffering from a failure of will and categorized as 'W' for 'Waverer'. Those affected were to be given a simple three-point treatment plan involving discipline, example and competitive games. If a man did not respond to such treatment, he would be permanently designated 'W', with a large red 'W' marked in the right-hand corner of his records. Officers lost their wings and decorations and were cashiered, NCOs reduced to the lowest rank of aircraftsman, second class, then either employed on menial duties or discharged. Once discharged, they were called up into the Army – the ultimate insult to an airman – or directed to work in the mines.

Charles Evans of the air ministry clarified the position: 'There will be a residuum of cases where there is no physical disability, no justification for the granting of a rest from operational employment, and in fact nothing wrong except a lack of moral fibre.' Thereafter all those suffering from temperamental defect were to be classified 'LMF' – Lacking in Moral Fibre. In other words, cowards. The repercussions of that document would be felt for the rest of the war.

It was an ironic situation: the RAF was viewed by the public as incredibly modern and technological, and yet here it was operating with this very old fashioned notion of courage and cowardice. The slap on the back, the congratulatory 'Good show, chaps' were what it was all about. Handlebar moustaches, smart blue uniforms and a jovial disposition was the classic image. The senior officers believed that breakdowns among their men were nothing to do with stress, they were all down to character, and that mostly meant what class you belonged to. Prior to the war and at the outbreak, the goal was to find as many public schoolboys of good breeding as possible. Recruitment interviews featured questions about sportsmanship and hunting. By the time the death rates had decimated the first waves of men and outstripped the available supply of public-school candidates, the RAF threw open its gates and new recruits lined up in droves. Despite the high casualty rates, the service never suffered from a shortage of new men, anxious to pass through its hallowed portals. Thereafter if anyone showed any signs of wavering, it was widely believed that they were simply the wrong sort of chap.

The commanders-in-chief remained defiantly resistant to any findings on the role of stress. That was something that happened in the Army, not the officer-class RAF. Internal memoranda recommended giving those returning from a mission a hearty breakfast of bacon and eggs, tea and doughnuts, as a good way of relieving stress in a group situation, followed by a long sleep, if necessary induced with 'whacking doses' of sodium barbitol. But to be asked to suppress the fear of death day after day for months was destructive, and simply couldn't be kept up for ever. Something was going to give.

MOs at air bases across the country began to notice an increasing number of 'early returns', instances in which crews aborted their missions and returned to base with technical troubles. When this began to happen more and more, questions were asked, which often put further pressure on the pilots. There were stories of crews collaborating together to stay alive, falsifying their log books and dumping their bombs over the North Sea, but such cases were rare and only caused further angst for those with a genuine problem, who then had to decide whether to continue to Germany with a leaking oxygen supply or some other technical problem, or to turn back. They had to weigh up what was best for their men and what was best for the team as a whole. If one plane turned back and the others were all shot down, the guilt became unbearable.

Stanley Freestone, a pilot who flew Wellingtons and Stirlings from Lincolnshire, recalled the trauma of flying a brand new plane that overheated badly in both engines half-way to Germany, forcing him to abort the mission and turn back. Tests were carried out on the aeroplane but it performed perfectly. 'Two nights later, I was off to Düsseldorf in the same aircraft. A complete repetition of the symptoms occurred. This time the debrief on my return took on a most serious complexion and was followed by an interview with the unit MO and the CO. I stuck to my decision, and to clear myself, suggested I go on the next offensive operation in another aircraft. Thus I was granted a "last chance" to prove myself. The trip went faultlessly.

'The aircraft I had previous trouble with was taken by a young sergeant pilot on his first trip. He never returned. We shall never know the truth of what happened but I believe that the trouble I experienced recurred and the young inexperienced pilot feared turning back and aborting more than the obvious danger of continuing into Germany with both engines almost on fire.'

In the early days of the war, the Battle of Britain had been the first real test of airmen under stress. Even though the eminent psychiatrist W. H. R. Rivers had told the Southborough Inquiry as long ago as 1922 that machine-gunners in observation balloons were the worst affected by shell shock, it was still thought that LMF was something to be stamped on. It was believed to be contagious, something that would spread and infect the other men. Such cases had to be got rid of and made an example. Those found to be suffering from LMF could be court-martialled, stripped of their rank and badge, even sent to prison and their lives ruined.

Wally MacFarlane, who flew Halifax aircraft on bombing raids to Germany, had a wireless operator who cracked under the pressure on his first trip back in an aeroplane after his previous one had been shot down. 'A shell exploded beneath us and before I know it this lad flashes past me. He was trying to bail out,' he remembered. 'I had one hand on the scruff of his neck and one hand on the controls trying to fly the plane. I settled him down and told him to sit down and try to rebuild the wireless. It kept him occupied for the four hours it took us to get back.

'When we landed, the lad was badly shaken and refused to fly again. He was shaking like a leaf and terribly upset. We were very sympathetic and had no intention of making a report about him whatsoever. We offered him a beer, but he went to the MO and told him he couldn't fly again and that was that. He was charged with LMF, drummed out of the RAF and we never knew what happened to him.'

Bob Armit, who flew Halifaxes, Stirlings and Lancasters on moonlit missions to supply resistance troops in France, lost two crews before completing thirty-two operations with his last crew. 'I had an unspoken idea about myself that I was a talisman. If they didn't go with me, then they wouldn't come back. This was an awful responsibility. As we got closer to the thirty tours I got very anxious. I started to smoke more and I swore a lot, which was very against type. The fear was throbbing. LMF created a certain amount of fear. I didn't want to get involved with that so I kept my pecker up. It acted as a deterrent because it was always at the back of your mind. If anyone was charged with LMF they were whisked away very quickly. So many men didn't make it back after each operation that for one more to suddenly go missing – no one would really have noticed.'

Arthur Smith, an air bomber and navigator's assistant on the twentieth mission of his first tour, was diagnosed as LMF after becoming ill on a particularly dangerous night-bombing raid on the Ruhr valley in Germany in bad weather. He described the fear creeping up on him, with each flight becoming 'a nightmare of tension' when every change in engine tone brought his heart into his mouth. 'It never occurred to me to talk to anyone about it, least of all the MO. I would only go to a doctor because I was physically ill, not because I was afraid,' he said.

When his courage snapped and terror took over, he understood for the first time what the term 'frozen with fear' meant. 'I couldn't do anything at all, I became almost immobile, hardly able to move a muscle or speak,' he said. 'My navigator realized something was very wrong because I wouldn't speak to him and I was shaking. He said to the skipper: "There's something wrong with Smithy. I don't know what. He can't do anything. He's ill in some way." After a little while longer, they said they'd better turn back because we hadn't even got over our coast and I might have been seriously ill for all they knew.

'I was taken to sick quarters and the MO examined me and found nothing physically wrong. I said, "I don't want to fly any more," and that was it. My illness was mental. I had gone LMF – none of us had ever met an LMF victim in all our years of RAF life. I was allowed no more contact with the crew and had to pack all my kit for immediate departure. No goodbyes or anything, and these men were like my family. Before leaving I was summoned before the CO for the severest dressing-down of my career when he left me in no doubt of the seriousness of the affair. I had let the side down and turned my back in the face of the enemy, an action for which soldiers had been shot in the First World War, he said. There was no going back for me now and it was a great relief to realize that I would never have to fly again.'

He was driven from the base under arrest in the back of a covered wagon and taken to an unknown destination to be interviewed by a psychiatrist. 'He was very sympathetic and friendly. He got me to tell him everything about my life. Then he told me exactly what would happen to me. I'd be stripped of my rank, lose my flying pay, be sent away to another station to do some menial job. Everybody would know what I'd done. My family would know and I realized that I'd be branded a coward for the rest of my life. The thought of this was absolutely shattering, but he said there was an alternative. I could go back to my squadron and stick it out until the end of my tour. I knew then that I had to take the latter choice, however hard it became. I was sure I could suppress my fear rather than spend the rest of my life as a coward. He called the CO who said he would take me back on my pledge that I would never crack again and only if my pilot and crew would have me. Their decision was unanimous. They said, "Yes, a hundred per cent." They wanted me back.'

Arthur lost the next five days in both his memory and the daily diary he kept, but went on to complete his thirty tours. 'I don't remember anything at all about the next few days, but I do know that we never talked about it. It was a closed book, it was something alien. You mustn't talk about it and it was never mentioned. It might never have happened. The flying didn't get any better; in fact it got worse and worse, but I had to divorce my mind from the fear and what was going on outside – the flak and the aeroplane jumping around in bad weather.' On his thirtieth mission, his aircraft crash landed and caught fire, killing two of the crew. He suffered severe burns in saving a fellow crew member who was trapped. 'Although it came to an end in a very sticky way, I was extremely relieved to realize that I wouldn't have to fly any more. I couldn't have done it, and luckily I was never asked to because after that we were all demobbed.'

A poem by Redmond MacDonogh, a pilot, brilliantly captures the mood of those who made it home after a sortie:

> We bomb, come home and end
> In the debriefing room, all smiles and mugs of tea.
> The stories mount to epics, lies abound,
> Are checked, debunked. We count the missing dead.
> The eyes are young now, thankfully, we know
> We have, each of us, two more days of life.
> To Germany, three nights a week.

David Stafford-Clark believes that the LMF label was grossly unfair. 'It was an administrator's term, not a doctor's term. I hated it. They didn't lack moral fibre. Maybe they were exhausted, maybe they had volunteered for something that they had underestimated in its demands and couldn't meet. It reeked of bureaucracy; it was a polite way of saying loss of courage, worn out, beaten. Doctors were expected to make the diagnosis of LMF and pass it on to the executive. But these men weren't cowards, and the labelling had a terrible stigma attached to it. Nobody who had done ten or twenty trips could be called a coward. A coward wouldn't have done more than one, believe me.'

Thanks to the sympathy and understanding of doctors like Stafford-Clark, there was a slight softening of attitude and a system whereby pilots could be saved from a court-martial by those tuned in to their problems. 'I learned to look out for the signs – a string of symptoms like sleep disorders, changes in personality, short temper,' said the doctor. 'They'd come and ask for sleeping pills. I watched them turn from eager recruits to unspeakably well-determined veterans. They lived with it and died with it. They never spoke of the following week because they knew it might never come. There had to be a way of surrendering which did not deny the fact that they had fought as long as they could, but had simply had enough, they had used up all their reserves of courage. My opinion would be respected; I could say that some-one who had done twenty-five trips ought to be taken off because I could see they were exhausted. I'd tell them that he mustn't be blamed, he mustn't be stripped of his rank and badge and all, and I'd be listened to.'

Doctors were under considerable pressure to keep as many air crews in the service as possible, because of the considerable cost and time involved in training new recruits. Anyone apparently exhibiting signs of stress would be picked out by the MO and spoken to. The doctor would carefully test the water, see how many missions had been completed, and try to persuade the affected man to carry on. What sent most over the edge was the experience of seeing fellow planes shot down and realizing that it could so easily be them next.

'I'd try and get them talking,' said Dr Stafford-Clark. 'I'd have to make up my mind if they really were at the end of their tether or not. I'd try and get a man to see that he would be cutting his own throat if he chickened out ahead of time when he hadn't fulfilled the contract he made with the community, with the government and his fellow human beings.'

Crew camaraderie played a big part in the persuasion process. The squadron leader would be asked to speak to the man personally, and the rest of the crew might be asked to 'look out for him'. There was the pressing issue of letting the side down, of breaking up the crew and making others wonder if they, too, might not crack soon. In some of the heavier bombers, like the Lancasters and the Stirlings, there would be seven people in the crew – pilot, co-pilot, front gunner, rear gunner, mid upper gunner, navigator and wireless operator – all flying out together three or more times a week. If they had all survived nearly thirty trips and one pulled out, it would make the others jumpy, not to mention the disruption of having to get to know a new crew member. It was all very personal, and if the crew a man had just left was then shot down, the guilt would often haunt him for the rest of his life.

'These people were inter-dependent. They all sank or swam together. The crew spirit was an enormously powerful cement that bound them together and the object was to all stay together and live together until the end of the tour. Each member would play a big part in keeping it together,' Dr Stafford-Clark said. 'They'd talk to each other of being scared shitless and if one said he was cracking up, the others would tell him, "Stop talking rubbish. We're all going to finish together." Obviously if someone still felt they couldn't go on then I'd hear what he had to say and if I thought he was done I'd say at the end, "Well, what you've told me convinces me that you've given your best and as a doctor I don't think I should try to make you do any more," and I'd tell the CO that the man was close to LMF and there was no point in pushing him over the edge. But I would tell the man to remember that if he could come back for another tour, then he owed it to himself and the service to do so.'

By the middle of the war, some recognition of the need for proper screening emerged from the air commodores, and the system was over-hauled. Thereafter the aviation candidate selection boards were instructed to classify recruits into the broad categories of P, N or B: pilot, navigator or bomber. Medical testing still focused on athletic prowess, and emotional evaluation was unsophisticated, but the major innovation to the system was the inclusion of practical flight testing before formal flying training, which was considered very effective. Under pressure from psychiatrist Wing Commander R. D. Gillespie, neuro-psychiatric techniques were gradually introduced to improve air crew selection. They struggled to convince the executive that internal factors such as timidity, lack of aggression or immaturity coupled with the stress of combat would lead to breakdown. If you could minimize the internal factors, they argued, then the emotional breakdown rate could be reduced.

By mid-1943, the powers-that-be were convinced that psychiatrists could be useful in the selection of air crew. But with such professionals in short supply, and most of them snapped up long ago by the Army or American air forces, there was little speedy change. A mental-health questionnaire was introduced for ground crew, and a memo issued to all flying instructors to advise them to recognize the symptoms of emotional disorder. Questionable cases were to be referred to psychiatric specialists, if available. Other than that, the air commodores considered that the continual presence of people like Dr Stafford-Clark and his colleagues at bases would be sufficient.

For those who suffered mentally from their experiences in the skies over Europe, treatment continued to be harsh. Many were treated as common criminals by ruthless senior officers who were not prepared to entertain the idea of low moral fibre in a time of war. As in the other armed services, such waverers were considered a menace to morale and likely to contaminate their colleagues. There were accounts of experienced airmen, on their second tours of duty, with medals to show for it, being publicly stripped of their ranks and flying brevets, before being discharged from the service as broken men.

Statistics are scant, but an estimated 5 per cent of the 125,000 air crew who served in Bomber Command between 1939 and 1945 were believed to have been affected – some 6,250 men – a rate four times higher than that of the entire Royal Air Force. In reality, that figure could have been much higher, due to the numbers treated sympathetically by their MOs or slipped quietly into instructor's duties by their squadron leaders. Air gunners made up the majority of the cases, with pilots ranking a close second. In 1945 the term LMF was dropped from common usage in the RAF, with precious little recognition that the policy may have been in any way misguided.

In the Royal Navy, yet another attitude prevailed. While the admirals realized – on the basis of the experiences of their counterparts in the Army and RAF – that war would produce a large number of psychiatric cases, their proposed therapy was a good dose of Navy discipline.

General naval hospitals were warned to expect new arrivals suffering from 'the special stresses and strains of war', such as those caused by the strain of protecting convoys and maintaining control of ports – British ships were constantly exposed to attack by enemy dive bombers – but there were few specialist facilities. One, the Royal Navy Auxiliary Hospital, Cholmondeley Castle, which offered physical and manual work, occupational therapy and psychiatric treatment, was set up as a receiving base for 'selected cases of good morale who are suffering from nervous breakdown as the result of operational stresses'. A War Office memo, about the types of treatment offered, said that the patients were given 'a special hardening course of treatment under strict Naval discipline'.

In a separate memo offering advice to medical officers on ships obout psychiatric cases and casualties, the admirals were gung-ho about their MO's ability to treat breakdown cases successfully without the need to refer to a professional psychiatrist. They suggested that those men working in prolonged situations of stress, such as mine-sweeping or on the Northern Patrol, were more likely to crack than those exposed to acute and dramatic stress in naval action. Symptoms listed included hysterical reactions in which the patient was said to be attempting 'to "escape" by the development of illness'. Twenty years on from the First World War assumption that any serviceman who allowed his mind to cave in to fear during warfare was trying to shirk his responsibilities, little had changed.

Chapter Six

We listen round the clock
For a code called peacetime
But will it ever come
And shall we know it when it does . . .
Or is it's message such
That it cannot be absorbed
Unless its text is daubed
In letters made of lives
From an alphabet of death
Each consonant a breath
Expired before its time.

'Code Poem', Leo Marks, Signalmaster,
Special Operations Europe

As the war entered its fifth year and the tide began to turn in the Allies' favour, the chiefs of staff decided to make one final decisive push into Hitler's captured territories. Ruling out a continuous push north from the Mediterranean, they would invade across the English Channel. The massive campaign that followed, Operation Overlord – later known universally as D-Day – began at dawn on 6 June 1944, and tested all participants to their limits.

General Dwight D. Eisenhower, of the American forces, was named supreme commander, with General Montgomery as commander-in-chief and British deputies for army, air and naval forces. The plan was to launch the largest ever amphibious assault, attacking on a narrow front in Normandy between the Cherbourg peninsula and Le Havre, initially employing five divisions on five beaches against the Germans' four divisions commanded by General Rommel and strewn along the coast. Artificial harbours were to be towed into place on invasion day so that the beaches could be supplied rapidly with forces and equipment, and the 12,000 Allied aircraft were used to neutralize the 200-strong German Luftwaffe and cut off its communications to the rest of Hitler's Army. The naval operation, codenamed Neptune, involved moving seven thousand vessels from around Britain to rendezvous areas where they crossed the Channel in great convoys.

Every able-bodied airman, seaman and soldier was needed for the fight and Vernon Scannell, incarcerated in his Alexandria military prison, was given a chance of freedom if he would agree to take part in the D-Day Normandy landings. It was not a hard decision. 'I'd have volunteered to be a human bomb to get out of that place,' he said. After six months' hard labour, and with no treatment for his mental breakdown, Vernon Scannell was put back in uniform and repatriated to England to take part in exactly the type of war conditions that had caused him to crack in the first place. 'This was it, I knew it was going to be make or break,' he said.

The invasion was originally planned for 5 June, but bad weather postponed it until the following morning. Vernon Scannell remembered the anticipation. 'The evening before, they gave us some pay and the beer tent was going, so we had a few pints and there was a general feeling of excitement. It was a question of terror held on a firm leash. When we got on the landing craft, we couldn't make the landing because the weather was so bad. The seas were very rough and everyone was being sick, and we were tossed around like that for a couple of days.

'The first lot landed and there were all these German mines just below sea level on great stakes driven into the sea bed, so the boats were blown on to their sides. There were a lot of bodies lying around on the beaches and we couldn't get in at first because of the wrecks. When we finally got to the beach, we were soaked to the skin, absolutely saturated, boots squelching, with full battle order on and I was carrying a Bren gun. We didn't get fully dry until two or three days later.'

Fighting was hampered in the Cherbourg peninsula by the ancient hedgerows, which made perfect tank barriers, a factor overlooked by the masterminds of Operation Overlord. Vernon Scannell found the countryside surreal. 'It could have been England, all those farms and soft pastoral country and orchards and trees. But I suddenly realized something was strange because although there were lots of cattle in the fields, they were dead. They'd been killed by a blast or shrapnel or something. There were cows and horses and sheep lying about in the fields, their stomachs distended, on their backs, with their legs sticking up in the air, like bagpipes. It was so strange and weird and when the guns stopped there was complete silence. That's when you realized there were no birds. Instead of birds, in the trees were German snipers.'

Although the Allies had secured the initial beach heads of Utah, Omaha, Gold, Juno and Sword by 7 June and had established positions by 11 June, progress thereafter was slow. There was some heavy fighting and the Allied forces made much slower progress than had been anticipated in the meticulous planning of the operation. The earliest assaults on the old city of Caen had to be abandoned and the arrival of an SS Panzer division, made up of idealistic Hitler Youth, inflicted heavy losses.

Caen fell eventually after it was flattened by 2,500 tons of bombs, the heaviest air bombardment in support of a ground attack to that date. In a graphic account of the bombardment, Lieutenant von Rosen, a German Panzer commander, recalled:

Early in the morning I was awakened by the thunderous sound of aircraft engines. As I crept out from under my tank, I saw the first bomber waves approaching. From this moment on our . . . area was subject to air bombardment, which lasted for two and a half hours without interruption . . . It was hell . . . Tanks weighing 58 tons were tossed aside like playing cards . . . It was like being in a very thick fog. It was impossible to hear anything because of the unceasing crashing of explosions around us. It was as if we were deaf. It was so nerve-shattering that we could not even think . . . The following silence was uncanny . . . Fifty men of the company were dead, two soldiers had committed suicide during the bombardment, another had to be sent to a mental hospital . . . the psychological shock of these terrible experiences remained with us for a long time.

Elsewhere in the battlefields of France, the marshy ground, thick hedge-rows and determined German defences prevented a breakthrough and threatened to re-create the trench stalemate of the First World War. Major D. J. Watterson, adviser in psychiatry to the second Army, wrote in his monthly report:

The high optimism of the troops who landed in the assault and early build-up phases inevitably dwindled when the campaign for a few weeks appeared to have slowed down. The gradual realization that the 'walk over' to Berlin had developed into an infantry slogging match caused an unspoken but clearly recognizable fall of morale. One sign of this was the increase in the incidence of psychiatric casualties arriving in a steady stream at Exhaustion Centres and reinforced by waves of beaten, exhausted men from each of the major battles.

During the initial ten days of fighting, almost a third of all British casualties were psychiatric. Because of the battle's intensive nature, there were at first few medical stations for the mentally wounded, and those affected had to find what help they could. But, for the first time, mass psychiatric casualties had been foreseen and were about to be catered for: within a few days, a proper military psychiatric system was in place, with a psychiatric hospital set up within ten miles of the front and a series of exhaustion centres to which men could be sent from the front line.

Dr Desmond Murphy, a psychiatrist who worked in a field dressing station at the front, described the stresses of the situation: 'We had a real baptism of fire when we set up in a field full of gliders that the airborne people had left there. That night the Germans bombed us, we had a very long hour of severe bombing and we lost two officers and four orderlies. That was followed by some very severe fighting, which was extremely frightening.

'I was a specialist and I had to look out for signs of stress and real mental wear and tear in myself. I was very conscious that I might not stand up to it. In these very dangerous situations one couldn't help but get tense and apprehensive. One hoped one was going to cope but sometimes sleepless-ness and irritability crept in. I had some anxiety dreams of being lost and helpless. When the stress disappeared one's equilibrium returned. I didn't ever positively treat myself. I think if the situation had reached the point where I had to give myself sedatives then it would have been a pretty grim situation. I was quite a religious fellow and I prayed quite a lot, which helped.'

In Holland, as the British forces chased the retreating Germans, Dr Murphy set up an exhaustion centre in a large café on a main road in a town called Helmond. 'It had two large rooms, one of which was where the men were given a good meal and sedatives and encouraged to rest on stretchers for the first forty-eight hours. In the other, men put on their uniform again and were encouraged to help out with tasks. The whole process usually lasted five to seven days, and by going back into uniform, the men were still identifying with their unit, which was generally just a few miles away. We must have returned sixty per cent to their units. The rest were evacuated by ambulance car back to the casualty clearing stations.

'The men were mostly young and presented different symptoms. Some were very agitated and tense, with a high, startled reaction, and would jump a mile if anything was dropped near them. You had the mute, tired soldier, who didn't say a word, and you sometimes had the hysterical person, who was gesticulating and shouting. Most of them would have fallen into the silent, depressed category. Some of them were ashamed of having broken down, others were guilty about their buddies who had been killed or wounded. One sergeant told me that his tank had been hit and he had got out by elbowing his way out of it, knocking his tank commander to one side. He was the only one who survived and he lay on the ground while his friends burned. People like that needed a lot of reassurance. It was really like a self-debriefing of intense human emotions – guilt and shame and sadness. We just listened in a non-judgemental way.' The patients were segregated to prevent what was called 'behavioural congestion'.

Dr Murphy said the military view was to save the men for another day, another battle, and he had to make clinical judgements about who would and who wouldn't survive another campaign. 'I was frequently uncertain, and I've no doubt I made the wrong decisions on some people, for better, for worse. It was very difficult to check on one's decisions because one often didn't see the soldier ever again. I know that I was always very fortunate to be doing the job I was doing, and I was glad I was a doctor not an infantryman subjected to the intense trauma of battle stresses. I doubt very much personally whether I would have stood them for long.'

Now that the psychiatrists were fully part of the military machine, they came under enormous pressure to return men to the fighting. They were placed in an unenviable ethical dilemma: which came first, their loyalty to the patient or to the military? Returning a few extra men to a battle could help it to victory and prove decisive to the outcome of the war, thus saving many men from further suffering, not just those who were sent back. In total, a third of all psychiatric casualties were sent back to fight, some 4,400 men thrown back into the breach.

In Britain, the first truly Army-run psychiatric hospital had been opened on a hill five miles outside Birmingham. The War Office considered that hospitals such as Sutton were not curing enough battle-shocked patients quickly enough and returning them to the front. Hollymoor, renamed the Northfield Hospital, was different. First opened as a mental hospital in 1905, it was taken over by the military in 1942 and received most of the psychologically damaged men from Normandy. With its distinctive copper-domed water tower acting as a landmark for miles around, its long stone corridors and forbidding appearance, Northfield offered two hundred beds for treatment and a further six hundred in the rehabilitation wing, making it the largest facility of its kind in Britain.

The hospital had a full military hierarchy, with a colonel as commanding officer and strict discipline observed, with saluting of officers by men. Those in the active treatment wing wore the ubiquitous hospital 'blue', and those convalescing in the rehabilitation wing wore khaki with a blue marker on the shoulder. The latter were given military training by combat-experienced officers, while remaining under medical supervision.

Turnover was high. By October 1944 nearly two thousand men had been admitted, including two hundred on one day alone. The average length of stay was seven weeks and there were often as many as seven hundred patients. Overcrowding led to tents being pitched in the grounds, and men sleeping in corridors. Huts had to be built to accommodate separate leisure activities.

Despite the regimentation, the use of locked doors, gates and wings, and the employment of military police to patrol the corridors, the chief aim was to use the hospital not as an organization run by doctors in their own interests, but as a community with all its members participating fully in its daily life. The idea was that no man is an island, and individuals were treated as part of a social group. The men had to take responsibility for themselves and for their own failings as servicemen. If they were allowed to wallow in their own misery and feel sorry for themselves, it was thought, they would never recover enough to go back to battle.

Social clubs were set up, and the men were expected to take full part. 'By tradition a hospital is a place where sick people receive shelter from the stormy blasts of life, but the concept of a hospital as a refuge too often means that patients are robbed of their status as responsible human beings,' wrote Lieutenant Colonel Tom Main, one of the chief psychiatrists, in the *Lancet*. 'Health and stability are too often bought at the price of de-socialization. Sooner or later the patient must face the difficult task of returning to the society in which he became unstable. Treatment of a neurotic patient who suffers from a disturbance of social relationships cannot be satisfactory unless it is undertaken within a social framework.'

Northfield was the culmination of the Army/Tavistock alliance and was putting into practice all the advice given by the likes of Charles Myers, W. H. R. Rivers and Richard Rows. However emotionally damaged they were, men were not allowed to forget that first and foremost they were servicemen. The psychiatrists saw their role as defeating the enemy neurosis, and through that, the Germans. They rejected Freudian techniques of delving too deeply into men's childhoods. Their sole aim was to make them effective soldiers once again.

After being wounded on D-Day in France, Stan Goldsworthy, from a Cornish mining village, was sent to Northfield to recover from trauma and stress. He had been conscripted into the Royal Warwickshire Regiment as a naïve eighteen-year-old and described the experience of being on the Normandy beaches as 'the ultimate theatre of war', which changed young men from the innocents they had been. By the time he arrived at Northfield, he was hardly able to speak because of a stammer and was at the end of his psychological tether. 'There were these huge iron gates,' he recalled. 'It looked like a prison or an old Victorian workhouse. It looked like something medieval, the sort of place where they lock you up for life. I was scared to death. The gates had a long drive behind them and they were locked. They sent for somebody to unlock them and we went up the long drive. They took our uniforms off us and issued us with the blue coats and blue trousers and the red tie and they didn't fit. None of them fitted. They just gave you one off the hook and that was it.

'It was a very bare sort of place, stone floors, no curtains and no central heating. We were taken to the wards and they were all dark with old iron beds and all these lads were lying in these beds after receiving this drug called Jungle Juice, a treatment which put you in a twilight world, a sedation period they called it. The lads were all like zombies, lying there, not speaking and looking at you. We all wanted to come away, we didn't want to be there, but we had to because we were in the Army.'

Stan said there had been no facilities in France and the first treatment he had was at Northfield. 'I had been very anxious and I lost quite a bit of my speech and had nightmares. It was all right in the daytime but at night as soon as I dropped off to sleep all these things reoccurred in my mind and I got these hot sweats. Then they woke me up and I couldn't get any sleep for the rest of the night. My body was all tensed up like a coil and I hadn't any control of what I did or said. It was a build-up of emotions in my body and my mind. I was just about ready to explode. But at Northfield I got this star treatment, all this therapy stuff, which was a great help. I improved considerably. It completely rested me, I felt much more relaxed, much calmer.'

The environment was disciplined, he said, with patients not allowed out and given cleaning chores around the hospital building. There were regular reminders that they were still in the services, and that they would be returning to their units, not to civilian life. Several male nurses provided constant supervision. 'The Jungle Juice was like syrup, but very bitter, given in a small glass. They stood by and watched you take it, you couldn't throw it away. Then you sort of passed out and went into a twilight world where you did everything automatically – you went to the toilet automatically and you ate your food automatically, and that went on for about three weeks. Then after that you went off to these different units where psychiatrists treated you and examined you and talked to you.'

He said he trusted the doctors who treated him. 'You had to believe what they said because they were the learned ones,' he added. 'I did sometimes think that they hadn't been through what we'd been through, but we still had to do what they said because we were in the Army.' Stan found drug therapy helpful because it made him feel renewed. 'It was a strange feeling because after a while you couldn't remember what went on before you went in there. It seemed as if you'd started off life anew, you'd started a new life.'

After his initial treatment, he was given manual work to do, stripping engines at the Austin Motor Company in the mornings, and occupational group therapy in the afternoons, making dolls for charity, taking carpentry lessons or learning embroidery. Many of the patients were, he said, 'too far gone' to recover from the effects of war and were sent on to mental hospitals, but generally the atmosphere was of group recuperation and a return of self-esteem. 'There was a community spirit because you were all in the same boat. Everyone knew what treatment everyone else was having and respected it. If there had been only one or two being treated for mental disorder, they would have been looked upon as crazy. This way, everyone had their own experiences and problems, but they were allowed for.'

Stan met his future wife Eileen when he sneaked out to a pub while at Northfield. Patients were not allowed to drink alcohol in case it affected their medication, and pub landlords were banned from selling a drink to anyone in a blue uniform, but the most wily of the patients used either to borrow an overcoat to cover their uniforms or persuade others to buy the drinks for them. Eileen took to the stammering young man immediately and invited him round for tea. 'It was smashing to be out of the hospital and do normal things,' said Stan. 'It was lovely, a sunny way of life, very different to that before. We ended up getting married and living happily ever after.'

One officer cadet was sent to Northfield after being so close to a bomb that his eardrums exploded and poured blood. He lost his memory after that but was put in charge of some new recruits, one of whom he tried to kill. 'I don't remember anything about it,' he said. 'I've known people go through three campaigns without a single memory. It's all obliterated.'

He remembers being taken to a cell at Northfield, which smelt of a combination of urine and disinfectant and had bars at the window. On wandering into a side ward, he was shocked to discover a room full of patients undergoing sedation therapy. 'It was very dimly lit,' he said. 'I could hardly see to start with. Then, as my eyes got used to the dark, I saw that it was full of fellows. Some were lying down in beds, some were sitting on the bed, some were sort of half-lying, some were snoring, some were moaning, some were crying out, some of them were twisting. It was a nightmare. That was where they went, the worst cases.'

He became so depressed that he contemplated suicide and thought of ways he could achieve it. 'Things closed in on me and I felt quite awful. Depression is a funny thing. It's fear really. I felt sort of terrified but I didn't know what of. I think the fear that every soldier had was going in again. You'd come out of it this time, but go in again and you were going to get killed the next time. That was the fear.'

He was given sodium pentathol and electric-shock treatment, neither of which he remembers much about. 'You'd go into the doctor's office and take your shoes off and he'd put a tourniquet on your arm and press the needle and away you went. We used to call it a cheap piss-up. You didn't remember any more until they were helping you up the corridor and back to your bed. But all the while you were under, he'd be asking you all these questions to try and unlock the things that were stopping you from remembering. Like everybody else in the place, I was very much enclosed within the carapace of my own misery and selfishness and egoism.'

Many of the patients remember one noisy inmate who believed he was Eisenhower and held an imaginary meeting of the generals in his ward every night. Then there was the Scotsman who claimed to hear phantom bagpipes calling him home, a patient who twitched and jerked so much he could hardly walk, and another who vomited every time he tried to swallow any food or drink. Another patient sent to Northfield from India with suspected hysterical paralysis of the leg was asked by doctors to think of the first thing that came into his mind. His reply was 'sore throat'. Upon further questioning, he explained that he had suffered from a very sore throat just before his leg became paralysed. The doctors then realized that he had had diphtheria with an organic neuritis. In other words, he was genuinely paralysed. They sent him back to the doctors who had sent him from India.

In charge of them all was an oddball collection of Britain's most radical thinkers sent to Northfield with a brief from the War Office to 'wage war on neurosis'. Like Maghull and Craiglockhart before it, Northfield became a hothouse environment for the staff as well as the patients. June Clayton was a fourteen-year-old assistant laboratory technician whose job included helping out on the wards. She saw several patients having deep-sleep treatment and was fascinated by it. 'They would sort of drip-feed them and put them to sleep for quite a long time and this sort of regenerated their body and their brain and I think it was a good thing,' she said. 'I used to go and see this one soldier in this little cell-like ward, I used to peep in at him through a round window and he was sleeping quite peacefully. When he woke up, came to, he tried to find out who I was and where I was. He told the nurses that he'd seen an angel.'

In the laboratory, she helped cultivate penicillin and looked after the rabbits and guinea-pigs used for tests. There were other, less palatable jobs as well. 'When a patient died they took the brain out and sent it down to the path lab for one of the girls there to take slices off it and look for certain things under the microscope. The brain was wrapped in muslin with the name and number of the patient and put in this big chest. After two or three years, the chief medical officer wanted all these brains sorted out and so we were wrapped in rubbers and wellingtons and hats and masks and had to sort all these brains out into buckets and take them to the furnace. It was awful.'

CHAPTER SIX

She had fond memories of the nervous patients, in their blue trousers, battle-tops and red ties, shyly asking her to dance at the regular Friday-night dances, which became the highlight of the week for the patients and the local women, starved of men. The idea was to prevent the men hiding away from the world, as they had been allowed to in other hospitals. At Northfield, however twitchy, stammering or nervous they were, they were ordered to the dances to mingle with the local girls.

For some, such social interaction became too much. 'There were one or two who hanged themselves and one who drowned himself in a little pool in a dell,' she recalled. 'Another one went missing and they found him in the snow.'

Beryl Sargent was a teenager when she attended the Friday-night dances at Northfield. 'We didn't think of the men there as being ill or anything. They weren't in bed, they were up and dressed and in their uniforms. Some of them were a little bit strange but most we treated as normal people,' she said. 'They never wanted to talk about their experiences. One chap I was seeing told my father that he'd had a mortar shell explode on his stomach, but he never told me that. I think he thought I'd be too embarrassed.'

Beryl remembers the huge ballroom where the dances took place, and the band, which was very professional and was made up of patients. 'A lot of the men were married and they were all shell-shocked, but they really enjoyed the dances, everyone did. One or two of my friends got quite attached to some of the men, and when they moved away and they never heard from them again, they were very upset. We'd be best of friends one minute, then they'd go away and we'd be forgotten. It was quite upsetting.'

Treatment at Northfield wasn't all dances and group therapy. Lieutenant Colonel Tom Main, a chief psychiatrist in the hospital wing, had a controversial technique for tank commanders who had broken down after seeing successive crews burned to death. Such men were particularly vulnerable to severe bouts of depression: standing at the top of the tank, they were the ones who, when their vehicle was hit, had time to get out as the explosion 'brewed up' beneath them. The statistics were dreadful, an estimated two-thirds of all tanks 'brewed up' when hit and 60 per cent of Allied tank losses were from a single shot from a 75-mm or 88-mm gun.

Getting out of the tank after a direct hit was not the end of it. Those who escaped had to watch helplessly as their second-in-command and those beneath him came out dying, often burning in front of their eyes. These were men who lived in a crew of four or five people, twenty-four hours a day for months on end. Losing a crew was like losing a set of close friends or relatives. If the commander was then appointed to another tank only to see the same thing happen again, he started to detach himself emotionally and became increasingly remote from the people with whom he was working. By the time it had happened a third time and he had suffered a sequence of bereavements, he would break down completely and arrive somewhere like Northfield, closed off from society, numbed by his grief.

SHELL SHOCK

Tom Main's idea was to tackle the problem head on. He called it 'compulsory mourning', and confined the affected man alone in a cell for three days, with one hour of daylight and one hour of electric light a day, and a diet of bread and water. It was a form of sensory deprivation. The patient would be left and ignored during that time, to give him the privacy to be angry and to grieve. He would invariably focus all his anger and grief on Main for locking him up, but the doctor didn't mind as long as it worked. He wrote: 'I used to say to them, "Well, you're a bit of a shit, you won't get any food, you'll get water." Then I used to shut the door and leave them in the dark for three days. They came out all right, you see it had to be left to them. They needed instruction – "You've got to bloody well cry, mate." It used to sanction their sadness. Whereas the Army never sanctioned sadness.'

Dr Patrick de Mare, who had treated shell-shocked men at Dunkirk and was later sent to Northfield, said: 'Compulsory mourning was experimental and rather brutal and was for patients who became clinically depressed. He believed that if you put them in isolation for several days with a Bible, you could transform the depression into something less savage. I don't think it worked. It was rather a cruel treatment.'

Vernon Scannell, the poet who was sent to Northfield after D-Day, wrote a poem called 'Compulsory Mourning' based on the experiences of the tank commanders he knew, which graphically depicted the treatment:

> Among the sludge and lumber in the mind
> An image, vast and vivid, of his face
> Plump, well-shaven, showing not a trace
> Of doubt or sympathy, this man who claims
> That he's not hoodwinked by my little games
> And sees with X-ray eyes through walls of bone
> Inside the haunted skull, and he alone
> Can teach me how to mourn as I should do
> The charred and blackened things that were my crew.
> . . . the man who thinks he holds a key
> To wind his soldiers up and then decree
> That they be used again in lethal games.

Despite some of his more radical treatments, Tom Main possessed remarkable enthusiasm for the science of psychiatry, and insight into the role of people like him in treating those affected by war. He wrote:

One campaign does not train a psychiatrist automatically for another. In the Middle East the great separation from home, the flat barren wilderness, the poor food, the rarity of action . . . contrast with the battles of Normandy which went on without remission for over two months in familiar green fields, with scarcity of sleep, the mortar and the continued carnage as the great stresses. In Burma it was not the explosions or power of the enemy weapons, but silence in jungle patrols, the fear of being seen without seeing, the difficulty of sleeping with a calm mind, and the long separation from home.

He showed great empathy with some of his patients, getting his pilot's 'wings', so that he could share their experiences, and pretending to be tougher than he was to bring out the anger in the shattered men he was treating. In one instance he ordered a self-styled 'macho' man to kill all the wild cats that roamed the hospital grounds, knowing full well that he was secretly an animal lover. The cats duly disappeared, and everyone assumed that the man had wrung their necks as he was told, but then it was noticed that he always left the dining room with leftover food. When it was discovered that all the cats were hidden safely away, and that this 'macho' man had been feeding them, Main let the information be passed round and the patient was able to behave as the gentle soul he was.

Dr de Mare described his time at Northfield as a 'very stimulating intellectual experience' even though some of the doctors were such innovative, powerful personalities who were often so out of step with the military that they were eventually replaced. One such was Major Wilfred Bion, the Tavistock Clinic psychiatrist, who had served in the First World War as a young officer in the Tank Corps and was still haunted by his experiences. By the time the Second World War broke out, he was suffering from regular nightmares and, on seeing history repeating itself, became despairing of the lack of awareness within the military hierarchy of the need for psychiatrists. He was contemptuous of those who made 'the hideous blunder of thinking that patients are potential cannon-fodder, to be returned as such to their units'.

Bion and his friend and colleague Dr John Rickman attempted to recruit their patients into what they called the 'battle against neurosis', setting up the first Northfield Experiment, an attempt to make sick men take back some control of their lives. They made bed-wetters wash their own linen and face the antipathy of the group about the smells and problems they caused. They allowed a group of about a hundred servicemen free rein in a hall to try to make them take control of their own situation. It was group therapy *en masse*. Rickman had come up with the idea after experiencing the leaderless, spontaneous meetings held by Quakers, and the men were virtually allowed to run riot, with no military discipline, reading newspapers, watching films and having ATS girls in. The hope was that when it got too messy or unruly, the men would organize themselves to clear it up and take back some control. Unfortunately, the experiment was not universally supported.

'The commanding officer, who was much more authoritarian, was treated with contempt by Bion and Rickman and he would feel very badly done by when he was trying to discipline people,' said Dr de Mare. 'One day the hall was left in a state of chaos; newspapers and used condoms on the floor. It was really upside down. And the CO went in there after the film was over and saw all this. He went straight back to London to the War Office to bring them down to see for themselves what it was like, and they came and were horrified and the next day Rickman and Bion were posted elsewhere.'

After their departure, Michael Foulkes, a German psychoanalyst who fought against the British in the First World War, took over and created smaller group-therapy circles, in which specific activities were held, like painting, drama or football – occupational therapy in its early stages. Foulkes's idea was to nurture a positive, creative atmosphere in which men could recover their senses and prepare themselves for a return to the outside world. 'Working for him was a kind of joy,' said Dr de Mare. 'It was fun – thoughtful, innovative and original. It was very exciting and he was very excited by it. He used to walk round very fast, trotting from one group to another, boosting morale and I don't think he ever had such excitement in his work again. Back in Civvy Street the work was much less inspired.'

Harold Bridger was the hospital's social therapist, and a major in the Royal Artillery; before the war he had been a mathematics teacher in Coventry. After working for the War Office selection board, he was posted to Northfield, and took charge of the rehabilitation wing in the late summer of 1944. Having read a paper on an experiment in Peckham, south London, in which residents were lured into taking part by the free use of a swimming pool which ultimately became a central feature of community life, Major Bridger decided to try something similar at Northfield.

'I got permission to empty one ward in the middle of the hospital and renamed it the Hospital Club. Its deliberate emptiness but allocated space for potential development, represented the patients' own personality,' he wrote. For days he sat in the ward alone and waited for something to happen. 'Everybody used to come along to me and say, "When is the club going to start?" and I'd say, "When you start it." After a week or two some of the patients got together and sent me a note ordering me to come and meet a group of them who wanted to know why this ward was being kept empty, 'wasting public space and money in wartime – space that could be put to so many good uses".' When he explained it to them, they suggested bringing things from their wards to put into the hospital club. One brought some chairs, another brought a table-tennis table and gradually the club built up.

Laurence Bradbury, a young sapper in the Royal Engineers with artistic talent, was recruited as an art instructor for therapy. In his own way he conducted a mini Northfield Experiment all by himself. 'I had this little hut of mayhem. It was really a sort of anarchy,' he said. 'There was no rank in there, we had officers as patients – one chap had the Victoria Cross. In a way it was a little like the selection-board experience. People could do as they liked, they came in if they wanted to, they went out if they didn't like it. I was just one of them, painting with them. No instruction was given, although if they asked, "How do I draw a nose?", I'd show them. They'd paint, or they'd sulk, or they'd fight and that was allowed. It got in the most frightful mess with paintings all over the place and the walls, and I suppose I should have been responsible and tidied it up, but I didn't. I'd wait until the tension was so great, and somebody said, "For God's sake we've got to sort this out. Let's get a sweeping brush." Then we'd all muck in, clean the windows and start again, so that we could mess it all up again.

'You could understand a regular RSM looking upon it as being virtually military anarchy. But the general attitude was that in this safe hut people could be themselves and God knows they needed to be, many of them still trying to cope with the guilt of killing or of not being killed when their chums were. All these things which were repressed came out in pictures, designs, slopping handpainted things or even just ripping up other people's works. They painted out the horrors and then tore them up and felt expunged of them. Some of the paintings produced there were really very interesting and brilliant free expression works, but most of the important paintings were destroyed, ripped up. The action was the point, the purpose.'

Some of the paintings he kept show the artists' pain. 'I still have one, done by a man who later killed himself, which is a marvel of paint, a wonderful piece of expressionism. I'm really quite jealous of it. Others show faces full of fright, sadness and anguish. They look at a condition of man and are pathetic. One shows the sadness of someone who is not physically injured and yet is mentally on fire, disintegrating. They are very poetic.'

There was little or no conferring with the psychiatrists about the patients' art works, although some doctors used to come and sit in on the sessions occasionally, and sometimes patients would volunteer their works to the psychiatrists for analysis. 'I was totally innocent and didn't pretend to know anything at all,' said Bradbury. 'I was just the chap who gave out the paper and the paint. I didn't go running back to the psychiatrists. There was no connivance there, there was never a question of my going behind a patient's back and saying, "You know there's something funny going here. I thought you'd be interested."

'I did occasionally have eyebrows raised about what was going on in the hut, some felt it was an indulgence, but it was no more outlandish than some of the other experimental treatments going on in the wards – experiments that they would never possibly have been able to put into practice in peacetime. Risks were taken at Northfield. There had never been anything like it because the circumstances had never been like it. I was on the fringe of history in the making, so many things happening, and in a modest way I think the art that we did was important too.'

Bradbury developed an amateur interest in psychiatry and used to sit in on the group therapy sessions with the patients and attend occasional lectures. 'I attended one lecture with great interest, only the doctor began by saying that the first manifestation of the inferiority complex is the growing of a moustache. I had a droopy little moustache at the time, which I had just grown, and I was shyly about to leave the room when I noticed that he himself had an even droopier one, which I found very amusing. After that I wore my moustache quite proudly as an offering of my inferiority complex.'

He described the charismatic Tom Main as every woman's ideal of what a man should be and look like – tall, brave, amusing, attractive, and with a remarkably magnetic personality. 'In battle, I imagine that men would have gone to the ends of the earth with him.' He agreed that Main's ritualistic mourning treatment could be brutal, but believed that it helped some of the men. 'They were allowed to wallow in their unhappiness, to believe that they were the dregs. They mourned for their friends, they felt the responsibility for their deaths, and they were allowed to sink almost to the point where they could decide it wasn't worth living. That would have been a terrible tragedy, but Main believed that the patient himself would eventually turn round, that the restoration would come from within, and that their dependency on the psychiatrist would be ended.'

Elsewhere in Northfield, other new methods of therapy were being tested. Group therapy continued to encourage the men to be responsible for a task and use it to mould the rest of the group together. There were ward meetings, psychodramas, work and leisure groups. At times there were open meetings in the main hall to involve the whole community in tackling a common problem like misbehaviour. In the regular group discussions, each member had their say in turn, or did not speak if they wished not to.

One patient recollected his attempt to bring a silent individual out of himself. 'He just sat on his bed and was no trouble to anybody, but he never spoke. This little lad came from an area where he would have had to know all about dogs and whippets, rabbits and hares. So we were on about something and I made up a little story about rabbiting, making some deliberate howler and he suddenly piped up, "You don't bloody well do anything of the sort," and he was off. After he bust loose, he chattered like a magpie, and I knew then that this group therapy thing worked.'

There were still those inside the hospital who favoured the organic or physical approach. Dr de Mare explained: 'There was a lot of leucotomy going on, which was generally accepted as a good thing, although it wasn't always done for the right reasons. I remember one person who was referred to me after he had his leucotomy because he had this delusion that he smelt. They did everything to try and change the delusion, but were met with no success whatsoever, so they finally gave him a leucotomy because it made him quite paranoid. He felt that everyone was sniffing when he was around. And he was sent to me to rehabilitate after the operation and the most terrible stench filled the whole room and he really did smell. Poor fellow, it was awful.'

As 1944 drew to a close, Northfield and the other psychiatric military hospitals received many former prisoners-of-war from the Far East. The campaign in Burma against the Japanese, fought from 1942 to the end of the war, confronted British soldiers with the harshest imaginable conditions, both physical and psychological. There were leeches, intense heat, monsoon rains and mud to contend with. In the Burmese jungle, units were isolated from each other for weeks at a time. Soldiers found themselves at the mercy of the Japanese suicide squads and their psychological games. They felt constantly watched, without being able to watch in return. Days of nerve-shattering silence would be broken by sudden battle.

The Far Eastern theatre of war became the only one in which forward psychiatrists were deployed to counteract the poor communications and long distances involved. It was radical but the military recognized the special problems its men would face far from home and in such an alien climate, where it was almost impossible to maintain any contact with loved ones, and illnesses like chronic amoebic dysentery, beri-beri and malaria compounded the psychological trauma.

In the RAMC journal, under the heading 'Psychiatry in Jungle Warfare', Major A. H. Williams, wrote: 'Chronic stress . . . is likely to predominate. During the most intense fighting, the stresses of climate, jungle and mountain, with rapid movements against an elusive foe, tend to produce types of anxiety state more like those seen in civil life. The exhaustion and panic states have an extremely good prognosis, the classical anxiety state a somewhat less good one.' He reported that psychosomatic illnesses occurred in about a quarter of cases, and gross hysteria such as night blindness in only 6 per cent. Depression and suicide attempts, he added, were common.

One nurse at Northfield recalled: 'Walking along the wards, particularly with the people who had come back from the Far East, the beds rattled. They rattled with fear. You could hear them. I was on night duty and this man came in and the sister gave me his papers and his age was about twenty-six or twenty-seven. I thought he was seventy or eighty, toothless. All he loved and cared for were a pair of slippers that he had. He said, "Those are my slippers. Please, you must know what I mean. They are my slippers." I just cried.'

Another said: 'The people who came back from Burma had been through such a terrible time they couldn't talk with a young psychiatrist golden boy, but they could talk to each other, so we put them in groups and the psychiatrist said practically nothing, just listened.'

Bill Hooper, who became a regular soldier in the South Staffordshire Regiment as an eighteen-year-old after an unhappy childhood, served almost the entire war in the gruelling Burma campaign, and was not so lucky. Instead of receiving any effective medical care, he was returned home, a changed man, to his young wife Betty. She had received no letters from him or from his doctors about his condition and when he arrived home, he weighed six and a half stone, could barely speak and had difficulty using his hands. 'My first reaction was utter shock because he was so thin, he was so haggard and I only just about recognized him. It was horrible to see him like that,' she said. 'He had been a very extrovert and outward-going person before he went off to war and he came back very different. We had no medical help. No counselling. It makes me laugh now to hear of men going away for three weeks and getting counselling. I don't know where all the counsellors were in our day, but I don't think they'd been invented, so we had to do it ourselves.'

Bill, whose limited training for South-East Asia included the advice from a sergeant not to worry about the Japanese because they were 'small blokes', was transferred to the Queen's Own Royal West Kents and sent to Bhopal, but went down with dysentery almost as soon as he arrived and was hospitalized for three months. Sent to the front line to fight the Japanese, he was ill-prepared for jungle warfare. 'It was hell,' he said. 'In the jungle you either survive or you don't. We weren't used to it, but the Japs were, it was their terrain. There were the monsoons and the diseases, the leeches sucking away at your legs and your arms. It's beyond belief what we had to face. It was enough to make any man crack, I don't care who he is. There were men there like zombies, they'd had the guts taken out of them. They're malaria-ridden, they've got leeches and jungle sores and they've been whacked to hell.

'You were in the soggy jungle half the time and the mud gives way and you are buried in mud and slime and water. It was like the trenches of the Great War – absolutely festered with it, up to your neck in it, pushing the jeeps and the guns out of it, pulling the mules out. You had no sleep and not much grub. They had food drops, but if the drops missed, the Japs got them.' Bill and his fellow soldiers learnt to live on snake, wild fruit, birds and boar. They lived in either complete darkness or bright daylight, with little respite from the sights and sounds of jungle life.

'Night-time was the worst. There were the monkeys and the frogs and the bats, all having a go, and you can't imagine the noise of a mortar shell or bomb in that environment. It was terrifying. It all plays on your mind. The Japs were crafty, cunning and ruthless. They used to employ these tactics where they found out men's names in the regiments and they'd call them out. They'd call, "Now come on, Johnny, you'll be all right. You come to us, Johnny." They used to wear the men down with it and some would just blow up. It is when a man loses his nerve and thinks, to hell with this, get this, and he fires – that's all they want, one shot and they've got you. They just wade in and wipe you out, simple as that. They are everywhere. You haven't got a dog's chance.'

He said that another common Japanese tactic was to entice Allied soldiers down into tunnels they had built deep into the jungle floor, calling their names and getting them to follow. Once inside the dimly lit tunnels, the Allied soldiers would hear a noise and panic, firing their guns into the dark. It was only when someone lit a torch that they would discover the Japanese had hidden local women and children down there as bait. 'Some of their tactics were absolutely vile. Some of the things we saw you couldn't even talk about. They didn't care what they did or how they got to you. It was a question of kill or be killed. We were thousands of miles from home, we didn't even feel like we were fighting for our country; we were fighting for our mates and we had to survive. If you can't survive, you go under,' said Bill.

In this previously placid and pleasant region of the British Empire, thousands lost their lives and hundreds lost their minds. The Japanese were well prepared for the conditions and had considerable support within the country. Their campaign was helped enormously by their attitude that to die for their country was the greatest honour. Suicide squads, similar to the kamikaze pilots seen at sea, were common, and by the end of the war in Burma nearly 85,000 Japanese servicemen had gone happily to meet their Maker.

Bill saw many British soldiers crack up under the strain of such deadly jungle warfare. He estimated that for every man physically wounded there were three or four psychiatric casualties. In Madras, he saw a whole hospital full of men who were so far gone that they couldn't be helped. 'There's nobody can foresee it. It just happens. A bloke don't plan it,' he explained. 'It just destroys you. The curtain comes down and that is it. In the First World War they called it cowardice, but it isn't. It is just when a man can't take any more and he breaks up.' Bill had seen his best friend Paddy shot dead in front of him and fall at his feet; he had almost cracked then, but managed to carry on. Not long afterwards he was wounded by a shell explosion in the battle of Pegu, Japan's last line of defence before the Burmese capital of Rangoon. He lost his sense of direction with the shock and ran towards the Japanese forces. He had to be rescued by his friends. 'I didn't know what happened. It just did, a devastating thing and it just fell apart. All I could see was bodies and all I could hear was tat-tat-tat. I'd been right through the whole lot, gone some thousand miles, and at that one particular point something went bang. That's it. Blank.' He was sent to a base hospital where he gradually lost his speech, then became paralysed. 'I'd hardly got any use of my legs or my arms and I couldn't talk much. I was a hell of a mess and I didn't know if I was coming or going. I'd completely lost my marbles. It was terrible; an experience I never want again. You feel absolutely drained and you've got no control at all. It was my Waterloo. A doctor came round and he told me, "You've been literally shattered and we've got to put you back together again." '

He was sent to a field hospital at Chittagong, and from there to five more hospitals where a succession of doctors claimed they could not cure him. His treatments ranged from sleep therapy to the truth drug. One doctor told him afterwards that the unresolved trauma of being tossed by a bull as a child had combined with the mortar-shell trauma to paralyse him. 'He said I was finished. I would never go back to the front line.'

Bill was put on a hospital ship back to Britain with four hundred 'head cases'; one man tried to throw himself overboard rather than face his wife and children. His comrades had to pull him back from the porthole. Bill was sent first to a hospital in Glasgow and then home where he continued to experience awful nightmares about what he had seen in Burma. 'I couldn't even talk about it, not even to Betty. I was almost at the point of blowing my top. I was afraid that my mind would just go completely and I'd end up in an asylum.

'Coming home, everything was dead quiet. I'd been used to a life over there being battered to hell. You didn't know one day from another. I'd settle in my house and the first thing I wanted to do was get out. I was boxed in. I told my wife. "If you've got a carving knife in the house, you'd better hide it." I was scared because in Burma we used knives, we used bayonets, so if you've got a knife, you use it. I didn't know what my reaction would be.'

For the first four years of their married life, Betty had to store all her kitchen knives with her neighbour, knocking on the wall three times when she needed to use them, then handing them back again. She had to nail up the windows after her husband kept opening them and crawling out because he couldn't be closed in. The couple could only rarely go to the cinema together because he would suddenly have to get out; he could only do outdoor work. They had to sleep in single beds because of his nightmares and shouting, tossing and turning. One night Betty woke to find him throttling her. 'I got used to his strange behaviour after a while,' she said. 'It was nothing for Bill, especially if it was raining, to be in the middle of his meal. He wouldn't say anything, he'd just put his knife and fork down, get up, go into the garden, stand in the pouring rain, come back in, sit down and finish his dinner. 'The only thing the doctor said to me when he first came to the house – and he only came once – was, "I'm not putting him on drugs because it will make him an addict. If you have to slap his face on occasion, do it. It'll do more good than my pills." And that was the only advice I received. So the whole of our first proper married life was ruled by trial and error. We'd battle through it together and if we didn't, we'd have both gone under, and we certainly had nobody to thank for that.'

Unable to cope, in 1946 Bill was sent to Netley in Hampshire, scene of the First World War shell-shock cases, where he spent five months. After two years, the Army stopped his pension, and he had to find work to support his family. 'I thought they could have done more,' he said. 'It took me four years after the war to get myself back to the way I was before and I still get occasional symptoms, but I intended to win. I thought, I've fought so far, I'll fight the rest, and I did. We just had to get on with it. It was the hardest battle I fought.'

The problems for those coming to terms with life after the Far East, especially those who were held prisoner-of-war in the notoriously cruel Japanese labour camps, were compounded by a Ministry of Defence directive not to speak about their experiences, lest civilians be upset. Most prisoners agreed that this was best at the time, but their enforced silence did little for their rehabilitation and readjustment.

In August 1944, the armed forces announced their intention to undertake the resettlement of ex-PoWs, who were being released or discharged to civil life. Those from the Far East had already started to flood in, but sick men from across Europe, Germany and Russia now needed to be catered for. Medical problems included chronic bronchitis in those forced to work in the German coal or salt mines, frostbite in those who had been forced to march from Poland and severe weight loss in most. The psychological problems from being held captive were equally debilitating.

Civil resettlement units were established, described as 'a half-way house to Civvy Street'. Psychiatric social workers were employed to help the men readjust to their new lives. Repatriates could stay for up to three months, during which time they were allowed 'job rehearsals' and supervised visits outside. But there were no such half-way houses for the majority of psychiatric casualties who, like Bill Hooper, were left to muddle through on their own.

The final few months of the war were marked by attack and counter-attack as the Germans and the Allies fought for every last inch of European soil.

Just when they seemed to be on the run, the Germans launched a surprise winter offensive on the Ardennes, sparking the bitter battle of the Bulge, in which 35,000 US soldiers were killed or captured before winning back their strategic position. When Eisenhower's forces reached the Rhine, Dresden was bombed in one of the greatest single acts of destruction of the war, the Japanese were defeated in Burma and the Germans were forced to give up Italy.

Bloodied and bowed, Hitler committed suicide on 30 April 1945, with a single bullet shot through his mouth. A week later, on 7 May, his chiefs of staff surrendered. Winston Churchill announced the news to the nation on the wireless. 'Yesterday morning at 2.41 a.m., at General Eisenhower's headquarters, General Jodl signed the act of unconditional surrender of all German land, sea and air forces to the Allied Expeditionary Force.' Europe was free, but it was awash with the dead, the dying and the displaced. Nevertheless, everyone who was physically able to do so celebrated VE (Victory in Europe) Day on 8 May.

It took a further three months to persuade the Japanese to surrender. On 6 August 1945, the *Enola Gay*, an American B-29 bomber, dropped an atomic bomb on the Japanese city of Hiroshima, killing 80,000 and injuring 40,000. A further 12,000 died in the following two weeks, and the radiation from the bomb continued to kill people for the next two generations. At first the Japanese refused to capitulate, and only did so when a second atomic bomb destroyed Nagasaki three days later, killing 25,000 people. A week later, Emperor Hirohito made his first public broadcast to the Japanese Army telling them to 'accept peace'. The formal surrender was signed on 2 September. The Second World War was over.

With the end of the war came the enormous task of clearing up and counting the massive cost of conflict. For the vast majority of those involved, it was difficult to see what benefit had been gained, with so many dead, wounded or scarred for life. But, as in the First World War, there had been hidden benefits of the conflict and valuable lessons were to be learned from the experience, not least in the military-medical field. The RAMC psychiatrists had proved that war could be fought effectively only with their help. A third of all casualties sent back to Britain for treatment had been psychiatric cases, and the full horror of combat and its effect on the mind had been recognized. Industry chiefs had already set in motion the process by which they would apply the psychiatric experience to their businesses. In medical circles, student doctors were clamouring to learn about the new psychiatry and how to apply it to a range of fields, including the treatment of the civilian population for neuroses many had never even heard of before the war.

For those still languishing in places like Northfield, there was a noticeable lack of direction. Most of the staff left, feeling that their work had been done, and the sense of pioneering importance vanished. New patients, still arriving from the front, found the place without purpose; some didn't see a doctor in six months. The general feeling was, that now the war was over, those men whose minds had been ravaged by their experiences should suddenly feel better. The doctors, whose *raison d'être* for the previous six years had been to make their patients well enough to go back to the front lines, were now faced with the unpalatable fact that many simply would not recover, and that the end of the war only marked the start of a lifelong course of treatment.

Among them was John Hanstock, the naval casualty who has suffered from psychiatric problems ever since the war. He still sees his GP once a month, but claims that his wife Marjorie has been his 'rock'.

Spike Milligan went on to an illustrious career in radio and television, becoming one of the members of the famous *Goon Show* with Peter Sellers, Michael Bentine and Harry Secombe. But unstable mental health has dogged his life. Now in his eighties, considered a national institution and an originator of modern comedy, he is the author of more than fifty books, even though manic depression has exerted an iron grip on him. He has had at least twelve nervous breakdowns, been married three times, and has spent much of his life in psychiatric hospitals.

Arthur Smith, the bomber pilot persuaded to return to his crew after going LMF, later developed a phobia of flying. He said he applied the lesson he learned in the war to his civilian life: he did not seek any position that was too high up or carried too much responsibility. 'I arranged my life so that I didn't get too stressed,' he said. He has had vivid, violent nightmares ever since, but is 'eternally grateful' to the psychiatrist who gave him the chance to overcome his fear and go back to his crew. He now lives with his family in Stevenage, Hertfordshire.

Bill Hooper became a lorry driver and was a founder member of the Burma Star Association in Southampton, where he lives with his family. He has been instrumental in campaigning for better recognition for 'the forgotten army', as those who served in the Far East have become known. He now believes his symptoms are under control, but he still has occasional nightmares.

Vernon Scannell, who was wounded at the end of the war and sent to a convalescent hospital, packed his bags and left when peace was declared. He spent the next two years on the run – not having been officially discharged – before being caught and court-martialled a second time. Considered psychologically unstable, he was sent to Northfield Hospital instead of prison, where he was kept in a closed ward with other deserters, many of whom received ECT treatment and drug therapy. Discharged, he went on to university and became a published poet. He suffered from recurring nightmares about the war and believes his experiences caused an adverse effect on his personality for many years. His works have been widely read by thousands of children studying war poetry in schools.

Stan Goldsworthy spent the first ten years after the war receiving hospital treatment for his physical and psychological condition. He spent almost a year in one institution, and found that the slightest thing could set him back. 'It's always there, it's always in your mind and there's always something happening in the world that brings it back,' he said. 'You pick up a newspaper and read about Yugoslavia or the Middle East and the bombs, and it brings back all these memories. You wake up at night and think about it, and fifty years on, it never goes away.'

Philip Gee, the pacifist who suffered a breakdown in civilian life, started work as a cost accountant and went on to work in finance. He has been on antidepressant drugs since the war and suffers from a heart condition. In the 1960s he became a vicar.

Major Wilfred Bion went on to chair the executive committee of the Tavistock Clinic, and from there his ideas spread into the world of business and management. He died in 1979. His son followed him into medicine and is a senior lecturer in intensive care at Birmingham's Queen Elizabeth Hospital.

Tom Main went on to the Cassel Hospital in Richmond, Surrey, where he built up a 'therapeutic community', in which inmates were not treated as ill but damaged, and were individuals rather than invalids. He died quite recently.

Between September 1939 and July 1944 there were 118,000 discharges from the British Army as a result of psychiatric disorder, the largest single category of injury. Nearly two thirds of these were considered war neuroses. During the year 1942–3, 2,989 airmen were adjudged to be suffering from LMF. In the American armed forces, 409,887 service personnel were admitted to military hospitals overseas as neuro-psychiatric patients. Twenty-three per cent evacuated from combat areas were psychiatric casualties. The figures failed to take into account the many thousands more who suffered in silence and remained undiagnosed. Once unfamiliar terms, such as battle exhaustion and combat stress, were now forever associated with the trials of modern warfare.

Despite the incontrovertible evidence of cases, there was continuing resistance to the new mood of sympathy for psychologically damaged servicemen, even in the highest circles. General George Patton remarked: 'Any man who says he has battle fatigue is avoiding danger . . . If soldiers would make fun of those who begin to show battle fatigue, they would prevent its spread, and save the man who allows himself to malinger by this means from an afterlife of humiliation and regret.'

In 1948 Northfield returned to civilian use and the last servicemen left. The giant apparatus set up to help those afflicted by the horrors of war was dismantled, even though many people still needed it.

The scientific optimism engendered by the war did not fulfil its promises, especially in military spheres. Psychiatry was still the Cinderella of medical specialities, whose concepts ran counter to the ethos of the military forces and encouraged insubordination and loss of morale. The concept of having psychiatrists travel with forces overseas, rather than follow them up, had been only partially embraced after six years of fighting. Those who had taken part in the uphill struggles against prejudice to try to help those suffering on the front lines had been whistling in the dark.

SHELL SHOCK

Even though all the evidence of the First and Second World War was to the contrary, the prevailing view during the late 1940s and early 1950s was that war veterans who resumed civilian status or were not hospitalized would either adjust without difficulty or recover physically and mentally with the help of their families. That may have been largely true, but at least 200,000 American and British survivors of the Second World War are still receiving psychiatric treatment today. Many broke down for the first time only after they retired from full employment and no longer had the diversion of a full working life; or when they were widowed and found themselves alone and unable to cope with the suppressed details of their past lives. Mental-health experts and voluntary organizations around the world report high levels of breakdown among veterans at retirement, which symbolizes their passing into old age and is coupled with the realization that the war robbed them of their youth.

One man, who, as a young private, helped to collect and bury hundreds of bodies of people who had been gassed by the Nazis at Belsen managed to suppress his mental horrors until he was caught up in the Bradford football disaster forty years later, whereupon he suffered a complete mental breakdown. Others exhibited long repressed symptoms of shock and trauma during the recent commemorations marking the fiftieth anniversary of the end of the conflict, with all the emotional memories it revived. Long-term studies of war veterans found that they generally retire earlier, are more likely to be on disability pensions, have higher rates of marital breakdown and that their children are more likely to experience emotional difficulties.

It was not until several years later, with the conflicts in Korea, Vietnam, the Falklands, the Gulf War and Bosnia that the harrowing experiences of those who took part in the Second World War were raised once more into public awareness – and in many ways, diminished by it.

Chapter Seven

The result of every land battle is determined by the number of people who run away, and by nothing else.

General Sir John Hackett

With every new war shell shock is 'rediscovered' by the military and medical establishment, who each time express their surprise and dismay that modern warfare has not eliminated it. In the years between conflicts, the condition – and the men suffering from it – slips from public consciousness and is largely forgotten. After the Second World War, a great deal more was known and understood about the advent and treatment of battle shock. After the First World War, the major milestone had been acceptance that it existed. Now, those at the forefront of psychiatry, keen to capitalize on what had been achieved, urged immediate action on its prevention and cure. They also wanted to take their expertise into the civilian field. Sensing a mood of change and optimism in the way the nation's health services were being organized, they demanded a key role.

The Tavistock set up a sister clinic called the Institute of Human Relations, to specialize in teaching and research. Wilfred Bion and John Rickman laid down the framework for the group therapy that was to take place there and introduced innovations such as one-way screens, tape recorded sessions and, unheard of previously, marriage-guidance counselling. Contact was made internationally with the World Health Organization and the World Federation for Mental Health, and the lessons learned from the war experience were all set to be put to good use.

The call to progress rather than regress was heard in America too. Alan Gregg, neuro-psychiatric consultant to the American surgeon general, urged for a greater value to be placed on the importance of psychiatry in light of the Second World War experience. He wrote plaintively:

An emotional bias against the psychiatric study of medicine frequently exists and owes its origins more to a self-protecting device of the physician. Psychological findings are as real and valid as those in any other field of medicine, even though relatively intangible. Unfortunately because of their training this fact is not accepted (or at least acted upon) by many physicians. The concrete nature of percussing the chest or examining the urine specimen seems more valid than investigating the emotions. In neurotic reactions, the time required to study the personality often acts as a deterrent.

The flowering of British psychiatry after the war was helped enormously by the introduction of the National Health Service in 1948, and the enormous contribution made by Sir Aubrey Lewis, chair of psychiatry at the Maudsley Hospital between 1946 and 1966. Australian by birth, Lewis advocated that mental and nervous disease should be given equal consideration to physical ills. In those days it was widely accepted that many organic diseases, such as stomach ulcers and headaches, were psychological in origin, and it was thus that psychiatry began to be embraced into general medicine under the NHS's grandiose scheme of care 'from the cradle to the grave'.

The problem was that, however much the doctors banged the drum for psychiatry, there was still a fixed idea in the public mind that mental illness was something frightening and incurable, which stood in the way of early voluntary treatment. If people suffering from psychoses were reluctant to come forward for fear of being labelled a lunatic and manacled in an asylum for the rest of their lives, there was little incentive for the medical authorities to provide a service that they knew would be under-used. Besides, greater principles were at stake. The new health service, the most sweeping reform introduced by Clement Attlee's Labour government, had promised free medical treatment for the entire population, with free medicines, dental care and spectacles, all coupled with a national insurance scheme and welfare systems to deal with the unemployed and the elderly.

In the great race to take control of the nation's hospitals and enlist thousands of medical doctors into the scheme, the need for the training and recruitment of psychiatrists was temporarily overlooked, yet official figures showed that in 1947 162,000 patients were in public and private mental hospitals in Great Britain and a further 2,000 were being supervised outside. There was a gross shortage of beds and manpower: in 1946, nearly 10,500 beds in public mental hospitals were still diverted to wartime uses, and four years later, nearly 2,000 had not been returned. At the same time 2,383 beds were unoccupied for want of staff and 1,703 were not fit for occupation. The resultant overcrowding was considerable.

In response to the problem, and because it now appreciated that psychiatry was highly relevant to preventive and social medicine, the Ministry of Health approached clinics like the Tavistock and hoped to enlist their key staff, but many declined to work in the NHS and left, including Wilfred Bion who returned to private psychoanalysis. Other clinics guarded their position fiercely for fear of being swallowed up by the Tavistock. Although state involvement guaranteed a certain level of funding and support for the new age of psychiatry, disillusion set in when additional funding had to be sought from America after it was realized that government money would not be enough.

Caught up in the bureaucracy of a brave new world, post-war progress was slow but steady in the field of industrial screening, bereavement, family counselling and individual psychotherapy, and paved the way for behavioural and social sciences, yet more than twenty years before the establishment of a Royal College of Psychiatrists, which converted from its previous incarnation as the Royal Medico-Psychological Association, 453 years after the Royal College of Physicians came into being. The formation of their own college finally gave psychiatrists the autonomy to frame their own practice, control their training and examinations and freed them from dependency on others. It would also allow them to monitor closely any future involvement with the military.

Out in the world theatre, war and conflict continued to erupt and be quelled and momentous events once again threatened peace and stability. In 1947 India and Pakistan became independent of Britain accompanied by appalling violence. The creation of the state of Israel, in the following year, proved a continuing source of bitter conflict in the Middle East; in the British colony of Malaya a ferocious and bloody jungle war broke out against Communist insurgents.

At the start of the new decade peace seemed as elusive as ever with the outbreak of war in Korea. In June 1950 US servicemen gathered arms to oppose the Communist North Korean troops, who had crossed the 38th parallel and invaded the south in support of their government's claim to national sovereignty.

The United Nations condemned the invasion and war was declared, effectively between the Communists in the north and UN troops – mainly American, but also British, French and Australian – in the south. It was a highly controversial war of containment that claimed more than 55,000 lives and saw many servicemen mentally and physically wounded. The nature of the conflict was guerrilla warfare in conditions alien to the troops sent to patrol the protected areas. The intense cold was such that rats crept under the ground sheets of the tents to keep warm. Atrocities and psychological mind games were carried out by enemy troops, and many of those captured were brainwashed.

It was in this conflict, and the one which followed, that American psychiatrists undertook the first large-scale scientific studies of how soldiers' minds stood up under combat. It has since been said that Korean veterans are the forgotten warriors of later twentieth-century warfare. The US armed forces at the time were largely made up of Hispanic or black troops of poorer socio-economic status. Combatants were found afterwards to be two and a half times more likely to have mental-health problems than their civilian counterparts; one study found that two-thirds of those interviewed were suffering from battle shock, yet these men were the least likely of all combat veterans since the Second World War to use the Veterans Association health services or receive disability pensions.

After a long and costly series of battles and the longest negotiated ceasefire on record, peace was finally declared in Korea in July 1953. Over a million people lost their lives in a conflict that did little but push America ahead of Europe in the business of combat madness.

*

In Britain in the 1950s, conscription was ended, and with it one of the major psychological problems of the Second World War: the apparent unsuitability of certain civilians to face combat. The new professional armed service, of young men and women who had enlisted by choice, was to be highly disciplined, motivated and well trained. Mental toughness was taken for granted, and the armed forces set about advertising themselves as reliable, worthwhile employers to attract the right sort of volunteer. As the British military establishment got to grips with the idea of being competitive in the field of commerce for the first time, the effect of war on men's minds was not a top priority.

With the early 1960s came a new mood of optimism in both civilian and military life in the West. It was felt on both sides of the Atlantic that enough was now known about the recruitment, screening and treatment of service personnel to reduce psychiatric breakdowns to insignificant levels in any future conflict. The dawn of the space age, the film and arts revolution, the advent of television and mass consumerism all added to the buoyant spirit. Martin Luther King offered hope to black Americans, John F. Kennedy came to power and earned unprecedented popular support, Britain's prime minister Harold Macmillan spoke of a 'wind of change' in Africa, and the Soviet leader Krushchev backed down from his hard stance against the Americans in the early years of the cold war.

By the end of 1964 all that had changed: Kennedy had been assassinated, Krushchev deposed and, with the outbreak of the Vietnam War, the predictions of optimists were proved dramatically wrong. When President Johnson first sought approval from Congress to take 'all necessary action' against the bellicose Communist regime in North Vietnam, he won it unanimously. Some members, however, felt duty-bound to express their fears that he would be committing US troops to 'an unwanted war'. Of all the conflicts fought this century, Vietnam was perhaps the most controversial and enjoyed, at best, ambivalent public support. In the eleven years of fighting that followed, 3.14 million American men served, approximately 58,000 died and 30,000 were wounded. Some say that as many as a million experienced serious emotional imbalance on their return.

Early predictions of limited psychiatric casualties were endorsed in 1966 by two psychiatrists, Tiffany and Allerton, who claimed in a lecture to the American Psychiatric Association that only 5 per cent of casualties in Vietnam were psychiatric, compared to 23 per cent in the Second World War. Others said that the problem of what was then called 'acute combat reaction' had been solved and that the mental health of US troops in Vietnam remained 'outstanding'. The mood was buoyant; it was felt that any psychiatric casualties could and would be cured with the necessary scientific research. But the Vietnamese combat involved unconventional guerrilla warfare in hostile conditions for which the young participants were untrained and ill-prepared. As in the Korean War, 20 per cent of soldiers witnessed atrocities or abusive violence, some even instigating it. The climate, humid atmosphere, and the widespread use of Agent Orange, a highly toxic organophosphate defoliant designed instantaneously to kill off the jungle vegetation that protected the Vietcong troops so well, added to the misery of the young men, who soon began to wonder whose war they were fighting on the other side of the world. There were just eleven US psychiatrists stationed in Vietnam to look after 200,000 men, although the Army distributed information on 'combat stress', and sent COs, MOs and chaplains on courses to teach them how to deal with it before and during the conflict.

Initially, few men were evacuated suffering from acute symptoms of stress, and by and large, they appeared to be coping well with their daily diet of death and destruction. But as the 1970s wore on and men returned home injured and shell-shocked, stories about Vietnam veterans began to circulate and cause concern. There were tales of serious readjustment problems, personality disorders and clashes with authority. Symptoms were said to include general anxiety, emotional numbing, and distressing flashbacks to the original battle or trauma.

However, the high numbers of men psychologically affected on their return may have had more to do with the background to conflict than the trauma itself. The average age of those who served in Vietnam was nineteen, and many had joined up in a wave of enthusiasm for military service against a clearly defined enemy: the Red peril, Communism. Their return home in the years that followed was a different story: the veterans were treated with disdain, identified in the public mind with the war itself, which in their absence had become unpopular. There were no parades, no welcoming speeches. Servicemen who had risked their lives and watched friends die were accused of being the puppets of an unpopular regime, or of failing to question the motives of war. They flew home from Saigon by commercial jet, a journey of a few hours, and no systems were in place to help them make the transition from warrior to civilian.

From the haunted experiences that subsequently manifested themselves in the hearts and minds of these men, a new term emerged, 'post-traumatic stress', to describe the condition in which symptoms erupted months or even years after they had come through combat apparently unscathed. The new label represented more than just an updating of language. It was born of the Vietnam War and has, in many ways, remained fixed there in a time warp in the public mind – the classic face of shell shock, 1970s style.

Harry Wilmer, a doctor who studied the sleep patterns of troubled Vietnam veterans at a hospital in Texas, wrote: 'In the tormenting nightmare images, the war lives on in the psyche as if Vietnam still existed, night after night. The combat dreams and the attendant insomnia are often the most disturbing symptoms. Such dreams may still occur nightly or weekly years after the war and the delayed stress reaction may not appear until many years after the war.'

A 1987 study found that Vietnam veterans were more likely to use mental-health services than their Second World War counterparts, but were associated with increased rates of violence, deliberate self-harm, divorce, social isolation and vocational instability. Korean veterans fell midway between the two groups. Twenty-five per cent of those who saw heavy combat in Vietnam were charged with an assortment of criminal offences on their return, and 33 per cent of the US federal prison population are veterans. Statistics have shown that the number of Vietnam combat veterans who have committed suicide since the war now exceeds the number killed during the conflict.

In recognition of the particular crises facing these men, the same US Congress that had sent millions of them to fight the Vietcong took the unprecedented step of agreeing to fund a service for those with readjustment problems. Research has shown that an estimated 450,000, or 15 per cent of all Vietnam veterans, were still suffering psychologically twenty years after hostilities ceased. Those physically disabled by the war were among the highest risk group: facing up to the loss of a limb or paralysis is difficult enough without the conviction that the injury may have been unwarranted. An additional 19 per cent were suffering from 'partial' psychoses, making a total of 830,000 Americans still suffering in some way from their experiences, an epidemic unforeseen by the authorities.

As the First World War did for Britain, the Vietnam War represented a major turning-point in US military attitudes. The bizarre and sometimes violent behaviour of its veterans raised public awareness of the disorder and presented the military with an unpalatable ethical dilemma about what to do in future conflicts. As modern warfare moved from trenches to tank battles to guerrilla engagements, and as the value attached to wars varied from valedictory to derogatory, the experience of soldiering and conditions of mental illness had also altered significantly, keeping pace with the changing face of conflict.

Those in the First World War had exhibited 'hysterical' paralysis at a time when it was difficult to tell whether or not such a symptom had a physical cause. At the outbreak of the Second World War, hysterical symptoms virtually disappeared in the face of medical science advances and technology that could quickly dismiss them as false. Sufferers instead complained of exhaustion, 'fugue' states of mind and unquantifiable, intangible symptoms that defied classification. Much the same happened in Vietnam but with a time lapse: symptoms of the mystery condition delayed their manifestation until the victim was at home and away from close scrutiny. The subconscious mind, torn by instincts of self-preservation and duty, appeared to be keeping one step ahead of those determined to expose it.

The British followed the American experience of Vietnam with mild interest, grateful not to be involved in another major conflict so soon after the Second World War and complacent about the possibility of war-related adjustment problems among its own service personnel. But on the doorstep, in the troubled streets of Northern Ireland, a time bomb was ticking away. The political situation heated up so fast that by the early 1970s British servicemen were facing life-and-death skirmishes that in many ways mirrored those on the other side of the globe.

In 1969, after a spate of political murders and violent demonstrations inspired by the American civil rights movement, British troops were sent in to keep order in the province. Their presence had been requested by the Northern Ireland government and welcomed by the Catholic nationalist minority, who had long complained of prejudice and discrimination against them. British soldiers were initially viewed as a preferable alternative to the wholly Protestant law enforcement agencies, but by the time they had disarmed the Royal Ulster Constabulary (RUC) and become the chief force for law and order, they had alienated the Catholics, who encouraged the rise of the terrorist Provisional IRA.

Soldiers sent on tours of duty to Northern Ireland faced unique pressures in the subsequent terrorist war. The IRA began its bombing campaign in March 1969, leading to severe rioting and violent clashes between the RUC and Catholic demonstrators. In 1971, troops were used to pursue a counter-insurgency policy, which included massive house-to-house searches and internment. Relations between the troops and the civilian population reached their nadir on 30 January 1972, when British soldiers opened fire on rioting Catholics in Londonderry, killing thirteen. In what became known as Bloody Sunday, the violence reiterated the view held by many in Northern Ireland that the British forces were now an army of occupation, and should be treated as such. An open season was declared on those seen to be representing the British government, and terrorist activities by Catholics and Protestants increased dramatically both in the province and on mainland Britain. No serviceman or his family was safe from IRA attack; even at German bases, car bombs were used to kill off-duty soldiers.

By the end of 1972, nearly 500 people had been killed in the political violence. At the peak of the crisis in 1973, when a state of emergency was declared, 16,500 British troops were deployed and IRA attacks were a steady and constant menace. Some barricaded no-go areas were patrolled and reached only by helicopter.

The participants in this very modern war were engaged in a completely different type of conflict from any previously experienced. They found themselves either patrolling the streets of British cities, surrounded by people and buildings exactly like their own, yet facing the hidden dangers of the sniper and the booby-trap; or caught in the middle of confusing sectarian rioting. Children as young as three threw stones at them and jeered; civilian women spat in their faces and banged dustbin lids; there were frustrating day-long patrols and endless nights. They saw friends blown to smithereens by bombs placed under armoured vehicles, or watched them fall with a sniper bullet between the eyes, or cleared up the debris after a city-centre bomb had blasted innocent civilians into little more than lumps of flesh.

Those who had seen service in previous conflicts had enjoyed a clear-cut sense of what was right and what was wrong. The enemy was the enemy: their bases, aeroplanes, ammunition stores and all their means of warfare could legitimately be taken out, even if that meant killing some of them in the process. In Northern Ireland, it was different. The enemy was all around them: the soldiers knew who the IRA were – they had to memorize their faces from photographs and saw them on an almost daily basis, walking down the street towards them, or smiling and joking over a pint with their mates. Yet, because of political expediency, they couldn't touch them. Military duty was all about surveillance and counter-intelligence, patrolling and peacekeeping. It was a game of watching and waiting – often just to be killed. The frontier between reality and unreality was fragile and the business of having constantly to differentiate between friend and foe encouraged widespread paranoia.

Inevitably, some soldiers developed psychiatric problems, by this time unofficially accepted in medical science as 'post-traumatic stress disorder' or PTSD. In the absence of any recognition that they were engaged in a war, or an understanding that the situation in which they were placed could produce the condition, their treatment was patchy at best. No specialist doctors were deployed by the military and there was no separate psychiatric care. If a man felt desperate he could ask to see the padre, but this would arouse so much ridicule and suspicion that they did not dare. A culture of machismo prevailed among this group of young men who had voluntarily put on a uniform and taken up arms. The way was set for some serious long-term side-effects in what for many became Britain's Vietnam.

As had happened in America in the years following Vietnam, throughout the 1970s, 1980s and 1990s British newspapers published stories of men whose background was military service in Northern Ireland and men who had previously been regarded as psychologically stable. Some had been given awards for bravery and acts of heroism, but now they had gone off the rails. It was a familiar pattern of post-traumatic decline.

One such soldier was Jimmy Johnson, now a middle-aged father of two, who served two tours of duty as a corporal in the Royal Tank Regiment in Northern Ireland in the early 1970s when the violence was at its worst and was decorated for bravery. He was one of the first to see service in the province and was caught in the middle of a bomb blast in Lurgan, near Belfast. The area was cleared because of a danger of other devices, but an hysterical man screamed at Johnson that his wife was trapped inside an underground toilet. 'I went in. I lowered myself down and found her,' Johnson said. 'There was blood everywhere. She looked just like my wife. I picked her up in my arms and got her out to the ambulance. I put her in the back and sat with her. The medic looked at me and shook his head.' Having realized that the woman was close to death, Johnson went into shock, shaking and breaking out in a sweat. His helplessness was further compounded by acerbic comment from a woman passer-by, a Protestant, who looked him in the eye and told him, 'Don't worry, she's only a Catholic.' He walked away from the bomb site and was found by colleagues much later in a nearby bar, not knowing where he was. After being given a sedative and put to bed, he was sent back out on patrol the next day. Not long afterwards, he was involved in a violent struggle during a riot, in which he nearly beat a man to death with the butt of a rubber-bullet gun. After another tour of duty in 1973 which he described as 'like going back to Hell', he left the Army in 1974 and started suffering from flashbacks.

In some, quiet English country lanes suddenly became sniper alleys, and in others ordinary crowds became angry mobs. 'You'd see a neighbour's curtain move. To anyone else it's just a curtain, but to me it was a sniper,' he said. One day he had accepted a lift from Keith Culmer, a security guard, and was travelling with him in his van when some children threw a ball or a rock that hit it with a bang. Johnson claimed he blacked out, flashed back to Northern Ireland and believed the van to be under attack. When he came to, he found he had carried his companion from the vehicle and had battered him to death with a pole, thinking all the time about 'hitting a bloke in Northern Ireland'. He admitted murder and was given the mandatory life sentence but was released on licence nine years later, having convinced the parole board that he was no longer a threat to society. After eighteen months of freedom he was given some odd-job work in the house of Robin Harwood, forty-one, a school laboratory technician, who knew his history but decided to give him a chance to earn some spare cash. In a completely unprovoked attack, during which Johnson claimed to experience another sudden flashback, he smashed Mr Harwood's skull, hitting him six times with a lump hammer. Then he collected legal documents belonging to the dead man and used them to arrange a £2,000 loan. Four days later he was arrested at a family wedding in Stockton-on-Tees, Cleveland. When he came to trial he pleaded guilty to murder and was sentenced again to life imprisonment, this time with a recommendation that he serve a minimum of thirty years.

In Frankland high-security prison in Durham, Johnson learned about PTSD from a fellow prisoner, a former doctor, and began to research it. He discovered case after case of soldiers cracking up, committing either crimes or suicide after serving in Northern Ireland. Looking around at his fellow inmates he discovered that a surprisingly high number were ex-servicemen – some estimates put it as high as 7 per cent, or 4,400 men. Johnson was eventually examined by Dr Morgan O'Connell, a former consultant psychiatrist with the Royal Navy, who believes that he carried out both murders while in 'a state of detachment or flashback to conditions of severe stress whilst serving in Northern Ireland'.

He has been granted legal aid for a test-case appeal against his conviction on the grounds that he committed manslaughter, not murder, and should have been able to plead diminished responsibility. It will be the first time that PTSD has been used in Britain as a defence against manslaughter or murder charge. Johnson's solicitor, Stephen Sullivan, said: 'If the appeal goes through it could open the floodgates to ex-soldiers suffering from PTSD who now languish in prisons.'

Robert Harwood, eighty-two, of Blackburn, Lancashire, the father of Johnson's last victim, has, however, decried the appeal and described Johnson as 'a brutal killer who should never have been released'. When the appeal was announced he told newspapers: 'I fought with the Fleet Air Arm in the Second World War in the Far East. I saw some terrible things and so did many of my comrades. We were traumatized and many veterans are still suffering, but how many of them became murderers?'

Among other cases that have made the national press was that of a young Army sentry who in 1979 went berserk with a rifle at a Belfast barracks and had to be shot dead by his colleagues after he killed one NCO and badly injured another. Edward Maggs, twenty-one, from Essex, was never able to explain why he fired indiscriminately at his fellow soldiers in the heavily fortified Woodburn barracks in West Belfast. Other members of his regiment, the Blues and Royals, raced from their billets in the darkness, believing that an IRA attack had begun.

After the incident Maggs's father said that his son should never have been sent back to Northern Ireland for a second tour of duty. 'My son spent four months in Ireland last year and he was terrified of going back,' he said. 'He loved the Army but he couldn't take any more of Northern Ireland. I only know this tragedy would not have happened if he had not been sent back. He was a victim of Northern Ireland just as surely as if he had been shot in the back by a terrorist bullet.'

In April 1990, an ex-Army corporal appeared before Ipswich Crown Court, pleading guilty to charges of criminal damage. Michael King, who had served eight years in the Army, bought himself out in 1988 and settled happily with his wife in the Suffolk village of Nayland. After a series of minor stress-related problems, he snapped one day after experiencing a flashback to his tour of duty in Northern Ireland during a quiet Sunday lunch, in which he believed he was being chased and cornered by the IRA. After running from the house, he returned and dragged out his military kit and a shotgun, setting up a firing position in the front window. Oblivious to his wife, who locked herself in a cupboard, he started shooting live rounds at the vicarage opposite. Surrounded by armed police, he shouted, 'Take me out!' realizing what he had done but not why. He was later captured without incident.

King made British legal history by entering a plea in mitigation that he was suffering from PTSD. In court, Justice John Turner accepted this and sentenced King to three years' probation, on the condition that he sought continued psychotherapy. He is since believed to have made a full recovery.

Among those Northern Ireland veterans who are still having problems, however, is John Flynn, of Gillingham in Kent, who was in the 1st Battalion Queen's Regiment and served two tours of duty in the province between 1978 and 1982. 'I nearly shit myself on my first foot patrol because I thought I was going to get pasted,' he said. 'Everyone feels like that – it's your first time out there and you feel they know who you are. You're a new boy, it's your first tour and you get this feeling they're watching you the whole time and you're waiting for something to happen. It's a different type of fear, not something you experience anywhere else. In war, you know more or less who the enemy are – they're in front of you. But in Northern Ireland, it's psychological war and there are all the rules you have to adhere to – the yellow card rule of shouting three warnings before you shoot – it's ridiculous. In a war if a woman or a kid gets killed, it's, "Oh, well, casualties of war", but in Northern Ireland you make a mistake and you're banged up. All those pressures add up on top of the stress of the job, and your mind is like a computer, with all the information in there for four or six months. Only you can turn a computer off, take the memory out and throw it away. With Northern Ireland, it's not switched off, you're stuck with it.'

Now aged thirty-eight, he lives with his mother and has been unable to work for some years. 'I started feeling funny after I came back from Ireland but I suppressed it,' he said. 'I got into trouble, I was drinking and fighting and I couldn't hold down a relationship.' He spent nine months in an Army jail, escaped and was recaptured – he was even confined in a straitjacket at one point – but still no one suggested he saw a doctor. Within a year he was back in Northern Ireland for a two-year tour of duty, after which he decided to leave. He bought himself out in 1983.

'In 1994 I had a big breakdown. I was crying, shaking all over, seeing images, thinking I was in Ireland,' he said. 'I had no shame whatsoever, I went to the hospital in tears. I went to pieces. I saw a psychologist, who suspected I was suffering from post-traumatic stress. He sent me to my own GP who eventually agreed to treat me. It was as though I was trapped. My mind was in Northern Ireland but physically I was back at home. I can't trust anybody, I can't use public transport. I get flashbacks and sleepless nights. I dive for cover when I hear a car backfire. When I first came out of the Army I got a job in a factory, but the lads there thought it was a laugh to come up behind me and slam trays down on the ground. I lost that job eventually because I ended up having a pop at the manager.'

Flynn said the Army doctors in Northern Ireland were only capable of patching men up – if someone was seriously hurt they went to a civilian hospital. 'There were certainly no psychiatrists. I think there was a padre you could see, but you would never ask. If you did, the officer would say, "Why do you want to see the padre?" You just couldn't really do it.' On the high-security military base, the men lived in tiny concrete rooms, six or eight in an area fourteen feet square. There was no privacy, no respite from the tension and the constant fear of death in riots, hoax bomb attacks and IRA mind games. His lowest ebb in the Province came when four friends were killed in a truck bomb explosion in 1982. 'The Army towed the wreckage into the base and kept it there as a reminder to everybody to keep on their toes. I saw it every day, it was awful. I couldn't get it out of my mind.'

Since his breakdown, the man who first joined up to have a career and avoid 'a life of potato peeling', has been unable to do more than menial work around the house and garden. He still suffers from flashbacks, is unable to sleep for more than a few hours at night and lives on a weekly war pension he collects from the local post office. A civilian psychiatrist whom he liked and trusted and saw regularly for a year suddenly moved away and Flynn has been unable to continue his therapy. 'At the end of the day, you just give up. You feel let down by everybody,' he said.

Another veteran, Graham Donaldson, thirty-seven, from Hull, is a former member of the Light Infantry whose problems started after his first tour of duty in the province in the early 1980s. He was involved in an accident in which three mates were killed when a lorry ploughed into them; a close friend committed suicide and thirteen members of the Cheshire Regiment were killed in a bomb explosion at the Drop Well Inn, including a good friend. In 1985 he had to attend the scene of a bus bombing in which eight soldiers from his old battalion had been blown up. 'It was carnage, I saw it all, bits of bodies,' he said. 'I went round picking up photos of mums and dads, I don't know why. I was picking up all the berets when someone said, 'You shouldn't be here, you shouldn't be seeing this'.

Sent to Berlin after Northern Ireland, he began to suffer from depression and nightmares, which he tried to combat with excessive drinking. A father of three, he took to sleeping naked in a box in the cellar of his house and regularly suffered flashbacks. Colleagues would realize he was missing and would find him in full battle dress feeding ducks in the local park when he was meant to be on duty. His wife Monica spoke to his CO and other senior officers to warn them that he was on the edge, but claimed that nobody listened. Placed in charge of the ammunition room one day, he grabbed a loaded gun and threatened to blow his head off. A fellow soldier jumped on him and stopped him. He was seen by a psychiatrist who placed him on light duties before transferring him back to Britain. Donaldson eventually left the Army after fifteen years' service. One night in November 1996 he went missing and the following night his wife watched the television news about a siege in a hotel in Hull. Shortly afterwards the police came to tell her that it was her husband who had taken three people hostage for more than two hours and threatened to shoot them, even though he didn't have a weapon. Armed police surrounded the hotel and eventually persuaded him to give himself up. In court, Donaldson's GP said he believed the defendant to be suffering from mental illness stemming back to his time in Northern Ireland. He had recommended that his patient be sent for treatment at a specialist clinic, but had been denied funding. The judge sentenced Donaldson to two years' probation, after telling him: 'You are a troubled and damaged man in desperate need of help.' He recommended urgent psychiatric treatment.

After a relapse, Donaldson threatened to kill himself by throwing himself off the Humber Bridge and was only talked down by his lawyer who spoke to him on a mobile telephone. He is currently serving a two and a half year prison sentence in Hull after walking into a Tesco supermarket, stealing a knife and pointing it at his own chest. Police arrived and attempted to calm him down, threatening him with CS gas. He was arrested, and told police that he had been depressed and suicidal for some time. Jailing him, the judge said: 'People like you are unpredictable. My duty to the public overrides your need for assessment and this offence is so serious that only a custodial sentence can be justified.' Graham Donaldson is still in the process of trying to get a pension for PTSD.

CHAPTER SEVEN

Darren Bartholomew, of Burton-upon-Trent, Staffordshire, served three tours of duty in Northern Ireland in the Royal Logistics Corps, and has since attempted suicide three times. 'I was a class-one soldier. I had been promoted and was due for another promotion,' he said, 'but then I had a bad tour in Northern Ireland and everything started to go wrong.' He went on to serve in two major conflicts, with only a short break between tours of duty, and ended up on a base in Germany, where his condition worsened. 'I didn't notice anything at first, but I was becoming a bad soldier in my attitude, and my dress, I was drinking too much and so on. It all came to a head when I went mad in the sergeant major's office and upturned the desk on to him. I was put in a military hospital and spent four weeks on an anger-management course. The wife eventually went to the military padre and fixed an appointment with the doctor. They diagnosed me as suffering from clinical depression, when they should have noticed I had PTSD. The Army tries to sweep these things under the blanket and I was strongly advised to leave. Elbowed out, more like.' Now he is suing the Ministry of Defence for lack of treatment. He says he still has 'good and bad days', but has managed to keep his family together and believes he can 'see light at the end of the tunnel'.

It was his wife who noticed the change in his behaviour, and who made him seek help. Military doctors and senior officers have long recognized the importance of partners in easing the readjustment of their men, and in listening to what they have to say. Jenny Simpson, an SAS wife whose husband Ian carried out some of the most dangerous and stressful undercover work of his long career in Northern Ireland, wrote graphically in her autobiography of the effect it had on their marriage during his brief periods of leave from 'across the water'. When he was home, he was moody, irritable and jealous, drank too much and eventually beat her so badly that she needed hospital treatment. She wrote:

> By the end of the week he was extremely uptight and I was a nervous wreck, wondering when all the frustration and jealousy bubbling inside him would erupt . . . I was tired of all the mind games he was making me play. If I could just get him through the week, I started thinking, then he would be back in Northern Ireland and he could take it out on some IRA terrorist and not me . . . I knew the signs to look for. Each night when I got home from work, I checked the look in his eyes. I knew from past experience that sometimes I didn't get much of a warning and that glazed look would be my last glimpse before the violence would explode. I felt on edge the whole time, as if I was constantly stepping around a land mine, that if I made one false move I would misjudge my footing and it would all blow up in my face.

Once when she made an innocuous, off-the-cuff remark about a television news bulletin on the murder of an off-duty RUC officer, her husband went for her.

> When it came, it came from nowhere. Before I knew it, Ian had leapt to his feet and was looking like a crazy man. He grabbed my neck and chin,

yanked my face inches from his own and spat, 'You haven't got a fucking
clue, have you?' His eyes were not his own . . . I saw a look of venom in his
eyes that I shall never forget as long as I live. His jaw was set and he was
glowering at me from above. It was the face of a man in torment.

After beating her black and blue, he returned to Northern Ireland for
another six-week tour, but within five days he was back, waiting for her on
the stairs, sorry for what he had done. He told her: 'I should never have hurt
you. Something just exploded in my head. It wasn't me, I didn't think of you
as you. I can't really explain it any better than that.' He had realized that he
had hit rock bottom, she said, and that unless he did something about it,
sorted his head out, he was going to lose his wife, and his mind.

Despite his continuing nightmares and occasional flashbacks, Ian did not
seek help from any professionals and it was left to Jenny to make him better.
'He had always been very dismissive of counselling,' she said. 'He was too
self-contained to seek help. He believed counselling was an American
phenomenon which revolved around – as he put it – people examining their
own navels.' She said that while he continued to walk his own 'mental tight-
rope', he resisted seeking help because – especially in the SAS – it would
have been seen as a sign of weakness, an inability to do the job. 'None of us
ever spoke of the psychological strain,' she wrote. 'It was strictly taboo, any
suggestion of being unable to cope. It wasn't just a question of macho pride,
it was more serious than that. Any member of the Regiment who shows a hint
of mental instability risks being binned, kicked out for good. So none of us
dared mention it – the truth that dare not speak its name.'

Military chiefs accept privately that they were wrong not to regard
Northern Ireland as a war zone in terms of what it could do to men's minds,
but they point out that the biggest concern at the time was Russia and the
nuclear threat, and they had no reason initially to think that the conflict in the
Province would be so protracted or bloody. To begin with, the freak incidents
of soldiers going off the rails could be explained away as unfortunate
tragedies, but as the dossier of human tragedy built up, questions were asked
about a possible link. When the link was made, it came from across the
Atlantic, where post-Vietnam studies had pushed US psychiatrists to the
forefront of the field.

It was in 1980 that the condition which had first been known as shell
shock, and was latterly labelled 'post-Vietnam syndrome', was finally
recognized as a universal disorder, named and classified. The term post-
traumatic stress disorder was officially accepted and appeared in America's
Diagnostic and Statistical Manual (DSM) III. A Bible of psychiatric disorders
used world wide, it defined PTSD as the experience of 'a certain set of
symptoms following a psychologically traumatic event that is generally
outside the range of normal human experience'. After Charles Myers's 1915
definition of shell shock, PTSD became the fastest growing and most
influential diagnosis in the history of psychiatry.

The manual went on to explain the factors that trigger the condition:

The stressor producing this syndrome would evoke symptoms of distress in most people and is generally outside the range of such common experiences as simple bereavement, chronic illness, business losses or marital conflict. The trauma may be experienced alone (rape or assault) or in the company of groups of people (military combat).

Stressors producing this disorder include natural disasters (floods, earthquakes), accidental man-made disasters (car accidents and serious physical injury, aeroplane crashes, large fires) or deliberate man-made disasters (bombing, torture, death camps) . . . The disorder is apparently more severe and longer lasting when the stressor is of human design.

More recent studies have shown that PTSD usually has three interlocking factors: threat, loss and horror.

The classification represented a watershed in accepting the inescapable fact that in modern warfare a proportion of men will be severely traumatized as a direct consequence of their military service. The official diagnosis included twelve symptoms, comprising its acute, delayed and chronic manifestations, which cannot be diagnosed for twenty-eight days, which is how long it takes for the trauma to be absorbed. The symptoms might include a psychological numbness after the event, but which may sometimes be delayed, and which can last for years. There may be a sense of guilt about surviving, anxiety, jumpiness, nervousness, depression, sleep disturbances, including nightmares and flashbacks, and lapses in concentration. Victims may find difficulty in developing or maintaining close relationships, and often resort to alcohol or drugs. For the rest of their lives they may be prone to depression, irritability and aggression, often at the cost of their closest personal relationships. They can be helped to live with their trauma, but there is no cure – a salutary thought for those responsible for the defence of the nation.

Less than two years after the official classification of the condition, another war tested the mettle of a highly professional army. The Falklands conflict changed everything in Britain with regard to the diagnostic understanding of how men react to combat. Defined by the military as a 'good war', with little psychological fall-out predicted, it began on 2 April 1982 when hostile Argentine forces invaded the British dependency of the Falkland Islands in the South Atlantic, surprising and overrunning the single company of Royal Marines garrisoned in the capital, Port Stanley. After a brief exchange of shots, the British troops were ordered by the governor to surrender. Although the Falklands had been a British colony for 150 years, the Argentinians – who called them Islas Malvinas – had a long-standing claim to them and timed the invasion to coincide with the 150th anniversary of British rule.

General Leopoldo Galtieri, head of Argentina's military junta, hoped the invasion would bolster his flagging popularity at home, where inflation was approaching 300 per cent, and the nation was on the brink of financial collapse. But just as the British government, under Prime Minister Margaret Thatcher, had failed to anticipate the Argentinian attack, so the Argentinians had failed to anticipate the hostile international reaction and British determination to retake the islands by force.

Within three days, amid a fervour of patriotic flag-waving and military music, Britain had dispatched a forty-vessel Task Force comprising 28,000 men and women, with land forces of 10,000 men. The frigates, destroyers and troop carriers set off on the 8,000 miles to the islands – a journey of two weeks. In the savage month-long fighting that followed, the Argentinian soldiers, mainly young conscripts, were unprepared for an all-out war against a highly trained and technically superior professional force, and suffered at their hands.

The British, in return, found their warships vulnerable to bombs and Exocet missiles launched from Argentinian ships and aircraft. The French-built missiles ushered in a new era in maritime warfare, bombing *HMS Coventry* and the *Atlantic Conveyor*. Britain sacrificed some of her international support by sinking the *General Belgrano*, the enemy's chief warship, with the loss of 368 lives on 2 May when she posed no real threat to British operations. Two days later the Argentinians retaliated with the sinking of the British destroyer *Sheffield*, the first major British warship to be lost for thirty-seven years. News of the attack stunned politicians and public alike, and service personnel waiting on ships elsewhere in the South Atlantic suddenly realized that they could be next.

On 21 May, British troops established a beachhead at San Carlos Bay, shortly before two Royal Navy ships, *Antelope* and *Ardent*, were sunk by Argentinian missiles. On 28 May, the British won the 'epic battle' of Goose Green and Darwin, but lost seventeen paratroopers and their commanding officer in the process. At the end of the battle, 250 Argentinians were dead and 1,200 captured.

On 8 June, two more ships, *Sir Galahad* and *Sir Tristram* were hit in Argentinian air attacks at Fitzroy, near Bluff Cove. Armaments stored in *Sir Galahad*'s hold ignited and the subsequent series of explosions tore the ship apart. Fifty men lost their lives and among the 143 injured was Guardsman Simon Weston of the Welsh Guards, a man whose badly burned face became an icon of the Falklands campaign. Describing the attack as his 'personal Hiroshima', Captain Weston later wrote:

> The bomb, a 2,000-pounder, had landed right in the middle of what, seconds before, had been a circle of happy, smiling faces. I can't have been more than twenty feet away from it when it exploded . . . Bodies were everywhere on the floor, on fire, or smouldering, and so still that they frightened me, but the colours, the vivid colours that the bomb had created were still magnificent – unbelievably intense, more beautiful than anything I had ever seen, dancing around my friends and then enveloping them in flames. Two lads in front of me danced reels in the rainbow, jerking and writhing to a silent tune of death, and there was nothing I could do.
>
> Men were mutilated and burning, and fought to rip off their clothing or douse the flames and beat at their faces, arms, legs, hair. They rushed around in circles in the roadway, screaming like pigs. A human fireball

crumpled just ten feet in front of me like a disintegrating Guy Fawkes,
blistered hands outstretched as he called for his mum. He fell flat and
horribly still; in the heat of the flames all around me, I watched transfixed for
a second or two as he died. Black, choking smoke engulfed the area and
I heard the voices of men I knew, friends who were crying out for help as
they died in unimaginable pain. It was the sound of hell.

Rescued from the burning ship and sent home, Simon Weston began the
agonizing recovery process that would include years of reconstructive
surgery and physiotherapy. He suffered from debilitating guilt, nightmares
and depression, reliving the moment of the explosion over and over again,
blaming himself for being alive while all his mates were dead. The *Sir
Galahad*, still burning two weeks after the attack, was towed twelve miles out
into the South Atlantic and sunk as an official war grave. With his physical
scars of bravery, its most famous passenger was given every conceivable
medical assistance, but little for his psychological injuries. For those like
him, with invisible mental scars as well as physical ones, there was little help.
  He wrote:

As the days went by there was a lot of pain: both physical and the pain of
grief, the horribly empty realization that the dead weren't coming back. I felt
as if my insides had been ripped out and I was hollow, raw; the special cord
that connected me to my mates had been severed, and I bled. I thought
there was no way I could get over the pain; the intensity of which I could
not explain to people at the time except to say that in my mind it was total
darkness, even in the middle of the day. Sometimes I went completely into
myself. I hadn't known that I could be hurt so deeply. I had never before
seen death with my own eyes, and of blokes I cared so much for. I felt
cheated. You live and you love people, and they die. I missed them more
than words could express. I wished I had had the chance to say goodbye.

By the time the Argentinians had capitulated on 14 June, 236 Britons
and 750 Argentinians had died. A further 777 British troops had been
wounded. The war was brief, the force was professional, motivated, and had
commanded widespread public support. But during the conflict, a so-called
'old-fashioned war' involving hand-to-hand combat, young men were
exposed for the first time to aerial attack and the sight of dead comrades,
experiences whose consequences appeared in the months and years that
followed.
  Prior to the war, the preparations made for psychiatric casualties were
based on expectations that this was going to be a short, sharp conflict with
clearly defined goals: the antithesis of the Vietnam War. Élite units were used
and strategic planning meant that combat engagements would be brief,
followed by periods of relative safety. Psychiatric problems were not given a
high priority in the Task Force, despite appeals from some senior medical
officers for battle shock rehabilitation units and field psychiatric teams.
Despite that request, no RAMC psychiatrists were invited to join the massive
convoy leaving Portsmouth, and only two Royal Navy psychiatrists were
sent, and they were on board ship, not sent ashore. There was no monitoring

or follow-up care. Early observations claimed PTSD rates as low as 2 per cent and confirmed anticipated levels.

Dr Morgan O'Connell, one of the two specialists sent, was the first psychiatrist ever to sail with a Task Force. He was on board the *Canberra*, the cruise liner hastily requisitioned as a hospital ship for the war effort. 'The history books say you need ninety days of fighting before you start to see psychiatric casualties, but we saw them before we even sailed,' he said. 'Officially you start counting when the fighting starts, but I didn't know when to start counting. The night before we got to the islands, a colour sergeant, a marksman in the Royal Marines, came to see me. He was supremely fit physically, but was in tears. Two years previously he had been diagnosed with mild multiple sclerosis and had been placed in a training role. He was within two years of leaving his company, but with the Falklands crisis, it was all hands on deck. "We thought we'd be sailing round the Isle of Wight and back again," he said. "It wasn't until they started bleeding people [blood donations were ordered ten days before so there was a fresh supply] that we had to accept it would end in a shooting match." His particular concern was that he would let his men down. In peacetime, these things can be fudged, but not in war. He should never have been passed fit. I had to downgrade him, and he stayed on board and served a useful function, but he felt very guilty. He was a casualty.'

Dr O'Connell saw another man, a merchant sailor. 'The men thought he'd all flipped because he always wore four or five layers of clothing, even in bed. But he had been torpedoed twice during the Second World War. He was the only one who knew what it was all about. He was totally sane, the only one who had a clue what it was going to be like, how cold it would be in the water.'

Some of the first people he worked with were the survivors of a Sea King helicopter crash in which twenty SAS lives were lost in rough seas on a routine hop between two ships. At first, he said, he didn't know what he would be expected to do and decided to wait to see what they wanted. Doctors screened the men as they came aboard, then forty minutes later they asked him for a debriefing. 'The impetus came from them. I'd never done a debriefing before, there were eleven survivors from thirty-one, including the pilot and another crewman. I went with my instincts, and asked someone to tell me what happened; I gave them a licence to share. It worked very well, and was, I think, helpful to the men.'

Dr O'Connell believes that debriefing should be done sooner rather than later, in groups, in the same scenario and by someone with credentials. 'When the *Ardent* was lost, the survivors were very angry because the ship had been used as a sort of goalkeeper. I went to see the CO and said I might be able to help, but I also didn't want to do any damage; there was so much anger. The CO said they'd been through so much already that I could go ahead, but in the end I didn't have to. One of the senior naval officers did a debrief over the intercom of what he'd witnessed of the *Ardent*'s demise from the bridge – it was common to report on the day's events. He told of what he'd witnessed, got to the bit where he described her sinking and then there was a long pause – he seemed to be sobbing. It was a marvellous example of leadership. It was saying it is okay to be upset. It cemented solidarity. He was interested in his men as people and had confidence in them. Morale and leadership was crucial in the Falklands.'

Dr Howard Oakley, a surgeon lieutenant of the Royal Navy during the Falklands, also served on the *Canberra*. He saw many of the injuries as a doctor, only two of which were psychiatric. 'One wanted to go home so he shot himself – gave himself a Blighty wound – and the other had a genuine breakdown,' he explained. 'The idea was to pass any psychiatric casualties back up the line to Morgan, but there really weren't that many. The loss of the *Sir Galahad* had a deep psychological effect; the *Sheffield* guys were all changed men, and there were other stresses – the loss of ships and the threat from the air. It was not pleasant but people came to terms with it.'

When the war ended and the Task Force headed for home, the men were ecstatic. The long journey back at least gave the Royal Navy psychiatrists the opportunity to debrief traumatized men, particularly those survivors from the *Sir Galahad*, who were especially affected. The ships arrived home on a wave of euphoria. The soldiers, sailors and airmen were greeted as national heroes and their achievements hailed, but once the honeymoon period was over and they began to question the usefulness of the war they had fought and to attend the funerals and memorial services of those who had died, the memories became harder to deal with.

Dr Oakley said: 'There was elation coming home, a sense of a job well done. The reception tided us over for a bit. Then we all had six weeks' leave and that was when people became aware that they had changed. It didn't always occur to them, but to their friends and families. "You're not the same man who went off to war", was a common complaint. I saw a few people around the place who told me they weren't getting on with their partners, that there was what they called an "invisible partition" between them, that they found it difficult to communicate and so on. That was when the first PTSD cases started coming through.'

Dr O'Connell added: 'Six weeks' leave for all the men afterwards was the worst thing that could have happened. It would have been better to have had a long weekend, and then been together for three to four weeks. During the conflict I had several weeks on a professional high, but when I came home I was very angry because I realized how thin the ice was that I had been skating on. I was angry because I hadn't been trained properly, despite all my previous work. Nothing had prepared me for the reality of war, but it was all there in the history books. It had all been written about. In the Falklands it could have gone either way. By sheer luck we got away with it.'

Despite his disillusionment, he believes that post-Falklands, the Navy was probably the most receptive to the lessons that had to be learned. 'They were frightened by how close they'd come to losing. The men were unfit, the ships unsuitable. They had spent too many years looking after the comfort of men in terms of clothing and furnishing, only to discover that in war they were not fire retardant. The Falklands really woke the Navy up.'

There were other realities to be faced on the Task Force's return. Before the Argentinian invasion, the British government had announced massive defence cuts. Whole regiments were to be merged, battleships scrapped, and thousands of men offered redundancy. Not long after the Task Force's return, the policy was implemented and many people were told that they would have to leave the service for which they had just risked their lives. 'There was a lot of distress,' said Dr Oakley, 'and it led to a sense of frustration at what had been experienced. There was no sense of people coming home and being able to do long-term follow-ups to see how men fared. The medical staff lost their jobs too, and there was no new exchange of information and ideas. PTSD was never welcomed as an opportunity, a challenge which could have been tackled. Once the war was over, it was all forgotten. No one ever spared a thought for the psychiatric casualties. It was a question of "If you're not happy, then get out, take the redundancy package and go". The government washed their hands of them.' What little statistics had been gathered before the sweeping cuts showed that the Special Services, the Paras and the Royal Marines had been best at coping with combat in the Falklands. They were small, intimate units, with much more mutual support, men who lived and drank together, with plenty of older ones to offer advice to the young. The Guards were hit the hardest because they were unprepared: most had been on ceremonial duties before.

As had so often been the case in the past, and which now became even more true, it was left to wives and girlfriends to offer support available to the men affected – men who were frequently irritable, often withdrawn and sometimes violent. Even those in the Special Forces were not immune: the SAS had suffered especially badly with the Sea King crash and the aftermath created a ripple effect in Hereford, home of the Regiment's Stirling Lines camp.

Ian Simpson, the Northern Ireland veteran whose wife Jenny had helped him through that trauma, witnessed the helicopter crash and the loss of his best friend Paul. Jenny wrote of her husband's return home several weeks later: 'He looked older and thinner and his eyes showed how very tired he was . . . I could see the pain,' she remembered. 'The fire had dampened in his eyes, which looked duller somehow and wearier, but he seemed to be keeping himself together well in those first few days, although I was not altogether convinced that it would last.'

Later, she wrote:

Having been upbeat for weeks, pretending that Paul's death was just another one of so many he had known, he seemed to lose some of his sparkle. His nights started to be interrupted by nightmares – vague, swirling visions of Argentinian soldiers, blizzards and helicopters – and his days were dogged by constant tiredness. Whenever I came home from work I would find him slumped on the sofa, his tasks for the day untouched, his speech slurred from exhaustion, his mind anywhere but with me. It took weeks of gentle coaxing on my part to get him to snap out of it. It was, I am sure, a manifestation of post-traumatic stress, post-Falklands depression, and sheer grief at the loss of so many friends and colleagues.

Gradually – and it took much of that long, hot summer – the Ian that I had known and loved started to re-emerge from the emotionally battered man I had been living with since June . . . I knew he was coming out of it finally when I came upon his diary lying open in the lounge. There had been no entries for several weeks, but suddenly, on 15 August, he wrote: "Jenny is my strength and I love her very much." '

Although the military had rightly anticipated few immediate cases of breakdown during the Falklands campaign – there were only sixteen psychiatric casualties from the entire conflict, a rate of 2 per cent – by the mid-1980s newspapers began to report a worrying trend of Falklands veterans encountering problems similar to those of Vietnam and Northern Ireland servicemen.

By 1986 a significant number of Falklands veterans were suffering from PTSD and accused the Ministry of Defence of complacency. James and Lovett (1987) published a series of case reports and concluded 'the comfortable conclusion that the Falklands war had remarkably few psychiatric casualties is not tenable'. In 1989 Captain Steven Hughes, an MO of 2 Para, who had fought at Goose Green, completed a study into PTSD in Paras from the Falklands, which found that 22 per cent of those still serving had it, and 28 per cent showed some of the symptoms – and this was among the forces group said to be least affected. He suggested that up to five thousand men might still be suffering. Of those diagnosed as having PTSD, the majority were younger, of lower ranks, and were more likely to have lost friends through wounding or death, or to have killed the enemy. They were also more likely to have actively assisted in the management of casualties.

The military was slow to pick up on the PTSD research. When the war ended it still had not recognized officially that the condition existed. Roderick Orner, a clinical psychologist who served in the Special Forces of the Norwegian Navy and has studied many veterans of the conflict, said: 'The media converted the Falklands into a national drama with all the cathartic effect of a Shakespearian tragedy. As if the performance was over, Britain walked away from considering the political, judicial, social and personal ramifications of war. In the euphoria of victory, those in need of help and those who were in a position to warn about the psychological effects of war appear to have been relegated to total obscurity.'

He criticized the 'shameful record' of after-care for ex-servicemen in Britain and described as 'inexcusable' the MoD's failure to implement systems for dealing with psychiatric casualties in the Falklands conflict, when the experience of those in Vietnam and elsewhere had been well documented by 1982. 'This may be a consequence of a conspiracy of silence and sanitation in relation to truths about wars and their aftermath,' he said, adding that the British government missed the opportunity to set up 'a task force for peacetime', in mobilizing professional care experts in the MoD, the NHS and other bodies, and had instead created 'a climate of distrust'. He added: 'If ever such a psychological and psychiatric task force was convened, it appears to have been operationally neutralized at a very early stage . . . All that appears to have happened, without systematic planning, was for O'Connell to provide informal briefings on the *Canberra*.'

Veterans who were angry at the lack of treatment argued that the MoD should have prepared better for the inevitable, and arranged appropriate treatment and aftercare where necessary. For those who found themselves psychologically out of control, the MoD's counter-argument that it could not help those who developed symptoms after they left the services, and that the NHS fully caters to the needs of ex-service personnel, offered little comfort. Among them was Lee Mosely, who, at the age of eighteen, was one of the youngest recruits in the élite 3rd Parachute Regiment in the South Atlantic and who saw action in some of the toughest encounters of the campaign. He was discharged from the Army a year after the conflict on medical grounds, his dreams of joining the SAS shattered. He turned to crime and subsequently helped organize military-style armed robberies on a jeweller's, a sub-post office and a home in Yorkshire before he was caught. He asked for twenty-one burglaries to be taken into account, and was jailed for nine years by a judge who told him he had taken into account that Mosely had been affected psychologically by seeing active service so young. The court heard that those who knew Mosely before the Falklands said he had been an ordinary person and they would not recognize him as the criminal he had become.

In July 1990, Alex Findlay, a former sergeant and Falklands veteran, was court-martialled for having run amok with firearms while on duty in Northern Ireland. He went beserk in Londonderry when he heard the sound of a beer can being opened, pulled a gun and took several fellow soldiers hostage. He was jailed for two years. His lawyer, John Mackenzie, based in Hounslow, west London, realized that Findlay displayed many of the classic symptoms of PTSD. On top of a drink problem and marriage breakdown, he suffered from frequent flashbacks of the carnage he had witnessed in the battle for Mount Tumbledown, in which several of his closest friends had died.

Mackenzie responded to the court-martial with a writ, which proved one of the most successful ever against the Ministry of Defence and the first for PTSD. Several years later, at the European Court of Human Rights Alex Findlay won an historic ruling against the MoD and was awarded £100,000 in compensation. The success of the action opened the floodgates: Findlay's lawyer has since been inundated with letters from ex-servicemen suffering similar symptoms, and has more than sixty on his books. Most claimed never to have heard of PTSD until the Findlay case and thought they had been suffering in isolation.

In 1995 Mackenzie issued high-court writs against the MoD for allegedly failing to detect and treat five cases of PTSD, four of whom came from the Welsh Guards and all of whom had been aboard the *Sir Galahad* when it was hit by the Argentinian Exocet missile. One of the men named in the writ was Simon Skinner, known as 'Kee Kee' by all his mates, who during the war had been just twenty-two. He was on board the *Sir Galahad* when it was hit and was promoted to corporal for his bravery that day. He returned to Britain a hero, one of 'Maggie's boys', but as with Simon Weston, the images of friends dying or melting before his eyes seared themselves permanently into his brain.

Skinner went on to serve in Northern Ireland and in Germany, but his behaviour grew increasingly erratic. He was admitted to a military hospital but his condition went undiagnosed. He absconded in 1985 while he was being sent back to the Royal Military Hospital in Woolwich, south London, and was eventually discharged from the Army. For twelve years he lurched from crisis to crisis, working as a security guard in South Africa for a while and marrying three times. He attempted suicide on several occasions and became an alcoholic, rambling incoherently about the war and suffering from vivid flashbacks. Once he got into a brawl with an Army recruiting officer in Swansea because he didn't think the latter should be encouraging young men to join up. Eventually he was sent to a specialist psychiatric unit in Wales, but too late. In January 1995 he had his final flashback, got out of bed, stood to attention and marched out of the room. He fell headlong down the stairs and died five days later of his injuries. He was thirty-five. At his funeral, which was attended by many of his mates, the priest told the congregation: 'I believe God has said: "Enough." Simon has had enough pain, enough misery, enough torment. Now he can come home.'

Chris Lewis, a former Welsh Guard and one of Skinner's fellow litigants, told reporters after the funeral: 'It's not the war we're protesting about, but what happened afterwards. As soon as we left the service, they didn't want to know. They just left us to rot on their own.'

Veterans and those campaigning on their behalf pressed the government for an answer on the question of those suffering from battle shock as a result of the war. In the House of Commons, Peter Blaker, the armed forces minister, reported only seventeen cases at the end of 1982. A few months later, Dr O'Connell, interviewed in the *Guardian* admitted to treating at least a hundred men since the conflict had ended. A survey of 924 officers and ratings that he later undertook showed that 113 were thought to have war-related psychiatric problems, a ratio of one in eight. And yet there continued to be a complicity of silence about the consequences of the war on its participants' minds, and the effect their suffering was having on their friends and families.

In the words of Simon Weston:

The world did not stop for the Falklands War. It hesitated, perhaps, for five or ten minutes each day as people switched on for the latest bulletin. The war changed the lives of the people who went down to the South Atlantic, it changed the lives of the families of those who are buried down there, but the world kept right on moving. We did not take part in a holocaust. It was not a war that will be remembered for ever. It was just another conflict, and now is just another already half-forgotten story, a more and more distant memory of Union Jacks and cheers of glory. But for many the price is still being paid; their war is still going on.

It was not until 1986 – four years after the Falklands War – that the British military recognized the term PTSD. Following on from the American example and in the light of incontrovertible evidence that some sort of condition existed, the disorder came of age, with its younger brother 'combat stress reaction', or CSR – short-term shell shock, which occurs during combat or immediately afterwards and is almost always temporary. The military had come a long way from the days of shooting cowards and malingerers. Along with recognition of the condition, came the ending of Crown immunity for the Ministry of Defence. The ruling in 1987 paved the way for a remarkable shift in emphasis. The armed forces were no longer seen as protector and provider to the nation, but instead as responsible for robbing several generations of their youth. Mounting discontent among those who had seen service in Northern Ireland and the Falklands and who were yet to receive financial or medical help for the condition they blamed for the break-up of their marriages or their inability to work resulted in a steady flow of claims for compensation. If PTSD was a definable consequence of war, veterans argued it should be compensated for, as if it was a physical injury.

A new mood of recrimination, blame and culpability emerged. Civilian society and the courts began to use the term that had originated in the battlefield as a synonym for shock or grief. People, it seemed, expected to be cushioned from all unpleasantness – in itself psychologically unhealthy – and compensated if they were not. It was the military's worst nightmare, a direct consequence of the official recognition of PTSD, and a potentially ruinous state of affairs for the nation's defence forces, especially with a new conflict just round the corner.

Chapter Eight

*You can hold back from the suffering of the world, you have
free permission to do so, and it is in accordance with your
nature, but perhaps this very holding back is the one
suffering you could have avoided.*

Franz Kafka, 1915

In the lead-up to the Gulf War, the British and American military had come
so far down the line of accepting that combat tested the endurance of
its participants to the limit that they mobilized psychiatrists as a matter
of course. It had taken nearly eighty years since the First World War, but
doctors of the mind were finally considered as important an element of
a soldier's needs as food and water.

Shortly after midnight on 2 August 1990, Iraq's Saddam Hussein took the
world by surprise when he ordered the invasion of Kuwait. In spite of the
tension of the previous two weeks, nobody had expected Iraqi forces to cross
the border into a country with such enormous British and American interests.
The dispute lay in Iraq's long-standing claim to Kuwait, which had been aired
sporadically since Kuwait had become independent thirty years earlier.
Latterly, though, the wealthy Kuwaiti oil princes had been accused by Iraq of
over-production and theft. Provoked into loss of reason, Saddam Hussein
sent 100,000 men to the Kuwaiti border on a tribal impulse: an act of defiance between one proud Arab leader and another. Within hours his troops
had captured the capital, Kuwait City, and declared the country an Iraqi
province. Hundreds of Western workers enjoying luxurious expatriate
lifestyles were taken hostage.

International condemnation of the invasion was swift and widespread. The
UN Security Council passed a resolution demanding an immediate withdrawal of Iraqi troops as the United States rushed military forces to Saudi
Arabia. While the majority of the Arab nations condemned Saddam Hussein,
others considered him a hero for making a stand against Kuwait, and the
nations chose their sides in what was fast developing into a possible build-up
to a Third World War. Unfortunately for Saddam, however, no international
conflict since the last world war had occasioned such consensus: even the
Soviet Union joined forces with the US in condemnation of his act of

aggression. The ensuing five months saw a massive build-up of British and American troops in the Gulf in what was dubbed Operation Desert Shield. Belligerent political posturing raged on all sides as a diplomatically negotiated settlement was attempted, and failed. Deadlines were set and passed, and by January 1991, coalition forces from almost thirty countries – concentrated mainly in Saudi Arabia – were set to strike.

The total number of men poised to attack Iraq's 550,000 soldiers, including 12,000 members of the élite Republican Guard, came to 700,000. More than 500,000 were American, but there was a sizeable contingent of 40,000 from Britain. There had been little time to prepare the professional soldiers and airmen for the conflict ahead, but the single most overriding fear was of chemical, nuclear or biological weapons, a form of attack Iraq had used previously in the Iran-Iraq War and against Iraqi Kurds. Servicemen and -women were injected with a cocktail of chemicals designed to counter the effects of any such attack, and were issued with IPE (individual protective equipment) suits to protect against NBC (nuclear-chemical-biological) attack and masks to protect their skin from blistering. Not since the First World War trenches had the threat of gas or chemicals caused such widespread terror. As the forces lined up in the desert and awaited the order to strike, the tension was almost palpable.

On 17 January 1991 Operation Desert Storm began, under UN authority, to use 'all necessary means' to liberate Kuwait. The war started with a massive air campaign using the most powerful air force ever assembled, including the giant American B-52 bombers, fighter planes launched from Saudi Arabia, and deadly Cruise missiles fired from the Red Sea. The main targets were airfields, missile sites and power stations. Iraq's capital city of Baghdad shook with the 'thunder and lightning' of Operation Desert Storm.

Despite Saddam Hussein's assurance that such an attack would bring about the 'mother of all battles', the Iraqi air force mounted only a minimal defence, mainly intent on saving aircraft, and there were astonishingly few coalition casualties. After two weeks of relentless bombardment and little resistance, the air assault was largely diverted against Iraqi troop formations and supply lines. Precision bombing had at last earned its name, and the vast majority of the attacks were performed with deadly accuracy.

Defenceless under such air superiority and in an effort to broaden the war by turning it into an Arab crusade, Saddam Hussein ordered the launch of Scud missiles against Israel, a non-participant of the conflict, but the hated enemy of the Arab world. A handful of the Allied servicemen and -women already living on their nerves and waiting for the green light to fight in the countries surrounding Iraq began to suffer from crippling phobic anxiety about impending Scud or gas attacks – phobia not seen since the First World War. There were forty-one full-blown cases among British troops, all but one of which were treated successfully with behavioural therapy and desensitization within seventy-two hours. Only one, a woman, was too overwhelmed by anxiety to remain on the front line and had to be sent home. Under heavy US pressure, Israel made no response. The Iraqis then pumped oil into the Gulf, threatening Saudi Arabian water supplies, and set fire to Kuwait's oil wells, causing massive pollution. Once again, the Americans advised patience.

The Allied land attack began on 24 February when – against all expectations of having to face the world's fourth largest army – it encountered only slight resistance. As the air attacks continued, killing an estimated four hundred fleeing Iraqis in one massive bombardment of a convoy on the Basra Road alone, Kuwait was swiftly liberated and part of southern Iraq occupied. Four days later, US President George Bush called a halt when Iraq agreed to carry out the requirements of twelve UN resolutions, including an unconditional withdrawal. In response to the sudden end of the hundred-hour ground war, rebellion broke out among the Shi'ites in the south and the Kurds in the north of Iraq, but both uprisings were crushed and Saddam Hussein remained in power, which angered and confused many who had seen the UN-backed attack as an ideal opportunity to rid Iraq of a ruthless dictator.

Casualties in the Gulf War numbered about 150 in the coalition forces. Seventeen British servicemen were killed in action, compared to 34 who had committed suicide the same year. The Iraqis lost an estimated 150,000 men, and some 7,000 Kuwaitis had been killed since the invasion. The war was brief, the coalition forces were highly motivated and enjoyed popular support, the enemy was clearly defined and the objectives were clear.

Nevertheless, some servicemen underwent potentially traumatizing experiences, mainly the constant threat of an invisible enemy: chemical and biological weapons. Wearing an NBC suit was described as akin to sensory deprivation. Some of those in charge of handing out the suits and warning of an imminent attack found themselves becoming paranoid about the responsibility.

Among those who saw direct action were the Grenadier Guards, who moved forward in tanks and armoured vehicles when the land war began and cleared the wadis of Iraqi soldiers. Andrew Stephens, who was just seventeen years old and already experiencing emotional problems when he found himself in the front line a year after joining up, described his experience as 'a nightmare'. He said: 'We were in action non-stop for one hundred hours, only stopping to have some grub and drink some water. My job was to clear the trenches, which involved firing thirty rounds into a bunker, probably killing four men in each, and firing phosphorous grenades which burn you alive. Basically we had to kill everybody and they were tough little bastards, never surrendering. There were bodies all over the place.'

When the war was over, he said they spent a week packing up at base, without any debriefing at all. 'Apparently there was a team of shrinks out there, but you would never have asked to see one, you would be considered weak, a coward. A week after it was over we were back in Germany. That was when the PTSD started – nightmares and flashbacks, so I started drinking.' Sent to an army psychiatrist at Woolwich Military Hospital, he was told to cut down his drinking, then sent off on a tour of duty in Northern Ireland. By 1995, he had left the Army, but was still drinking heavily and getting into trouble.

When he went to a petrol station and threatened to set himself alight the night after the anniversary of the Gulf War, he was sectioned under the Mental Health Act and has been receiving psychiatric treatment ever since.

Combat paramedics serving with the artillery also suffered psychologically. Tom Ford, whose task it was to clear the Basra Road of bodies from the burned-out vehicles, has never really recovered from the experience. 'There were lots of dead Iraqis, people blown to bits,' he said. 'Some of the soldiers used human heads as footballs.' When he returned home to Manchester, his wife Angie threw a party for him, but he couldn't cope and walked out to spend the next three days and nights on a beach. 'He is often suicidal,' she said. 'He has trouble coping and gets into terrible fights. He smashes things up. On the anniversary of the Gulf War he just blows up. There was no aftercare for him although he did see a psychologist eventually. The courts were kind and we had a good barrister. It took us seventeen months to fight for a war pension, but we got one in the end.'

The British Special Forces, sent deep behind enemy lines to find and destroy Scud missile launch sites, faced some of the worst fears and dangers, especially after several were captured and killed. Specially trained to cope with the unique stresses of covert warfare, they none the less found themselves fighting to quell their anxieties, and sympathized with the regular servicemen waiting in Saudi territory behind them for their chance to attack. 'We found the conditions and the territory hard-going enough,' said one senior SAS officer, who was mentioned in dispatches for his assault on a Scud missile site, 'and we had all been trained for it. It was those poor bastards back at base I felt sorry for, waiting for us and the pilots to finish, unable to take any direct action, feeling like sitting ducks for the Scud attacks and anything else Saddam's boys cared to chuck at them. Their nerves must have been frayed to the edges by the time they were told to get in their tanks and go, go, go.'

Above all, it was the British airmen based in Bahrain who had been forced to deal with the stranger extremes of modern combat: one day sitting in an air-conditioned hotel watching the latest bulletins on Cable News Network, the next flying low over enemy territory, dropping bombs and running the gauntlet of the deadly anti-aircraft fire. They worked with the very latest 'smart' weapons and a daily fear of death. When two of their number, Flight Lieutenants John Peters and Adrian Nichol, were shot down in their Tornado and were captured, then appeared bloodied and bruised on Iraqi television appealing for an end to the hostilities, the fear of the same thing happening to them made the nightly flying missions a torment for their friends and colleagues.

Dr Keron Fletcher, an RAF psychiatrist at the time, treated one Tornado pilot who suffered from debilitating panic attacks during his service in the Gulf and was sent back to Britain. 'After a brief period of treatment he was fine,' he said. 'He went back to the Gulf and had a few more problems with anxiety. He was stigmatized and chopped from flying, even though he was rated as performing above average as a pilot. His panic attacks were under control and he could have been supported out there. But the other side of the coin is that the squadron bosses wanted everybody fighting fit, so the attitude was "get shot of him".

'This can be devastating to the man who gets the chop but it highlights a very interesting problem. If you think of it in a really balanced way then you can't take sides. You can't get rid of everybody showing signs of worry, stress and anxiety, because in combat that is normal, but you also can't carry men who have lost the confidence of their colleagues or who are affecting the capacity of the unit to function at its best. This is the military's constant dilemma.'

Wing Commander Geoffrey Reid, consultant adviser in psychiatry to the RAF, believes that moderate levels of anxiety actually enhance an aviator's performance, but that when the anxiety leads to an acute stress disorder, an airman should be regarded as 'temporarily overwhelmed' and allowed to rest. After seventy-two hours, he said, most cases will have recovered and be able to return to flying duty, although he accepts that some will not. 'Post-war psychiatric syndromes are not uncommon,' he added, 'They include PTSD, depressive disorders, adjustment problems and chronic fatigue syndrome. Sadly, ignorance, mistrust and the fear of stigma often prevent appropriate help being either sought or given.'

Psychiatric casualties in the Gulf were initially low, as expected, but there were a few, and more emerged once they had returned home, which disturbed the military, who had done all they could this time to prepare for and prevent this. One study found that of 4,500 returning US veterans, 9 per cent were affected, rising to 34 per cent reporting significant psychological stress in the months immediately following their return. One year later, 19 per cent reported moderate to severe family adjustment problems, and 40 per cent marital discord – one of the best measures of adjustment.

Dr Fletcher treated one RAF cook in Germany who became ill during a base barbecue a year after the Gulf. 'He was spit-roasting a pig for the officer's mess summer ball; the pig fell into the charcoal and he got the most horrific flashback of the time he'd carried the charred and burnt body of a small child from the Basra Road,' he said. The experience reminded him of the period after the Falklands conflict when the government offered free health assessments to servicemen who had been Far Eastern prisoners-of-war (FEPOWs) in the Second World War. 'It was amazing,' he said. 'Forty-five years after the war I'd ask a question like "What was the worst part of your wartime experience?" and they'd break down and cry. They were still getting sleepless nights. I reckon that over half had significant symptoms and I saw well over a hundred.'

Dr Fletcher believes that modern-day treatments can help people with PTSD, although those FEPOWs from the Second World War have been left too long to help. 'Counselling is generally of little use for them. They get help from being with their peers, but things run too deep and it's really too late. With the more recent ones, we can help them to experience a marked reduction in symptoms, which has a beneficial impact on their everyday lives. They sleep better, and are less irritable. They get on better with their families and have fewer flashbacks. Although they may live with some symptoms of the condition for much of their lives, they can gain some relief; we can help people function again. In ten or twenty years' time, people will look back on our efforts to treat PTSD and reflect the same way we do now on how the military handled shell shock in the First World War. I sometimes wonder how the future will judge us.'

More peculiarly, and unique to Gulf War veterans, an estimated 43,000 US and more than four hundred British soldiers have since reported a variety of ailments in what has become known as Desert Storm or Gulf War syndrome. Symptoms are diverse and apparently unrelated, including chronic fatigue, myalgias (aching muscles), poor concentration, memory impairment, respiratory, cardiac and gastrointestinal complaints. In some cases relatives also claim to have been affected. Theories have abounded as to a possible cause. Gulf veterans were exposed to numerous potentially toxic hazards – multiple immunizations, medication against nerve agents, pesticides, dust from tank shells containing depleted uranium, and fumes from burning oil-wells. Many have spoken of alarms going off after missile attacks during which they were assured that there had been no release of nuclear, biological or chemical weapons. Now, in light of their many symptoms, they are not so sure.

Whether or not the symptoms relate in any way to Gulf War service is a highly contentious issue and is currently denied by the MoD. Psychiatrists studying the condition cannot help but note that many of the reported symptoms are reminiscent of the neurasthenic symptoms first described by soldiers in the American Civil War, and repeated in every conflict thereafter. According to Martin Deahl, an Army psychiatrist who served in Operation Desert Storm, Gulf War syndrome may well include some cases related to combat stress and may in future be viewed as yet another failure to learn from the lessons of history.

To its credit, the military had geared itself up well for psychiatric casualties in the Gulf War and had undertaken considerably more preparation for it than its predecessors, including specific stress-management training, which involved imagining what battle would actually be like. But it is never possible to prepare servicemen for some of the gruesome realities of the war: there are no dead or dismembered bodies in exercises, and the most basic of preparations can fall foul of the best intentions. The sight of hundreds of black plastic body bags being loaded on to the aircraft was enough to send some senior NCOs into a deep depression.

The organization of psychiatric services in the Gulf was complex: at its heart were battle shock recovery units (BRUs) and field psychiatric teams (FPTs), both located as near to the front as was practically possible. The FPTs included a psychiatrist, nurses and orderlies equipped with vehicles. Their task was to assess servicemen who were in no shape to continue fighting, to evacuate them from the immediate battle area but not so far away that they would disappear in the one-way medical evacuation chain taking the physically wounded back to the UK. In the field, psychiatrists were instructed to treat their men as servicemen, not patients. The plan was to get them fit to fight again. The BRUs were never afforded Red Cross protection because they were considered logistical and not medical units, in other words, a source of reinforcement.

Brigadier Peter Abraham, director of army psychiatry in Britain, explained: 'The idea was that, as much as possible, soldiers were treated in the theatre of operations. They were kept as near as possible to their unit locations while being removed from the worst effects of battle.' Pre-war estimates suggested that half of those affected would recover in forty-eight hours. Those who did not would be moved to a second station further back from the front line, where 70 per cent were expected to make a full enough recovery to be returned to the front lines. A further 10 per cent were expected to be able to return to other duties, and less than 20 per cent passed back to longer-term care, mainly in military hospitals and rehabilitation units.

More than in any other war, both field commanders and defence medical services were aware of the risks of battle exhaustion and subsequent PTSD – and of both the personal suffering and the manpower consequences. Treatment of the forward medical teams was commonsensical and speedy, and utilized the PIE – proximity, immediacy and expectancy – model first propounded seventy-five years earlier by the likes of Charles Myers.

Lieutenant Colonel Ian Palmer, senior lecturer in military psychiatry, a fan of Myers and William H. R. Rivers, and the man to whom Gulf War and now UN peacekeeping forces turn to for help, sees great similarities between the work of the First World War psychologists and the present day: 'Before the First World War psychiatrists worked in asylums and there was no therapist/patient relationship that we would recognize today. To see a psychiatrist would mean being "committed" – sent to a "bin" – and it was believed widely in society that "Once a lunatic always a lunatic." Any nervous breakdown could only be thought of in terms of lunacy – an inherited degeneracy or cowardice, lack of moral fibre or backbone. As the First World War progressed, the idea that it was therapeutic to talk about, "relive", the experience, became common as an understanding of unconscious mental processes developed to explain such breakdowns in previously healthy soldiers. Rivers was of the opinion that you had to go back to the experience to master it, to take some nugget of goodness out of it, some silver lining to this terrible cloud, and get on with your life. It still works that way today. The experience of having your best mate blown up next to you was pretty similar in 1914 to what it was in the Gulf War in 1991.

'What the First World War really taught was that everyone has his breaking point – the difficulty is knowing who, when, where and why. Subsequent wars have taught us to understand the who and the why, but when and where are more problematic.'

He believes that it is a rare human being who is not affected by the unique experience of war; some are just more susceptible than others. 'One of the conundrums of selection of conscripts is that the very process will select the nation's finest to fight and possibly die first. But psychological selection then as now is a very inexact science, and after excluding the most obviously vulnerable it is unlikely to tell you who will function best in battle. Sometimes people who look best in training are the ones who break down first.

'Death is a constant feature of the battlefield, and grief in battle is seldom expressed until afterwards. Sometimes there is no body to bury, or your best mate has been horribly mutilated. Who lives and who dies can seem unfair, and the relationships formed in training, preparation for battle and the hardships of the battlefield can be of extraordinary strength, which can make the pain of the loss harder to bear. Those "pals" who happily went off to war in 1914 and survived made acquaintances but few friends because they didn't want to repeat the mourning process. Fear is ubiquitous and has many faces – fear of death, of injury or mutilation, of blindness or gas attack; fear of being afraid, fear of self, of what you'd become. Every soldier is changed by the experience of war.

'The extraordinary thing is that most people don't break down. Everyone is different and it is quite difficult to imagine why more people don't break down,' he added. 'The thing which really keeps soldiers together and keeps them fighting is the group process, their mates. It keeps them together so they can fight together, live together and perhaps even die together. The group, family, is the psychological protection for individuals. The power of the group cannot be overstressed.'

Those servicemen who felt close to breaking point in the Gulf were given the chance to sleep, rest and have plenty of warm drinks. Unlike their predecessors, the uniformed psychiatrists were wary of prescribing drugs, but like their predecessors in both world wars they treated their patients in the way their forebears would have recognized. The men were put to work as soon as possible, and encouraged to talk about their experiences with fellow servicemen while performing useful tasks. The battlefield is a place for simple 'here and now' psychotherapies and not the analytical type. Psychiatrists were warned to watch out for those servicemen who were at the end of their tether, tired beyond imagination and suggestible, who might 'catch' symptoms from one another until they sparked off some sort of mass hysteria, which might escalate if not handled properly. Faced with the prospect of getting away from the scene of stress, those affected by battle shock often hang on to their symptoms as a sort of standby ticket out of the trouble zone. The dilemma for every soldier, from the First World War to present-day conflicts, is whether or not they use the 'ticket' to escape the danger or stay and risk death with their mates and the group.

To help them choose the latter course of action, daily debriefing sessions were ordered, encouraging free emotional expression and the accurate recounting of experiences and events. Grieving for dead comrades was also encouraged, with letters or telephone calls to the bereaved relatives; attending or watching funerals and memorial services was considered appropriate. Individual counselling was on offer for those who felt the need, including the relatives of those returning from the theatre of war. There were even psychiatric staff for the psychiatric staff, with counselling and rest recommended for those dealing with the stressed.

Colonel Sebastian Roberts, an MO in the Gulf, took decisions about sending men away from the front on a pragmatic basis. If a man really didn't want to fight, he took the view that it was probably better if he didn't. In one incident, a tank commander, who was famous as the hardest man in the regiment, started hallucinating about bathing his baby daughter just before the big push across the desert which he was supposed to be leading. Until then neither he nor anyone else knew he had emotions. The doctors took the decision to send him home, claiming some physical problem so as not to destroy morale. It was thought best not to test his emotional resilience in the heat of a battle when others' lives and confidence depended on it. It is a difficult decision for a doctor to make. In many cases it is a psychological advantage if men are sent to the front: they do badly if cut off from their unit and the relatively low level of carnage in the Gulf produced more depression than any other symptoms.

Morgan O'Connell, the Royal Navy psychiatrist who served in the Falklands, said that the Gulf was a very different war for the Navy. 'In the Gulf they expected large numbers of psychiatric casualties if ships sank; they even looked to Cyprus as a debrief station. Everyone was frightened. I stayed behind to defuse the hype that was being generated. I got a call from one hospital to say that they had cleared their psychiatric ward and could offer us two hundred beds. I said that if we needed all those beds for psychiatric casualties then the physical casualty numbers would be so great that it wouldn't matter a damn about anyone else. It all got totally out of control, but there was this constant fear of chemical warfare and weapons of mass destruction.'

TA psychiatrist Martin Deahl, who was mobilized on four days' notice along with many other medical personnel, said that servicemen in the Gulf did not have the luxury of a long ship journey to acclimatize to their war role or to adjust to what they had seen and done before reconfronting the civilian world. 'It is sudden change that can be so damaging,' he said. 'Desert Storm pilots described the surreal pressures of high-tech, push-button war, where the consequences of their actions were not seen until they watched them later on CNN, and how at the end of the war, some returned home to their families in a very short time, still high on the adrenaline of battle.'

Despite the technological advances of more recent wars and their effects on the troops, those who have been comparing the Gulf War with previous conflicts, like US naval surgeon Craig Hyams, say that it is often almost impossible to tell the two apart. Dr Simon Wessely of the Maudsley Hospital, who has been comparing shell shock cases from the First World War with PTSD cases from Vietnam, said: 'If we put some of these cases side by side, I suspect no one will be able to tell which war which case came from,' he said. 'The symptoms and supposed causes, the characteristics of post conflict syndromes in any given period, depend on the character of the war fought. The predominant image of World War One was of shells exploding, hence shell shock, but of Vietnam it was a nation's guilt and trauma towards its soldiers, hence PTSD.

'The essential condition varies less than the names we apply. There has also been a great change in society, the rise of the victim as hero, ever since Vietnam. Because of guilt and shame over that war, servicemen were told for the first time that their condition was not their fault. PTSD is the first guilt-free diagnosis – someone or something did this to you. It is an acceptable psychiatric disorder, with no guilt attached. But what is often overlooked is that the traumatic event is only the trigger, not the sole cause. In reality, there are preconditions for PTSD and they are similar to those for other psychiatric disorders, such as depression and anxiety.'

In the modern age, he said, people have too much general knowledge about health and health issues. They see themselves as 'consumers' who expect a 'product' or diagnosis from their doctors; everything has to be given a name or receive some sort of treatment. He described counselling as 'a job creation scheme for people who have a need to be around others less fortunate than themselves'. He believes that debriefing has yet to be shown to be effective, and the evidence is that it may be harmful to some because it interferes with natural coping. The practice of compulsory debriefing – as in some British police forces and fire services – should, he said, be banned. 'It may instil the idea that it is normal to develop psychiatric distress, whereas the opposite is true. To be upset is normal, but these symptoms are catastrophized. It is okay to be more open and discuss feelings, but they don't have to be medicalized. The vast majority of those who take part in a war do not break down – for some the excitement makes it the best days of their lives. Now that trauma has been scaled down to the point that it is used to describe a minor road accident or similar, much smaller, life event, not things outside the range of normal human experience, it devalues it.'

Dr Stephen O'Brien, author of *Traumatic Events and Mental Health*, agrees. 'One man's trauma may be another man's hard day's work or even an exhilarating event,' he said. 'The normal vicissitudes of life, including distress and the normal response to events, are generally to be borne without compensation. If PTSD is a normal response, then it is not eligible for compensation. If it is an illness, then it may be.'

By the time the Gulf War was over, the psychiatric services were in place to deal with any aftershocks. Those returning were issued with leaflets outlining the possible symptoms of PTSD and urged to seek help if necessary, their families too. Counsellors were made available at every base camp in the country, and if that was too close to home, other organizations were recommended.

One official leaflet, entitled *Stress after Combat: Coping with a Relative*, advised on the range of symptoms a combat veteran might experience – anger, guilt, shame and sadness among others. It added: 'These feelings are normal for anyone who has been through any kind of traumatic experience such as combat and personal injury.' Spouses or partners were advised to allow the sufferer to express emotions and show grief. It called for patience and understanding during a readjustment period, warned against excessive use of drugs or alcohol and urged spouses to encourage their partners to face the reality of what had happened, by attending funerals, memorial services or having reunions. It listed organizations such as Combat Stress, run by the Ex-Services Mental Welfare Society, the Traumatic Stress Unit, the Trauma Aftercare Trust, Victim Support, Relate and the Salvation Army as possible sources of help.

For the minority who were affected by their war experiences, a repeat of the defence cuts that followed the Falklands conflict did little to ease their pain. Many servicemen who were disillusioned with the armed forces and were offered a redundancy payment, left before their symptoms came to the surface. As civilians, they slipped through the net and felt betrayed by the organization for which they had laid their lives on the line. There was considerable anger about the way men were treated when they got home, not even knowing if their regiment was going to survive the latest round of government spending cuts. Most agreed it was not the most sensitive way to treat heroes.

Money, or the lack of it, continued to feature largely in the care and aftercare of veterans after the Gulf War. With peace declared and increasing pressure from the Treasury to save taxpayers' money in all departments, the Ministry of Defence decided that in the future it could offer help only to current servicemen, not those who had left the armed forces, whether voluntarily or not. Ex-servicemen would have to rely on the medical services provided by the NHS. For those still in uniform, a much reduced system of support would be on offer, as medical units closed or were merged, even though statistics still showed that combat veterans were going off the rails in considerably higher numbers than their civilian counterparts.

Some of those who served in the Gulf, and before that the Falklands and Northern Ireland, are now facing the tough new demands and unique pressures of their role in the United Nations peacekeeping force, sent to places like Bosnia and Somalia, countries ravaged by centuries-old conflict or famine, where they are under attack but helpless to fight back or to defend properly those they have been sent to save. A good war from a psychiatric point of view is short, has a well-defined enemy, clear objectives and expectations of the servicemen. Peacekeeping is often the antithesis of that: men often have to witness atrocities and are powerless to intervene. It is work that is increasingly common and the way of conflict in the future for the modern-day serviceman, who has little sense of mission and purpose and whose experiences are those of a tiny, isolated minority. Proud to become professional soldiers and keen to fight a war, they are, however, distanced from death and the reality of killing. They are members of a society that finds fatalities unimaginable. When presented with the unimaginable, they crack.

Gary Bohanna, a young signalman who served nearly eight months in Bosnia in 1992, saw action there for the first time in his Army career. 'I thought a peacekeeping role would be good. I thought it would be better than war, where your friends get killed and stuff like that. No one wants to see that. But I didn't understand,' he said. After months of work with hardly a day off, and being treated with disdain by the civilian population, who had wanted UN intervention sooner, he got lost one day in the middle of a war zone. 'I saw women getting killed, people getting blown up, families, kids. I had to give first aid to people. I was basically caked in blood. I drove through four towns. That was definitely the worst day. I saw the worst of it there. I saw two women getting raped, brutally raped and attacked, and I had to shoot the fellows. I was completely on my own.

'There was this young girl and she had shrapnel wounds in her head, half her head was blown away. Her eye was coming out of its socket and she was screaming. She was going to die, but I couldn't bear her pain. I put a blanket over her head and shot her in the head. That was all I could do.'

On his return from Bosnia, he went to see a military doctor who diagnosed depression, nothing more. 'I was having cold sweats, I was irritable, I was having nightmares. There were people in the unit who said I was a totally different person, but they told me that it would ruin my career if they put anything but depression on my medical records.' After an argument with his girlfriend, he was put in a military prison, where he asked to see a psychiatrist. 'They knew they'd messed up but they wanted to palm me off. They were trying to get me to carry on. "Don't worry, it'll go away," my sergeant said. The doctor said he wanted to help me but his hands were tied. Two days after getting home I had a nervous breakdown. I couldn't sit with anyone, I couldn't watch television, I was having flashbacks all the time. Whenever I was asked a question I snapped. To suppress the bad feelings, I was going down town and drinking.' He left the Army, got himself a flat, but became so ill that he was eventually referred to Combat Stress, which he describes as 'a huge relief'. Diagnosed as suffering from PTSD, he finally received a 60 per cent war pension after three years of treatment with the organization, whose motto is 'People who care about those who gave more than they could spare'. He is still receiving counselling.

Among others no longer in uniform, the picture is often bleaker. A 1994 survey for Crisis found that up to a quarter of Britain's homeless were service veterans. The charity said that many end up sleeping on the streets because they have left a job that provided them with a home and lifestyle. After years of institutional life, they are often unable to cope in the outside world. One man, Andy Howarth, thirty-one, a former lance corporal in the Royal Engineers, told the charity's researchers that he had served two tours in Northern Ireland and had seen people die. He was sleeping in doorways in the Strand area of London and drinking six bottles of Thunderbird wine a day. 'I got a medical discharge from the Army because they said I was a little bit nutty,' he said. 'I had a psychiatrist.' Care agencies believe that under-privileged and emotionally disturbed people are often drawn to the security of the armed services and are the people least able to cope when they leave.

In August 1995, the psychiatric services of the Army, Navy and RAF merged into the new Defence Services Psychiatric Centre (DSPC) at Catterick, in North Yorkshire. The decision represented a major cut in the overall psychiatric provision at a time when the doctors whose services had been so needed in the Gulf War were fighting for their jobs. By 1997 staff cuts of 40 per cent and hospital closures had been implemented, which were intended to save £600 million a year, stemming from the MoD's belief that with more and more troops based in the UK and an adequate NHS, it was wasteful to offer servicemen what seemed like a private medical system that duplicated the facilities already available. A House of Commons select committee strongly criticized the policy and urged action to reprioritize psychiatric services. In response, the defence minister promised to investigate, and there has since been a gradual return to dedicated psychiatric units at Haslar, the Royal Navy hospital in Portsmouth, and at RAF Brize Norton in Wiltshire.

Cost-cutting had its advantages: when doctors lost beds elsewhere, they set up day services, discovered that the majority of patients didn't need to live in, and their way of working changed dramatically. It was subsequently decided that only one hospital – Catterick – was to have beds; £100,000 was set aside for a residential unit, and within three months it had been established with ten beds for each of the three services.

Ever since, Catterick's main purpose has been to provide psychiatric inpatient treatment for those who are severely traumatized, principally current servicemen. The treatment is primarily psychological, based largely on cognitive behavioural psychology, as well as therapy for the allied problems of PTSD, such as alcohol abuse, war pension and financial worries. Although the doctors working there would be happy to see more veterans, the government has insisted that resources would only be made available for the treatment of current servicemen. Compared to the Department of Veterans Affairs (VA) in the United States – a legacy of the Vietnam War – which funds world-leading research into PTSD and provides comprehensive medical care to thousands of current and former servicemen, it is a poor substitute.

The VA provides the world's most comprehensive and diverse programmes of benefit for veterans and dependants. It is the second largest of the fourteen US cabinet departments and administers to a veteran population of 25.6 million, spending $40.4 billion annually on compensation, pensions, education, medical care and cemeteries. Among those it helps, 32 per cent are survivors of the Vietnam War, 27 per cent of the Second World War, 17 per cent of Korea, and 6 per cent of the Gulf. The department operates 206 veteran outreach centres to provide readjustment counselling to veterans of every conflict since Vietnam, and has extensive programmes to deal with PTSD and homelessness.

Roderick Orner, clinical psychologist, believes that the Vietnam War did for America what no war has yet done for Britain: 'It forced a silent majority of Americans into a recognition of the massive material, personal, social and political costs of denial about its military involvement in South-East Asia,' he said. 'It led to a world-wide recognition of a syndrome of human reactions to traumatic stress . . . namely that it is negligent to fight a modern war without full regard to the scientifically documented need to make comprehensive care provision for surviving war veterans and their families.'

The military in Britain would argue that even when it made adequate provision in the Gulf War, the casualties persisted and in the same numbers as in previous conflicts. Despite a hundred years of experience, they seemed to be no closer to solving the problem. The simple fact is that men are crushed by the strain of warfare. There is no such thing as getting used to combat, or preparing for it. All men are at risk of becoming psychiatric casualties and most will collapse given enough exposure to battle stress. The question now is who is responsible for coping with it when the men affected have volunteered for the work? In modern society, that is a legal and financial issue of enormous implications, and one that the British government has long been reluctant to address. Even for those they agree to help, that offer is not always appreciated. One of the problems encountered at Catterick has been the discovery that while some of the most distressed men need the precision and security of its strict set-up, many who are traumatized reject the military and its restrictions as a symptom of their condition and do not therefore respond to treatment offered by it. A cardinal symptom of PTSD is anger – bitterness about how terrible everyone and everything had been: 'They didn't do anything' is a common complaint about the armed forces.

Finding the balance has been difficult, but has been largely achieved by the setting up of a number of other slightly less militaristic establishments elsewhere. One is Audley Court, in the heart of a residential area in Shropshire, run by the charity Combat Stress, which has mainly older veterans as its patients. It is still quite militaristic and does not suit all patients, especially those with behavioural problems, but it is one rank lower than Catterick in terms of military strictness. Run by Colonel Larry Brown, who had a long and distinguished Army career including active service in Northern Ireland, Audley Court is chiefly funded by the war pensions department. 'Half the battle of getting treatment is accepting that you need help,' he said. 'That is the hardest hurdle. Once here, people can stay for two to four weeks. Each man can have a total of six weeks here a year.'

Dr Martin Davis is a psychiatrist at Audley Court. He said that survivor's guilt is the biggest problem facing his patients and that being with fellow servicemen is a great help. Longer stays than three weeks are not encouraged because the men are too long away from society and lose touch. 'The treatment we offer is a complementary addition to the treatment a local health authority might already be offering. We aren't competing with the local psychiatrists, and don't want to say that we know better. It is just that, for these men, being with their peers is crucial.'

Cases that Audley Court and Catterick would probably reject – or who would have rejected their offers of help – are sent to the Ty-Gwyn nursing home, near Llandudno on the wild North Wales coast. The privately run unit takes almost any case which might be related to PTSD, including those of alcohol and drug abuse. Ty-Gwyn's inmates are often the angry young men of the most recent conflicts. Dr David Alun Jones treats servicemen of different generations there, men who have fought in conflicts from Korea to the Gulf, and he believes that men today are incapable of fighting war without psychological damage. 'Masculinity, with society, has changed too much,' he says. 'Men today are too vulnerable.'

A civilian psychiatrist, Dr Jones first set up the unit to take in traumatized men after meeting a former pilot in the 1970s who had been shot down over Holland during the Second World War. 'He'd clearly suffered, and it dawned on me that what happened in the war was relevant to his condition. I wrote to the war pensions people and they wrote back, and it really grew from there. The more I got involved, the more I realized that I'd seen men whose condition harked back to military times.'

He set up the twenty-bed unit to give ex-servicemen an improved quality of life. 'It's always the women, the wives and girlfriends, who tell me, "My man didn't come back," and we go from there. There is so much despair. The men are on their own, they realize they're not well and don't know where to turn. The Army is not the social services, it is an organization for killing people. They are not very good in the way they deal with post trauma conditions. It is often a battle for recognition that it won't go away, that it can blight a person's life, the acceptance of a diminished way of life for many of them.'

Every admission to Ty-Gwyn has to be authorized and funded by a local health authority, some of which are grateful for its specialist services while others refuse to send people there, arguing that as the sufferers are now civilians they can be treated under the NHS. Dr Jones feels that this overlooks the need for men to be with their peers, other ex-servicemen with the same life experiences. He accepts that he is viewed with suspicion by the War Pensions Office because he is constantly demanding more money for the men in his care, but he said that he will not take sides: 'I am a clinician and I deal in facts. The facts of these particular cases speak for themselves.'

Former RAF psychiatrist Gordon Turnbull has impeccable qualifications in the field of PTSD. He counselled Lebanese hostages John McCarthy, Terry Waite and Jackie Mann, Andy McNab of the SAS, John Nichol and John Peters, the pilots taken prisoner during the Gulf War. He has also worked with the RAF personnel drafted in to clear up the human debris at Lockerbie, survivors of the Hillsborough disaster, oil workers from the Piper Alpha oil-rig fire and travellers caught up in the King's Cross Fire. He now runs the PTSD unit at Ticehurst Hospital amid forty-four acres of Sussex parkland, and was among those who fought for PTSD to be recognized in Britain. He is anxious that it should not be regarded as an illness. According to him, up to 80 per cent of people who suffer some calamitous event will develop its symptoms after an incident; 10 per cent will be crippled by it. 'No matter what the event – war, train crash, rape – the symptoms are always the same: flashbacks, hallucinations, over-alertness caused by overworked adrenal glands and leading to cardiovascular problems and high blood pressure, nightmares, the avoidance of anything which might bring back the memory. Sometimes the flashbacks are so vivid that the person affected is convinced they are real and that the event is about to happen all over again. They feel they are losing control of their minds, but are reluctant to admit to it in case the doctor confirms that they are. The label of schizophrenic is very hard to overcome.'

Dr Morgan O'Connell, who left the Royal Navy frustrated at the lack of funding, now runs a private clinic offering therapy for those suffering from PTSD. He is angry that the military has failed to realize how much can be learned from veterans. 'The NHS has no adequate system for treating men because they usually need to be with their peer group and relate to people who understand the realities of war and service life,' he says. 'Most people feel immediately at home again within a military atmosphere. When men feel in chaos, they need reassurance and structure around them.'

Dr O'Connell tries to get sufferers to accept that their reaction to trauma is normal. 'What is not normal is how they are coping in the long term. They are stuck in recovery. It seems that what stops these people from recovering is an earlier trauma. This has often occurred with people with PTSD, but it is impossible to test for predisposition because these types of earlier traumas are usually very deeply hidden within the psyche.' His treatment is all about the senses – touch, taste, smell, sound and vision. 'Often men can see or hear or smell something which will take them right back to the trauma, and unless they can relate to it and understand it, they will revert to aggression or alcohol or drug abuse.' He believes servicemen are over-represented in prison and that many have some form of psychiatric disorder. 'They should have their own support group in prison staffed by ex-servicemen. This would be cost-effective and reduce damage to the buildings, violence and alcoholism. I suggested it to Her Majesty's chief inspector of prisons, who wrote back and said he saw no need whatsoever for such a programme. The government's uncaring attitude, and its policy of ignoring the fact that PTSD is affecting their soldiers, is inflicting more damage on their own men than any foreign power or terrorist organization could hope to achieve.'

Dr O'Connell believes that, with careful planning, Britain could become a worldwide centre of excellence in preparing military doctors for war, training civilian counterparts, treating servicemen and veterans and sending staff abroad to learn from foreign workers in the field, but that it will never happen because of a shortage of funding. 'Psychiatrists are even more important now because the military has fewer reserves. In other words, you need men to be able to go back to the front because there are not enough men to replace them. A good military psychiatrist can return eighty per cent of men to the front. This is invaluable in wartime. Recruitment is not a problem, but retention is. I know a guy from Bosnia who says thirty-seven men on his unit are leaving. No one wants to stay.'

The problem with recruitment is an eternal one: how to encourage people to join when you have to warn them of the possible consequence. The people who are wanted – the intelligent, thinking men and women – are the very ones who will ask the pertinent questions and realize the significance of the answers. Even if they get past that stage and into the recruitment process, there is no guarantee that the rigorous screening will spot those likely to crack.

CHAPTER EIGHT

New screening techniques may include a two-thousand-point question-and-answer session that takes three hours or more to complete; subjects are asked questions such as whether they liked to be in charge, what impression they thought they made on others, in what way they had ever let down themselves or others, what they thought of their father, what their mothers were like, whether they thought teachers should be paid more, how naughty they were at school and whether putting a fish hook in a worm would make them shudder. Body language is carefully scrutinized throughout and a detailed assessment drawn up on the basis of the answers given.

However rigorously the answers are analysed, by the time an individual is in uniform and out in a combat situation, he or she will have matured and changed. A tough, gritty twenty-five-year old in Northern Ireland who had a fantastic record and had never shown any symptoms of stress, cracked up when he was caught in a mortar attack. When debriefed afterwards, it was discovered that a few days before his wife had given birth to his first child and fatherhood had changed his views on life and death. The problem for the military is that there is no legislating for something like that.

Dr Martin Baggaley, former consultant Army psychiatrist in charge of Catterick, said: 'One of the realities is that you cannot prepare someone. When men go to the Job Centre to find out about jobs in the Army, they don't get shown pictures of heads blown off or carnage, they get shown tanks crashing through woodland and people trekking through forests with twigs sticking out of their helmets. It is hardly realistic of how combat really is. The reality of discovering that your actions as a soldier have terrible consequences on others can be very distressing. Remember that these are young men who may be dysfunctional [59 per cent come from single families], who train for war as part of a team. When they go somewhere like Bosnia and their role is much less clear and cohesive, they may not handle it.'

Modern weaponry, too, is so accurate and unpleasant that it is highly stressful to operate. Technology, many believe, will distance them still further; hence the development of computerized virtual-reality battlefields and super 'Doomsday weapons' such as the new hand-held laser gun, already in production, which can kill its target half a mile away by locking on to co-ordinates. At such a distance, there would be no risk of the operator witnessing the exploding of flesh or loss of blood that might otherwise cause him nightmares. Some even believe that the Americans are in the business of developing drugs to create fighting automatons, the 'chemical soldier' with no sense of fear, having taken men to the limits of endurance.

Psychiatry is doing its best to keep pace with the stresses of modern warfare and is more sophisticated than ever. The latest thinking about how to prevent battle shock deteriorating into PTSD includes 'the buddy system', in which men pair up to support each other and others step in for a 'buddy' when one is killed. The salutary facts of combat-stress reaction are learned as part of basic training and Army medical services are now backed up by mobile psychiatric teams who can administer psychological first aid in the heat of a battle.

For those in whom symptoms present and in whom PTSD has been identified, one-to-one counselling sessions with trained therapists are tape recorded and the patient listens to the recordings almost daily for several weeks to try to gain an insight into his condition. As the sessions progress, the patient is expected to 'rewind' and press the pause button on the most distressing events, freezing a distressing image in his mind but seeing it in the greater context – not forgetting it but rationalizing it, and making the fear of it manageable. The therapist creates an atmosphere of confidence and safety in which the traumatic event and subsequent feelings can be exorcized. A modern-day compulsory mourning.

The fashionable trend towards compensation and victimization has done little to help those trying to come to terms with their experiences of war. In a culture of complaint and indifference, the experiences of real victims of real tragedies are belittled and counselling is freely available for anything from pet bereavement to minor theft. More than half of the population of the USA and Western Europe are now believed to be suffering from some type of depression, personality disorder or psychosis. Too many people are jumping on the trauma bandwagon in a society where to be a victim confers upon people a state of innocence. What they don't realize, psychiatrists warn, is that it also saps them of the ability to take responsibility for their own lives and actions.

The word trauma comes from the Greek for 'wound' and those affected claim that they are, indeed, wounded and need to be healed. A high court judge recently threw out a claim of 'secondary trauma' made by people who had watched the Hillsborough disaster on television and insisted that they were as affected as if they had been there. The flurry of cases has signalled a move away from sympathy for genuine sufferers, and a view that not every bad emotion has to be put down to PTSD.

If fourteen policemen on duty during the Hillsborough disaster whose task it was to rescue and retrieve trapped and dying strangers from the stands are eligible for £1.2 million because of the stress they suffered, then why not servicemen who watched close comrades die in battle or the stretcher-bearers who cleared a battlefield of hundreds of bodies? One of the police officers involved in that successful litigation defended the claim. 'It is not blood money,' argued PC David Frost. 'It is what anyone damaged, mentally or physically, in the course of their work should be entitled to.'

The climate has changed radically from the days when gibbering teenage soldiers, battered and bombed for months on end in the trenches, were shot at dawn, although sympathetic campaigners and distressed relatives who demanded a posthumous pardon for 307 of those executed in the First World War on grounds of cowardice or desertion have been told repeatedly that an apology only is on offer and that it would be 'inappropriate to rewrite history'. What is seen as common humanity at one extreme becomes the thin end of a dangerous wedge at the other.

British authorities are anxious not to follow the United States down the ruinous road to litigation. PTSD has been used in a plea of not guilty by reason of insanity on at least twenty-eight occasions in American courts, with the defendants claiming that their offences occurred during flashbacks, because the plea carries a relatively light sentence there. It has rarely been used in British courts because the resulting sentence carries the term 'confinement in a mental institution at Her Majesty's Pleasure'.

The US is already at the stage where a jury recently awarded £90,000 to a woman who claimed to have suffered acute anxiety when her landlady destroyed a wren's nest outside her window. In Britain, a cancer patient was granted legal aid to sue his doctors because he did not die, but believed – from their gloomy diagnosis – that he would. In such a climate, some envisage a future society in which insurance companies and taxpayers will suffer heavy losses, where PTSD becomes expected, stress-counselling becomes obligatory and where every individual and institution will be culpable. In such a climate, it would be impossible for the armed forces to function properly.

When the High Court awarded Alex Findlay, Scots Guardsman and Falklands veteran, £100,000 compensation for his court-martialling without due attention to the psychiatric evidence about the effect of his experiences in the action of Mount Tumbledown, there was an outcry. It largely disregarded the fact that men like Findlay and those who followed him to the Courts were handicapped and dysfunctional, many unable to work, and that their compensation was mostly for loss of earnings with only a small part for suffering. Their argument was and is that their employer fundamentally failed to detect occupationally acquired ill-health or to offer the appropriate treatment. As one senior former Army psychiatrist said, 'At least if you're shot you see a surgeon.' After the ruling, the eminent military historian John Keegan wrote: 'What, I wonder, would the psychiatrists make of the condition of men who fought continuously from 6 June 1944 to 8 May 1945, some of whom returned to duty three times after wounding? Every D-Day veteran I have ever met reckons himself lucky to be alive. Most of them are still only seventy or so. They could break the bank if they made a mass claim and yet they are, in one way, as normal a group of people as it is possible to meet, yet almost paranormal in their modesty and self-deprecation.' He said it was wrong to assume that war is something unbearable. 'It is clearly wrong, or those who survived the Second World War would have done so only as nervous cripples, which the vast majority clearly are not.' He concluded: 'Responsible states have tasks to perform. Those of their citizens who volunteer to implement such tasks do so in the full understanding of the personal risks entailed. They want encouragement and a modest rate of admiration, not mummying from the dangers they have chosen to face.' Keegan criticized the professional over-protectiveness of brave men and added: 'It may well be that human ingenuity will succeed in making the battlefield uninhabitable by anything but robots. Until that time, common sense realism demands that we should recognize war as almost unendurable – and honour those who bear its horrors all the more.'

Others concur, particularly in the light of claims for compensation for Gulf War syndrome. The cap badge says, 'Death or Glory' not 'or Compensation', they point out. Dr Morgan O'Connell believes that the process of suing the MoD will do little to help veterans in any event. 'I tell every patient I see that there is no compensation on earth for what they have been through. Damages for pain and loss, maybe, but not compensation. If people seek legal redress, that isn't going to cure them. For most there is no cure – all we can do is help them live more comfortably with their scars.'

Field Marshal Lord Carver, a member of the Royal Tanks Corps and former chief of defence staff, 1971–3, argued in the *Daily Telegraph* that compensation and counselling were undermining the armed forces. He wrote:

Is the so-called Gulf War Syndrome a genuine medical condition, a psychological delusion or a ramp to extract money from the Ministry of Defence?

He said that until recently, the risks and hazards of life in the military were accepted as an inevitable element of the chosen career and indeed, for many, were considered an attraction that would otherwise had to have been found in a dangerous sport. If someone was injured, then it was considered little more than bad luck, as it would be in dangerous sport.

The soldiers, sailors and airmen of today have to operate against a rather different background. This has been encouraged by instant media reporting, which plays to a sentimental public, and has been exploited by a certain type of lawyer. It provokes the relations of a serviceman or -woman, and a limited number of service personnel, to expect and demand counselling and compensation for any adverse effect they claim originates from their military service.

Such effects could be mental or physical, and range from sexual or racial discrimination to death and injury, he said, fostering an attitude of hesitancy and caution in the face of danger that was detrimental to the greater cause and greatly blunted the effect of the armed forces.

Early recognition of psychiatric trouble by commanders, comrades-in-arms and doctors is vital. Everybody, even the bravest of the brave, has his breaking point . . . but the idea that the answer to stress is professional counselling may tend to undermine support for the serviceman's own strength of will to overcome his anxiety to fears, so retaining the respect of his comrades.

Everyone joining the forces realizes that they must sacrifice a degree of personal liberty. If they are not prepared to make such a sacrifice, they should not enlist . . .

He concluded with a warning against 'the insidious influence of today's compensation and counselling culture'. Despite this, in January 1995, five *Sir Galahad* servicemen announced their intention to sue the Army for £1 million. Two years later a group of seven Bosnia veterans also announced their intention to claim compensation for PTSD.

The official government response is that when servicemen have left the armed forces or if they do not present any symptoms to military doctors and divulge their problems, there is little the authorities can do. 'It is nonsense that no counselling is provided, but it has to come to light while someone is serving,' a spokesman pointed out.

Dr Baggaley said that the dilemma for the military is that people do not come forward for treatment when they are still in service: 'The main problem is that men avoid treatment. They become withdrawn and don't like talking about what's happening to them. Avoidance is a key factor in PTSD, exacerbated by the male-orientated environment of the services. In society as a whole, people still do not like to admit that they need therapy – there is still an old-fashioned image of men in white coats dragging people away. Counselling has a much better press than psychiatry.

'It is not just an Army problem, but across the board. Those affected will always say afterwards that "no one listened" but the truth is they didn't talk. Some people who have the symptoms of PTSD don't want help, or may not even need it. They may be unhappy at all the prodding and poking that screening might involve, exposure of private things they might not want to disclose. They become resentful of interference by the military they have turned their back on. They are so sensitive to all the triggers of memory – uniforms, smells, noises – that the man affected wipes his hands of the Army, not the other way round. Having had enough, they come to hate the Army and want to get away. They think that leaving will make it better, but it doesn't. At least in the Army they get paid, they get rest, treatment and attention. Leave and you're on your own. NHS treatment is not nearly so good or as quick. Despite what the men think, the support services are terrific in the Army.'

According to Dr Baggaley, COs are not the problem. 'The stereotype is that the Army is full of pompous Colonel Blimp types, telling men to pull themselves together – but it's the men lower down the ranks, warrant officers and the soldier's own peer group, the *Sun* readers, who the sufferer is first and most often in contact with. They are less sensitive, and add to the difficulty. The major message is that the Army cannot be complacent. They have got to try harder. It is much more difficult to intervene when men have left.'

TA psychiatrist Dr Deahl saw service in the Gulf War when he debriefed members of a seventy-two-strong war graves registration team, responsible for collecting, identifying and repatriating enemy and Allied dead. Only half asked for debriefing after they had finished their gruesome task. Those who had been debriefed believed it had helped, but a year later, no difference was found between the groups in terms of psychiatric symptoms: 50 per cent in both groups showed signs of PTSD. 'It's good to talk', says the BT advert, but it may not be: it may simply keep the person locked in the same time warp, repeating the experience over and over again, fixating them on their distress, instead of letting them get on with their lives.

SHELL SHOCK

Dr Deahl has been to Sarajevo and claims to recognize 'disaster junkies' in the military, the aid agencies and the world's media. He sees people trying to outdo each other in terms of ghastly experiences; individuals who fall apart with the Red Cross and who then turn up at a rival agency like Médecins Sans Frontières. Some people, however, are 'super-copers' who adopt an 'It has made me value my life more' approach, viewing the crisis optimistically. 'The only reliable way to avoid PTSD completely,' he said, 'is to avoid potentially traumatizing life events. The resilience of so many servicemen is remarkable, and research is starting to ask not why so many break down, but what makes so many stay resilient in the face of such adverse conditions.'

Modern-day sergeants grumble about how recruits get softer by the year: they join the military in search of safety and stability but once on the battlefield they feel betrayed. Dr Deahl believes that recruitment is still very much part of the problem. 'The Army is five thousand men short, so it is understandable that it may take men it shouldn't. The ethos and values of the military are alien to modern society. After the Second World War virtually every family in the country was related to at least one serviceman. Now they represent only a tiny minority. Many of those in the military are from service families anyway, or they come from broken families, are only children, or join up to avoid unemployment. The Paras have been jokingly called the Aldershot Orphans and many Sandhurst cadets have divorced parents. This can lead to huge tensions, and the Army ethos and structure, based on the public-school system, is often alien to those who choose to join it. The wider loyalty is breaking down. Today's soldiers have none of the sense of God, king and empire, mission and certainty.'

To add to the confusion, the old regimental system has crumbled. In the old days the subaltern would be responsible for welfare; his wife would help the soldiers' wives like a social worker, and the CO's wife would be the senior social worker for the battalion. Social life was organized for the men; being in the Army was a twenty-four-hour vocation, not just a job. 'In the last five years, young officers increasingly clock off at five p.m., leaving men behind with nothing to do but spend their time in the junior ranks club drinking cheap booze. Officers' wives are often professional working women who don't have the time or the inclination to play a social-worker role. Abroad, the soldiers' wives are frustrated at only being able to get menial jobs. It leads to huge dissatisfaction. Service marriages have a very high breakdown rate – many collapse in the first three years because of the pressures. Families are caught up in the despair of disaffected men. It becomes a vicious circle of a degenerating condition.'

According to Dr Deahl, the 'typical squaddie' joins up at seventeen or eighteen years old, is often sent quickly to Germany, has money for the first time so he spends it on alcohol, gets home leave, is the only one with any cash so he attracts the girls. He often marries an equally immature girl, who may also be pregnant, who joins him in Germany. He is then sent to Bosnia, Northern Ireland, or on some other operational tour almost immediately, leaving his young wife alone in a foreign base camp far from home and with little support for her and the baby. He has to queue for half an hour to speak to her by telephone once a week and when he does she's in tears and he's worried she might be seeing someone else. 'He comes back from the danger zone very stressed, and she's uptight. Wife and child abuse are well recognized in service families. These young men and women have little emotional resources for dealing with what would be a difficult situation for anyone. Most of the peacetime work of military psychiatrists is dealing with unhappy wives and men who drink or threaten suicide, ground down by repeated tours of duty overseas.'

Within the existing regimental system, the entire unit is moved around every two years, unlike the US Army in which individuals move but the unit remains static at the same base. British troops are also sent on unaccompanied tours, to places like Northern Ireland and Bosnia, for several months at a time. It is recognized by the professionals that if a serviceman spends more than six months away in two years his family is at higher risk of breaking up.

'The changing nature of warfare is also crucial. In the old days, the front was five kilometres deep and fighting stopped at night. You could retire behind the lines and be relatively safe. Now there are no lines to retreat behind – deep and rear battle. War is fought twenty-four hours a day, weapons are ferocious and are equally deadly at night. There is the additional threat of chemical warfare, bringing with it the fear of the unknown and unseen'.

Recent experience suggests that in such circumstances, battle shock accounts for approximately a third of all casualties in a conventional war, with even higher rates in mass casualty situations. The figure is likely to be considerably inflated in the presence of heavy and sustained indirect fire or with the use of nuclear, chemical or biological weapons. The combination of 'carrot-and-stick' has long been used to persuade servicemen to stand and fight – the 'carrot' being the sense of loyalty and duty to comrades, the 'stick' being the threat of punishment and harsh discipline for those deliberately failing in their duty.

In the light of modern experience, however, new carrot and stick techniques are employed. The one thing most strongly and desperately pleaded for by all combat men is a break from the fighting. An American study reported that the most effective goal a commander could offer his men was the promise of an honourable release from combat duty at a definite time, the thirty-tour rule in the RAF, for example.

The insoluble problem, however well shell shock, PTSD, combat stress or battle shock is prepared for, responded to or treated, is how a nation can properly defend itself with a professional armed force at the same time as protecting its servicemen and -women from lasting damage. It is an ethical dilemma of insurmountable proportions. The old dichotomy of sanity and madness simply cannot address the questions of the age: how the individual fits into the larger machine, and what should be done when he breaks down.

Fear cannot be eliminated from the battlefield, but the incidence and effect of battle shock can be minimized. Order, discipline and operational imperative has to be pitched against compassion and humanitarian concern. How much trauma can a nation reasonably ask its men to suffer in its defence, and how much should the men expect to suffer when they sign up? The moral issue is always easier to solve in a combat situation: it is a question of the group's need over the individual – but in modern conflicts such an easy answer quickly comes unstuck.

Dr Jonathan Bisson, a former Army psychiatrist, says the difficulty of his profession is the military part. 'It is the fact that you are a part of the war machine, which needs a healthy, active, fit person. They don't want someone who is crying and skiving off duty. The majority of people stigmatize mental health – that is true of society in general – but in the military it is more pronounced. I suspect that the military is maybe a decade behind the rest of society.

'The Army finds it very difficult to prioritize and look after the mental welfare of its soldiers when it's got a big new missile it can buy, but it does have a duty of care for its employees that is very straightforward. I would argue that you do need a bunch of fully fit men in the Army, but I would argue very strongly for screening people and offering appropriate aftercare. What you shouldn't be doing is watching people get into trouble, losing their marriages and getting into substance abuse. That shouldn't be happening, it is not ethical.'

Half the battle, many believe, is education. Psychiatric casualties should be regarded as inevitable as gunshot and shrapnel wounds and treated accordingly. Fear in a combat experience enhances it; it is only when the fear becomes overwhelming that combat efficiency is undermined and may jeopardize the safety of others. Officers need to be educated so that battle shock is the first, not the last, thing they think of when someone is behaving strangely, and the sufferers need to be told that it is okay to seek help. Such an approach would form a two-pronged attack.

At Catterick and elsewhere, the message is that the military can prepare servicemen for almost anything except the sight of a charred body or freshly maimed friend – the very conclusion reached by William H. R. Rivers at Craiglockhart Hospital in 1917. For a professional serviceman in a combat situation, the horror of war is part of the job but it is also the part that people find hardest of all to deal with. In the years since men like Private Harry Farr and Captain Leland were forced to face their own personal demons, the military has now come to recognize that, under acute stress, everyone will develop battle shock: nobody is immune from it. Only the individual threshold differs. Malingering has nothing to do with it: the behaviour of battle-shock casualties paradoxically often puts their lives at greater risk. Anyone can develop it, but predisposing factors do exist, and the circumstances of the combat can greatly exacerbate it.

Unlike most civilian trauma, servicemen face multiple, interacting and prolonged traumatic events. They are uprooted from their normal role and environment, thus losing the support of their family. They face daily uncertainty about the nature and duration of combat, which adds to their sense of helplessness and inability to control their fate. Other contributory factors are fatigue, a hostile, uncomfortable environment, lack of privacy and personal space, a threat to personal safety, witnessing atrocities and body handling. The conditions of the First World War trenches filled all the classic criteria for battle shock and its most seriously affected victims would today be evacuated from the scene of battle, allowed to rest and recover, before being offered a lifetime of therapy and care.

In the light of the modern experience of war and the freedom democracy has given people to question it, battle shock has been described as a reaction by sane men to insane circumstances. The fact is that, no matter how many psychiatrists are mobilized to offer counselling to those who have been seriously affected by their combat experiences, the armed forces have simply been unable to prevent a rise in the number of cases.

Anthony Babington, who won a Croix de Guerre in the Second World War and was twice wounded when serving with the Royal Ulster Rifles and the Dorset Regiment, is now a respected judge, who has studied the history of shell shock. He wrote recently: 'Some people might say that this was because modern men are less selfless and resolute than their forbears. Others might contend it is due to the fact that they have become more percipient and more conscious of the imbecile futility of war.' It is something to which the military-medical establishment is going to have to give serious moral and ethical consideration as it enters the new millennium.

Bibliography

Books

Addison, Paul and Angus Calder, *Time to Kill, The Soldier's Experience of War in the West 1939–45*, Pimlico Press, 1997

American Psychiatric Association, *One Hundred Years of American Psychiatry*, Columbia University Press, 1944

Barker, Pat, *Regeneration* trilogy, Penguin, 1995

Babington, Anthony, *For the Sake of Example: Capital Courts Martial 1914–20*, Leo Cooper, 1983

Babington, Anthony *Shell Shock, a History of the Changing Attitudes to War Neurosis*, Leo Cooper, 1997

Bowyer, Chaz, *The Royal Air Force 1939–45*, Ian Allen, 1984

Brown, Ben and David Shukman, *All Necessary Means: Inside the Gulf War*, BBC Books, 1991

Dicks, H. V. *50 Years of the Tavistock Clinic*, Routledge and Kegan Paul, 1970

Elliot Smith, G. and T. H. Pear, *Shell Shock and Its Lessons*, Longman Green, 1917

Feudtner, Chris, *Minds the Dead Have Ravished*, Historical Society, vol. 31, 1993

Franks, Norman, *RAF Fighter Command*, Patrick Stephens, 1992

Fussell, Paul, *The Great War and Modern Memory*, Oxford University Press, 1975

Grant, Neil, *The Illustrated History of 20th Century Conflict*, Hamlyn, 1992

Hastings, Max, *Bomber Command*, Michael Joseph, 1979

Keegan, John, *The Second World War*, Pimlico, 1989

Laffin, John, *The Western Front Illustrated 1914–1918*, Alan Sutton Publishing, 1991

McCarthy, Chris, *The Somme, The Day By Day Account*, Arms & Armour Press, 1993

McCarthy, Chris, *Passchendaele, The Day By Day Account*, Arms & Armour Press, 1995

Milligan, Spike, *Mussolini, His Part in My Downfall*, Penguin, 1978

Moran, C. E., *The Anatomy of Courage*, Constable, 1945: Sphere Books, 1968

Munk's Roll: Lives of the Fellows of the Royal College of Physicians of London 1826–1925, RCP, 1955

American Psychiatric Association, *One Hundred Years of American Psychiatry*, Columbia University Press, 1944

Owen, Wilfred, *The Pity of War*, Phoenix, 1996

The Penguin Book of First World War Poetry, Penguin, 1979

Putowski, Julian and Julian Sykes, *Shot at Dawn, Executions in World War One by Authority of the British Army*, Wharncliffe Publishing, 1989

Sargant, W., *The Unquiet Mind*, Atlantic – Little, Brown, 1967

BIBLIOGRAPHY

Sassoon, Siegfried, *Memoirs of an Infantry Officer*, The Faber Library, 1930
Simpson, Jenny, *Biting the Bullet: Married to the SAS*, Harper Collins, 1996
Slobodin, Richard, *W. H. Rivers*, Columbia University Press, 1978
Stone, Martin, *Shell Shock & The Psychologists*, in Bynum, W., Porter, R., Shepherd, M., (eds) *The Anatomy of Madness*, vol. 5, Routledge, 1985
Tucker, Spencer C., *The Great War 1914–18*, University College London Press, 1998
Selwyn, Victor (ed.), *The Voice of War, Poems of the Second World War*, Penguin, 1995
Wells, Mark K., *Courage and Air Warfare, The Allied Aircrew in the Second World War*, Frank Cass, 1995
Weston, Simon, *Walking Tall*, Bloomsbury, 1989
Winter, Denis, *The First of the Few: Fighter Pilots of the First World War*, Allen Lane, 1982
Yealland, L. W., *Hysterical Disorders of Warfare*, Macmillan, 1918

Journals and articles

American Psychiatric Association, *Diagnostic and Statistical Manual of Mental Disorders*, vol. III, Washington, DC, 1988
Bogacz, Ted, 'War Neurosis and Cultural Change in England 1914–1922', *British Journal of Contemporary History*, (1989) vol. 24
Clarke, David and Harrison, Tom, 'The Northfields Experiments', *British Journal of Psychiatry* (1991), vol. 160
Cohen, David, 'A War of Nerves', *New Scientist*, March 1991, vol. 129
Deahl, Dr Martin, 'The Effect of Conflict on Competence', in Dom Black *et al*, *Psychological Trauma: A Developmental Approach*, Gaskell Press, 1994
Hanigan, William C., 'Observations on the Wind of a Ball', *Journal of Military Medicine*, August 1994
Journal of the Royal Society of Medicine, (Feburary 1998) vol. 91, pp. 99–100
Neuroses in War-Time: Memorandum for the Information of the Medical Profession, HMSO, 1940
O'Brien, L. S. and S. J. Hughes, 'Symptoms of Post Traumatic Stress Disorder in Falklands Veterans Five Years After the Conflict', *British Journal of Psychiatry* (1991), vol. 159
Orner, Roderick, 'Post-traumatic stress disorders and European war veterans', *British Journal of Clinical Psychology* (1992), vol. 31
Randell, G. and S. Brown, 'Falling Out: A research study of homeless ex-servicemen', Crisis, 1994
Reid, Wing Commander Geoffrey, 'Aviation Psychiatry', notes from a talk
Sargant, MD, William, 'Psychiatry and War', *Atlantic Monthly*, May 1967
Shephard, Ben, 'The early treatment of Mental Disorders: R. G. Rows and Maghull 1914–1918' in *150 Years of British Psychiatry* (1995) vol. II
US Department of Veterans Affairs, VA Fact Sheet, January 1998
Wieneke, Sonia, 'An investigation into the recognition and treatment of shell shock in the British Army during the Great War', unpublished thesis, October 1993
Wilmer, Harry A., 'Vietnam and Madness: Dreams of Schizophrenic Veterans', *Journal of the American Academy of Psychoanalysis* (1982), vol. 10, no. 1

Archive material

Bion, W. R., 'Psychiatry At A Time of Crisis', *British Journal of Medical Psychology*, vol. 21, part 2, 81–9

British Medical Journal archives: 12 December 1914, pp. 1005–6; 25 March 1916, pp. 441–3; 2 January 1943, pp. 1–6; 22 July 1944, pp. 105–109

Bion, W. R., 'The Leaderless Group Project', *Bulletin of the Menninger Clinic*, May 1946, vol. 10, no. 3

The Buckle: the magazine of the Craiglockhart College of Education, 1968

Craiglockhart War Hospital Admission and Discharge Registers, Public Records Office, Kew, PRO MH 1887–1902

Grinker, Lt Col. Roy, and Capt. John Spiegel: 'War Neuroses in North Africa: the Tunisian Campaign Jan–May 1943', Josiah Macy Foundation, Wellcome Institute Library

The Hydra, April 1917–July 1918, magazine of the Craiglockhart War Hospital, Owen Archive

The Lancet: 13 February 1915, pp. 316–20; 14 August 1915, pp. 349–59; 27 March 1915, pp. 663–4; 2 October 1915, p. 766; 17 November 1915, pp. 1201–2; 1 January 1916, pp. 15–17; 8 January 1916, pp. 65–9; 5 February 1916, pp. 306–7; 12 August 1916, pp. 264–8; 6 October 1917, pp. 518–20; 26 January 1918, pp. 127–9; 19 August 1922, pp. 399–400; 6 July 1940, pp. 2–4; 25 January 1941, pp. 107–109; 22 March 1941, pp. 393–6; 12 August 1944, pp. 218–21

'Neuroses in War-Time', Ministry of Pensions Memorandum for the Information of the Medical Profession, HMSO 1940

Psychiatric Disorders in Battle, War Office, August 1951, WOP 35260

RAMC Court of Enquiry report, 'Shell Shock: failure to carry out an attack', July 1916

Royal Army Medical Corps Journal: Penrhyn Jones,Capt. G. 'Impressions of a Medical Officer to a Civil Resettlement Unit', vol. 4, April 1947, pp. 161–4; Major A. H., 'Psychiatry in Jungle Warfare', (August 1949), vol. 8, pp. 75–9

Rowlands, Dr John, K., 'A Mental Hospital at War', notes from a lecture given to the Liverpool Medical Historical Society, 1985

Southborough Report of the War Office Committee of Enquiry into Shell Shock, London 1922

Index